GW00535861

SIMON AND SCHUSTER

NEW YORK · LONDON · TORONTO · SYDNEY · TOKYO

embrandt's Portrait

A Biography

Charles L. Mee, Jr.

Copyright © 1988 by Charles L. Mee, Jr.
All rights reserved
including the right of reproduction
in whole or in part in any form.
Published by Simon and Schuster
A Division of Simon & Schuster Inc.
Simon & Schuster Building
Rockefeller Center
1230 Avenue of the Americas
New York, NY 10020
SIMON AND SCHUSTER and colophon are
registered trademarks of Simon & Schuster Inc.
Designed by Edith Fowler
Illustration research by Jeffrey Hantover
Manufactured in the United States of America

10 9 8 7 6 5 4 3 2 1

Library of Congress Cataloging in Publication Data

Mee, Charles L.
    Rembrandt's portrait : a biography/Charles L. Mee, Jr.
        p.   cm.
    Bibliography: p.
    Includes index.
    ISBN 0-671-62213-7
    1. Rembrandt Harmenszoon van Rijn, 1606-1669.
2. Artists—Netherlands—Biography.   3. Painting,
Dutch.   4. Painting, Modern—17th–18th centuries—
Netherlands.   I. Title.
ND653.R4M356   1988
759.9492—dc 19
    [B]   87–28356
                                                        CIP

Acknowledgments

I am deeply indebted to Walter Strauss, editor of *The Rembrandt Documents,* and to Dr. Walter Liedtke of the Department of European Paintings at the Metropolitan Museum of Art, for their readings of my manuscript, and to my editor Alice Mayhew for her unfailingly true judgment and guidance.

For my son Charles

Contents

Prologue

THE VERY FIRST glimpse that we have of Rembrandt is a self-portrait—one of his earliest surviving etchings, done when he was twenty-four years old. He is facing directly forward. His hair is long and wild, as though he had just been struck by lightning. His eyes are fierce and blazing, and one of them has a slight sideways cast to it. He is frowning. He has a stubble of a beard, and a big gob of a nose. He looks dirty, as though he had been sleeping in his clothes, and he is wearing what seems to be a filthy fur. This is an ugly derelict of a young man—dirty, sweaty, smelly, a determined outsider—and he looks as though he would not step aside for anyone passing him on the sidewalk.

In another etching that Rembrandt made at about the same time he is abruptly different—a sweet, soft, sensitive young man. A delicate shadow falls across one side of his face. He gives a come-hither look.

In another etching, he's making a face: He has that same shock of hair again, the same big nose, a thick, workingman's neck, a bit of baby fat still in the cheeks. His brows are drawn up, his lips are pursed, his eyes are wide with mock horror and real insolence.

In another, he laughs—or else, maybe, the way his mouth is drawn up, he sneers.

In another, he looks as though he might be hurrying along the street, a man of purpose, and has just turned to shoot a penetrating, irritated glance at us, as though we had bumped into him or stepped on his toe.

In another, he is monarchical, with a great soft sack of a hat that might (or might not) be a crown, and a collar that might (or might not) be ermine.

In another, he is bland, insufferably self-possessed, sure of himself, a young know-it-all.

In another, he is a grandee, a self-admiring young man of the court.

In another, he is a beggar, neglected and hungry.

In another, he cries out like a wounded animal.

In another, he is a simple young man, not posturing but trying to seem just as he is—frowning, as though he wishes to see more deeply and directly into the mirror he is using for these self-portraits.

Theatre people often call Rembrandt the Shakespeare of painters—for his ability to penetrate character, his compassion for everyone he portrays, for his sense of seizing the dramatic moment and presenting it with stunning effect, and because in his art he was one of the very few who was Shakespeare's equal—a phenomenon of creation, like Mozart, or the Grand Canyon. But sometimes Rembrandt seems to be a whole Shakespeare play all by himself—one moment a young prince, the next moment a suffering beggar, then a clown pulling faces, then a hostile drunk, a monarch, a sensitive young poet, a man of action, a lost soul, a simple, honest man.

The question is: Somewhere in all these pictures is it possible to find the authentic Rembrandt?

Rembrandt Angry. Etching, 1630

Rembrandt Open-mouthed, As If Shouting. Etching, 1630

A Three-Hundred-and-Fifty-Word Biography

THERE IS NOT much to work with. Even the lives we know best, even our own lives, are full of probablys and perhapses—and Rembrandt's life is more a mystery than most. Like Shakespeare, Rembrandt left almost nothing behind except his work, and not even his work can be counted on. Of the seven hundred accepted Rembrandt paintings of 1900, only three hundred have survived twentieth century scholarly study, and many of those are still being questioned by one art historian or another. He left no diaries or collection of letters; his friends and acquaintances kept no journals and wrote no memoirs. All that we have from his own hand are a few scraps of paper, seven letters to one of his patrons—begging, as artists always do, for money.

In addition to these scraps, there are a few scattered phrases and paragraphs in documents of the seventeenth century that refer to Rembrandt, a will, a lawyer's brief for a libel suit, a couple of paragraphs written about him by an early patron, a notarized complaint against him by a former mistress, a bundle of documents that come from his futile efforts to avoid bankruptcy, birth records in the town archives, the complaint of a man who said Rembrandt had cheated him—and not a lot else.

But there is a logical piece of evidence with which to begin. The first biography that was ever written of Rembrandt is a scant, 350-word essay. It was written in 1641 by an ambitious pushy writer, bookseller, and local historian named Jan Orlers, who worked his way up to become, eventually, burgomaster of the small city of Leiden, Rembrandt's home town. His profile of Rembrandt appears in a guidebook that Orlers wrote, printed, distributed, promoted, and, as burgomaster, gave his boosterish blessing to—a book that includes a history of Leiden, a tourist guide, notes on the city's leading citizens, and little potted biographies of the city's artists.

Rembrandt van Rijn

Son of Harmen Gerritszoon van Rijn and Neeltgen Willemsdr. van Zuytbroeck, born in the city of Leiden 15 July 1606. His parents sent him to school, so that in the course of time he would learn Latin and thereafter could enter the Leiden Academy [that is, the University of Leiden], and that eventually, upon reaching maturity, he would with his knowledge be best able to serve and promote the [interests of the] city and the community.

But he had no desire or inclination whatsoever in this direction because by nature he was moved toward the art of painting and drawing. Therefore his parents were compelled to take him out of school, and according to his wish they brought and apprenticed him to a painter from whom he would learn the basic and principal rules of art. As a result of this decision, they took him to the good painter, Mr. Jacob Isaacsz. van Swanenburg, to be instructed and taught by him. He stayed with him for about three years, during which time his

progress was so great that art-lovers were most amazed,
for it was clearly evident that he would one day become an exceptional painter. . . .

This is not the sort of fat, detailed document Agatha Christie
would hope to find about a subject's childhood, but quite a lot
can be teased out of these few facts if we look at them closely.
First of all, the name Rembrandt was an old-fashioned name,
and it was an odd choice for Rembrandt's parents, who (according to the town archives) named most of their other children
for aunts and uncles with such common names as Willem and
Adriaen and Elysabeth. Not to make too much of it, but a child's
name is often an important element of his sense of who he is.
Rembrandt was a name that would have stood out among the
boy's playmates from the first day of his life. And it was a name,
too, that Rembrandt would grow into: not only because he would
be a man who stood out, but also because he would be in certain essential respects an old-fashioned man, who liked familiar
old buildings, history, and mythology—even old hats.

The last name, van Rijn, was not one for which Rembrandt
had much use in his early life, even after he had begun painting.
His first paintings are most often signed with the initials RH:
Rembrandt Harmensz. or Harmenszoon, that is, Harmen's son—
not a world-famous painter, just a local boy.

His father Harmen, Gerrit's son, must have been a hard-driv-
ing man with a firm grasp on the value of money. He was a
miller, as his father (Gerrit, Roeloff's son) had been, and his
grandfather (Roeloff, Gerrit's son) and his great-grandfather
(Gerrit, Roeloff's son). Tradition, in this family, was ironclad.

Harmen's older brother (Roeloff, Gerrit's son), would doubtless have been a miller, too; but he died at the age of ten, and
broke that chain of first-born heirs, permitting the family mill-
ing business to pass to the second-born Harmen. Harmen's windmill was just at the edge of town, where there was a good wind,
on a branch of the river Rhine: It was called the Rijn mill; and
so the miller was called after his mill, van Rijn.

To own a mill was to own a substantial piece of property and
machinery; it did not put Harmen at the very top of the social

Rembrandt's Father. Drawing, about 1640

The Windmill. Etching, 1641

structure of Leiden, but it made him solidly well-to-do. And he was not a man to sit back and rest with what he had. In addition to the house adjoining the mill, he owned six other houses in town and a quarter-acre of land outside the city walls—a tiny plot by most standards, but not by the standards of the Dutch who coveted such little suburban plots for flower gardens. He seems to have had a powerful drive for money, and a disciplined sense of how to manage it. One can see in this nothing but greed—or one can see in it a wish to do better, even to excel.

The river ran through the center of Leiden, and was split into several major canals from which dozens of small canals radiated. A wall and a river-fed moat surrounded the town, and at intervals along the wall, on little fortified embankments, where another city might have placed its cannon, sat windmills. Just across the moat was open country, divided into hundreds of small plots of cultivated land, flat to the horizon, punctuated only occasionally by a tree, a farmhouse, the steeple of a distant village church.

Leiden was a textile town, as it had been since the fourteenth century. During Rembrandt's youth, almost ninety percent of Leideners worked in the textile trade. Business had been good in the very early years; then Leiden's heavy broadcloths fell out of fashion, the Leideners scrambled to make a lighter cloth, and business revived. The city was prospering when Rembrandt was a boy, but the prosperity lasted only a decade before the town began to slip again—though not before it had attracted thousands of immigrants. With the news of Leiden's prosperity, country people had come to the city looking for work, along with former soldiers, small farmers bankrupted by failed harvests, foreigners, escaped convicts, old whores, refugees from wars farther south. Housing was scarce (only seven thousand houses—little houses of red brick, with red-tiled roofs, for 45,000 people). Landlords split houses up into smaller and smaller apartments. Women and children were more and more drawn into the labor force. The gap between rich and poor grew. By 1622 the town council appealed to the central Netherlands government to grant a reduction in taxes for 15,000 impoverished Leideners—a third of the population. By 1633, nearly half the population would be on relief. Leiden was thronged with the poor. Squatters' houses sprang up around the town walls. The homeless wandered the streets. The municipal authorities came up with an unprecedented attempt to solve the problem: They tried to rehabilitate the poor by teaching them trades. But there were not enough jobs even for trained workers, and so the authorities tried the next best thing: They imposed jail sentences on beggars and vagabonds and told themselves that poverty was a God-given condition.

In this context, Harmen van Rijn, who was doing quite well, may have been a man without much generosity of spirit, a man who looked single-mindedly to his own interests. The town archives of Leiden contain a document noting that Harmen requested to be discharged from the civic guard—saying that he had injured his hands when his musket misfired and that he could no longer use a gun. The civic guard declined to release him altogether, though they did place him on inactive status and did excuse him from night duty—the hours of the evening breeze, when a windmill operated at its best.

Rembrandt, meanwhile, would do sketches of the beggars he saw on the streets—old men in rags, their toes sticking out of their shoes, bent over, exhaustion in their faces, looking for a handout; an old woman with a cane; a young couple with a small child begging at a doorway. He drew them without comment, showing life as it was, nothing criticized, nothing beautified, nothing glossed over. He was mastering the facts.

If Rembrandt ever painted a portrait of his father no one can prove it. When he was in his early twenties he did do a number of paintings of an old man with white hair and a long white beard, a man who sometimes seems worn out by hard work and rage, a bag of flesh and mental confusion, but a man who is occasionally able to rise to powers of lucid concentration and intelligence. One of these drawings has Rembrandt's father's name written on it: "Harman Gerrits vande Rhijn." Unfortunately, the name was added later—in handwriting that is not Rembrandt's. On the other hand, it was not added later than the 1600s. Possibly it was added by someone who knew who Rembrandt's father was, though that is hardly certain. But, if Rembrandt ever did draw his father, this is the man: quite old, worn out, though still with a broad, powerful frame, his head bent forward and down, his brow furrowed in deep thought, a man treated with respect by the artist.

Rembrandt's mother Neeltgen, Willem's daughter, came from a family of bakers—and so made a natural match for a miller. Nothing else is known about her. In his twenties, Rembrandt would paint and etch the portrait of an old woman almost a dozen times—indeed, this would be the only old woman from Leiden that he would ever depict, and most Rembrandt scholars feel secure in assuming that this is his mother. At the time these portraits were painted, she was in her early sixties—a toothless old woman, serious and thoughtful, perhaps a touch sad, certainly worn out, dried up, and a trifle remote, even cold. She was also, either in reality or in Rembrandt's wishful imagination, the female bearer of culture: Devoutly praying in one painting, quietly reading the Bible in another (in truth, to judge by legal documents in the archives, Rembrandt's mother was illiterate; she signed her name with a ' + '; it was Rembrandt's father who could read and write). Like his mother, Rembrandt would spend much of his life with the Bible. Not much, however, can be divined of the relationship between mother and son. There is not a great deal of warmth here; but there may be what could be called a longing for warmth.

She was already an old woman, at age thirty-eight, when Rembrandt was born. She and Rembrandt's father were both twenty-one years old when they married. They had no children for a half-dozen years—whether these were years of difficulty, or prudent postponement, or passionate love, no one knows—and then they had ten children in quick succession. Three of the children died in early childhood, but seven of them grew up together in the mill house. The youngest child was Rembrandt's sister Elysabeth. Rembrandt was the ninth child, and the youngest boy.

However Harmen may have prospered with his mill, he did not acquire many luxuries. His religious convictions were against it. One cannot imagine Rembrandt's mother dressed in silk or fine lace or his father sporting a large white ruff collar or embroidery on his sleeves, or conceive of a home furnished with an

Rembrandt's Mother: Head. Etching, 1628

abundance of pewter and crystal, a library of fine books, cellos and lutes, silver bowls with fruit, or expensive wallmaps or globes of the world. Certainly Rembrandt and his family did not live the simple life of a poor miller in a dirt-floored house or a tailor in a sparsely furnished workshop-home; but even so Rembrandt did not grow up a rich boy or an aristocrat. He grew up in a comfortable home with parents trying to teach him the virtues of hard work, thrift, simplicity, and conformity.

Children of the Netherlands were notorious all over Europe. Turned out of the house and into the streets in the early morning, the children ran wild through the day, playing, yelling, fighting, jeering, even throwing stones and lumps of dirt at strangers. At home they addressed their parents as 'Sir my father' and 'Madam my mother,' but they assumed otherwise an air of complete equality and liberty, and, as Jean-Nicolas Parival, a professor of French at Leiden University, wrote, "It is . . . surprising that there is not more disorder than there is. . . ."

Most of their games—rolling hoops, walking on stilts, spinning tops, riding hobbyhorses, playing with dolls—are still familiar, though the appearance of the children is not. In the paintings of the day, the children all look like little adults. They are dressed like little adults (there was no such thing as children's clothes). And they were expected to work like little adults.

From the age of three to six, Rembrandt would have attended nursery school, and then, from the age of six or seven to nine, a city school. There was nothing soft in this system: The city school opened at six o'clock in the morning in summer, seven in winter, and closed at seven in the evening. Children attended 313 days a year, including Saturdays. They were let out for two hours at midday to go home for lunch, and again for an hour from four to five for dinner. They learned sacred history, reading, writing, and arithmetic. Most of this was learned by memorization, and by way of problems that referred to the daily life of future burghers ("Two people have together bought eight pints of malmsey wine, which they want to divide up into two equal quantities. But to accomplish this they have available as measures only a five-pint bottle and . . .").

If school was anything like Jan Steen's painting *The School-*

master, it was bedlam. One or two of the children, it is true, are actually looking at books—or, anyway, one is just looking up from a book, and another has fallen asleep on one. The others are lying on the floor, standing on a table, throwing things at one another, shouting, calling across the room. Or, possibly, the painting of *The Schoolmaster* by Adriaen van Ostade, in which the children seem merely stunted and depressed, is more realistic. In this painting, the schoolmaster holds a wooden spoon, which calls to mind the view of the theologian Batty who held that the wisdom of God had so formed the human buttocks that they could take a severe beating without serious injury. Schoolmasters who scorned the wooden spoon sometimes resorted to the perforated wood block, which was attached to a pupil's leg for a time—sometimes for several days. The reward for doing well in such a school, for a student whose parents were ambitious, was to be sent on to Latin school, where one was educated in the classics and trained to take one's place among the elite of the nation.

In keeping with tradition Harmen named his first-born son and heir Gerrit and raised him to take over the mill. The second-oldest boy was also raised to be a miller and a shoemaker. Another son became a baker. Certainly not much in the way of inheritance remained for Rembrandt. It was a blessing not to be the first or second born in this family.

And so Rembrandt was sent to Latin school at the age of nine—presumably because he was bright, if not necessarily brighter than his brothers—but also because there was nothing else to do with him except to entertain some hope that he would be able, as Orlers said, to serve the interests of the community, that is to say, have a career as a civil servant—perhaps even, if he were smart enough, a grand career in The Hague, the capital of the Netherlands. Perhaps even some sense of familial pride had become attached to the promising boy.

The Latin school was just seven blocks from Rembrandt's home. It was a substantial building, with an imposing, classically pedimented front door, wide enough to accommodate four windows across the front of its first and second floors (and three, two, and one window on the upper floors as the building grew narrower up to its peaked roof). Latin was the principal subject taught there; it occupied about thirty out of thirty-four hours a week of classes. The method of teaching was memorization. The other four hours were taken up with religious instruction and calligraphy.

Rembrandt seems not to have liked school—and historians (who usually do like school) have labored ever since to explain just why. Gary Schwartz, a politically sensitive art historical detective, who wrote a book about the political interests of Rembrandt's patrons, blamed it on politics. A religious controversy, it is argued, forced the ouster of the headmaster of Rembrandt's Latin school, and the same controversy must have caused the withdrawal of Rembrandt from the school.

Whether intense politics or intense indifference is to blame, Rembrandt was taken out of Latin school before he had graduated. And then he was registered at the University of Leiden— perhaps not so much because of his love of studies as because university registration carried with it several privileges: a certain ration of beer and wine without excise taxes and, more crucially, freedom from guard duties. (Rembrandt seems to have had no more sense of civic duty than his father—either at that time or later in his life.) Then, as Orlers says, his parents, "according to his wish" (is there another discreet hint here of a willful adolescent able to get his way with his parents?), apprenticed him to the painter Jacob van Swanenburg. He was thirteen years old, and he stayed with Swanenburg for three years.

Swanenburg was the son of a former burgomaster of Leiden and so a man of recognized social standing—an asset, perhaps, in the mind of Rembrandt's father if not of Rembrandt. Swanenburg's burgomaster father, who had died just five years before, had also been a painter—indeed, he had been the best-established painter in Leiden for fifty years. Rembrandt's family evidently had some instinct for quality. Furthermore, as Schwartz has noticed, Jacob's son Johan was married to the secretary of the stadtholder in The Hague, and Jacob had managed to get several commissions for paintings from The Hague. If Rembrandt could not be a courtier, perhaps he could be a painter to the court.

As an influence on the young Rembrandt, Swanenburg has

been given short shrift by most art historians. Few like Swanenburg's paintings, or know much about him, so it seems easiest to belittle him and move on. But Swanenburg must have been an impressive figure to a thirteen-year-old boy, if for no other reason than that he had been outside of the Netherlands, to Italy, and lived there for twelve years, and seen the paintings of the renowned Italian masters. Swanenburg was a man of the world, sophisticated, he had married an Italian woman, and was doubtless full of stories of young artists pulling pranks and flouting convention all over Italy.

Swanenburg himself loved to do dark nocturnal scenes and visions of hell inspired by Bosch and Brueghel, and he had had a wonderful scrape with the Inquisition when he painted a witches' sabbath and offered it for sale in a church. The love of daring, the darkness of his canvases with the central characters picked out by dramatic light, the inspiration from Italy: These would be characteristics of Rembrandt, too.

A young apprentice was ordinarily required to live with his master (though Rembrandt may have stayed at home), to sweep out the workplace, stretch canvas, prepare the colors, clean the brushes, and otherwise do what he was told. For this, his parents might pay the master fifty or one hundred guilders, an amount of money about equal to what a small family would spend for meat, fish, and bread over the course of a year—or, if they were not so well off, they might give the master a barrel of herring or cod each year. The apprentice, for his part, would be fed, and given lessons in drawing and painting. He would be taught how to compose a picture; how to work it up in charcoal, chalk, and pen; how to draw with pastels; how to draw from plaster casts of heads and arms and noses and ears and from studio models; how to mix colors; how to render flesh, drapery, feathers, fur, stone, gold, and clouds; and above all how to copy the work of the master.

Eventually, the apprentice might be expected to fill in parts of his master's compositions—do the clothing, say, or the stone floor, or even produce complete copies of a master's piece. Often a portrait would be ordered with several copies for relatives or friends. Pictures of celebrities were always in demand, or simply *face paintings,* portraits of anonymous people who looked interesting: Turks, for example, or soldiers, or old men. If the master was particularly known for, say, flower paintings or winter scenes, the apprentice might turn out endless copies of a masterpiece, which the master would touch up, sign, and stockpile for sale in the open market. To be sure, a promising young man would not want to stay forever in someone else's picture factory. He would want to set up on his own, and produce his own masterpieces.

Before Rembrandt took that step, however, someone decided—possibly Rembrandt or his parents but probably Swanenburg—that he ought to be passed along to an even more accomplished master, to put the finishing touches on his education. No one in Leiden was deemed good enough for this job: It was necessary to reach out into the larger world, all the way to Amsterdam, the Netherlands' greatest city, where the very best Dutch artists were to be found, to get just the right master. Evidently Rembrandt was already considered that good, at least by his parents, or by himself.

The Landscape

A HALF-DOZEN little bridges radiated out of Leiden, over the town moat, into the countryside, and travellers from Leiden to Amsterdam had a choice of land or water routes to take. The land route went up north through farmfields and marshes and small villages, on paths running along the sides of canals and ditches, where horses' hooves and carriage wheels left deep impressions in the sand. The water route went up across the lake of Haarlem, the largest lake in the country. Although the roads of the Netherlands were a marvel to most Europeans, the Dutch generally spurned them for all but local travel. Boat travel—though high winds on the inland Haarlem Sea could sometimes make the passage rough, or even dangerous—was more comfortable and faster than travel by land; and the journey was short: Amsterdam is only twenty-five miles from Leiden.

Between Leiden and Amsterdam the landscape is not simply flat; it is concave, and the view to the horizon is one of a great sinking sensation, its plainness broken by the occasional sand dune that rises up and subsides again into the low moors and marshland, swamps and ponds. It is a drenched, drowned country, whose lands rise just marginally above the water and whose waters rise just marginally in turn above the sand, a vast river delta of innumerable little streams and inlets and collapsing sand banks, with water up to its roots and roadways and doorjambs. It is, truly, the nether world, soaked from below, covered in clouds and mist from above.

The soil is sandy, not good soil for growing cereals, and indeed the Dutch imported much of their staples from abroad. The farmers did cultivate small vegetable gardens between their ubiquitous ditches, however, and they were efficient at producing such things as potatoes for the local village markets. The soil was good for pasture land, too, and the Dutch became known for importing thin cattle every spring from Denmark and Holstein, fattening the cattle in their pastures, and exporting fat cattle in the fall. And, of course, the Dutch made cheese.

But the Netherlands was not an agricultural country; it was a country that depended on the water—on the shoals of herring in the Atlantic; on cod, whiting, and sole; on eel; even on the salmon in the Rhine. But even then, the explosive prosperity of the country did not begin until 1385, when an unknown Dutch fisherman invented a process for curing and barreling herring. From that humble discovery came the growth of a large herring fleet—ultimately of nearly five hundred ships—and a Navy to protect that fleet; and then, from the accretive experience of the sea and of ships and navigation, came vast wealth by way of trading through the Dutch ports that were so well protected by sandbanks and, fortuitously, so centrally located for the conduct of the European traffic in grain. The Dutch became traders of other people's grain, and then of other people's spices, wood, weapons, furs, timber, beer, cork, figs, oil, fruit, wine, slaves— most of the trade conducted out of Amsterdam, which happened to be the best port in the Netherlands and which became the leading port in Europe by default, when the Spanish bottled up Antwerp in the course of chronic European warfare. By the time Rembrandt set out for Amsterdam, the Dutch East India

Cottages Beneath High Trees. Drawing, about 1657–58

Company and the Dutch West India Company had come to lead the way in a commercial empire whose presence was felt on all the oceans. The Dutch had, or soon would have, established trading outposts or solid colonies on Manhattan Island, Formosa, the Virgin Islands, Martinique; in Connecticut; along the Delaware River; in Java, the Moluccas, Tobago, Brazil, Mauritius, Ceylon, South Africa, and they brought a fortune home. Within fifty years, the Dutch merchant marine would be larger than that of England, France, Spain, and Portugal combined. Not for nothing was this known as the Golden Age of the Netherlands.

Predictably, the Netherlands became the publishing center of the world for maps, atlases, charts, travel books, books on shipbuilding and navigation, and newsletters. Sixty or seventy percent of the news that appeared in English journals came from the Netherlands, some of it dutifully labeled "Truthfully translated out of the Low Dutch copies printed at Amsterdam." And collectors commenced to put together libraries of atlases and maps (the secret maps, if they were lucky enough to get hold of them, of the East India Company), city plans, and paintings of cities and towns.

In these years, a painter could make a good living, if he was commercially inclined, doing pictures of the ocean and the fishing boats and naval vessels that had brought such a fortune to the Dutch. In previous centuries painters had done landscapes in the backgrounds of battle scenes or portraits; now, in the Netherlands, the landscape emerged as a subject in its own right, and the Dutch turned out paintings by the score of towns and villages and rivers; of canals, lakes, farms, and sand dunes; of roads in summer, winter, and spring—with ice skaters and without; of sailing boats in a brisk breeze, in heavy weather, with low hanging clouds, in the evening calm, with fishermen laying nets; on a Sunday afternoon, with church spires and little bridges, with watermills and windmills, duck hunters and lovers, harvests and spring plantings—in an extraordinary sort of celebration that often comes of a country doing well and loving to look at itself.

The ocean was ever present, not simply as an idea or an

Windmills on the West Side of Amsterdam. Drawing, about 1654–55

avenue to the riches of the world. Every year from November to February, waters infiltrated the eastern provinces of the country, and turned the whole landscape into a vast sheet of water, or ice, with houses and dunes rising above it like tiny islands. From time to time a tidal wave or hurricane or other disaster would strike, and the ocean would wipe away a section of houses, or flood cellars and destroy stores of food before the Dutch were able to pump the water back out with their windmills—the greatest technological device of the age, one that produced an inexhaustible supply of energy.

The western provinces, which lay slightly below sea level, were protected by the dunes along the coast, and by the supplementary dikes that the Dutch built and kept adding here and there, and by the dams and lock gates that had been constructed along the rivers until the whole country had been brought into a single continuous network, and a singular equilibrium with the sea. In the Netherlands the ocean itself was removed from the country, bit by bit, until finally thousands of acres of land were reclaimed from water. It is a piece of human ambition and engineering that makes the Great Wall of China seem trivial.

The dikes were made of vast mounds of grass-covered sand. On the water side, a wall of huge wooden beams, fastened together by iron clamps, was driven into the mud to act as breakwater. Behind the breakwater was the dike itself, and in some of the more exposed sections of coastline, dikes several lines deep were built. To stabilize the mounds against erosion, a new technique—the use of a mixture of kelp and earth—came to be seen in the 1600s. But the dikes were dreadfully fragile, continuously eaten away by the sea, and needed constant, tireless checking and tending and rebuilding.

It was, and is, a small country, a little more than two hundred miles along the coast, no more than one hundred miles wide. The distance from Amsterdam to Haarlem is only ten miles. From Amsterdam back down past Leiden to The Hague is just over thirty miles. From The Hague to Delft is less than ten miles, from Delft to Rotterdam less than ten. It was a remarkable country in this respect, too: that there were more cities per acre in the Netherlands than in any other country. Rembrandt saw a good deal of his own country, although in his whole life he never travelled more than sixty miles from home.

Until recently, this country, along with other territories that had been called the Netherlands—Belgium, Luxembourg, and a piece of northeastern France—had belonged to the Holy Roman Empire. Charles V, Holy Roman Emperor and King of Spain, had united what had been seventeen provinces into a single, unified possession in the 1520s and thirties. In 1555, due to ill health, Charles stepped down in favor of his son, Philip II, and Philip became King of Spain, although the electors of the Holy Roman Empire denied him the imperial title. The seventeen provinces of the Netherlands, then, came to belong to Spain, not the Holy Roman Empire.

Philip appointed viceroys or stadtholders to administer all his provinces. The stadtholder of Holland, Zeeland, and Utrecht was William I, prince of Orange. And, in 1564, William led the nobles of the seven northern provinces of the Netherlands in a move for independence. In 1579, the northerners signed their own articles of confederation, and began the so-called Eighty Years' War of independence from Spain—which vastly disrupted European trade and finances, sent refugee populations scurrying from country to country, unleashed devastating famines here and there, and generally played havoc all across the continent—a war with occasional truces, and frequent second thoughts, and very mixed motives on the part of those northerners who joined in, or opposed it.

Some of these northerners—members of the House of Orange, for instance—had ambitions beyond mere independence. The Prince of Orange wanted not just to free the seven northern provinces from Spain, but to reconstitute the Netherlands of the seventeen provinces under his sway. Others—the Amsterdam merchants, for instance—were against going on with the war for that purpose, since it was easier for Amsterdam to dominate the seven provinces than to dominate all seventeen, and since unification of the seventeen provinces would throw together people with fierce differences over religion.

With the passage of time, leadership of the House of Orange passed from William to Maurits to Frederik Hendrik. These

Sunlit Cottages Under Stormy Sky. Drawing, 1641

stadtholders had something of the position of princes, although they had to vie for political control with the other nobles of the other former imperial provinces, and with local politicians, and, in particular, with the merchant princes of Amsterdam, all of whom were represented in a parliamentary body called the States General.

The seven provinces of this new, smaller northern Netherlands consisted of Groningen and Friesland in the north, Overijssel, Utrecht, and Gelderland in the center, and Zeeland and Holland to the west, along the coast of the North Sea. They were united by a loose confederation, and each province, or state, sent representatives to the States General at The Hague. Of these seven provinces, however, Holland was the richest and most populous. The Hague was in Holland. The two largest cities, Amsterdam and Leiden, were in Holland. International trade was conducted mostly out of Holland. Indeed, the country was dominated by Holland: presided over by the court at The Hague, heavily influenced, not to say ruled, by the merchants of Amsterdam. And so, to the intense irritation of the citizens of six of the United Provinces, most Europeans simply called the Netherlands Holland.

Ambition, persistence, thoroughness, luck, a fluke of geography, bad soil for grain, good fishing waters, an anonymous workman's invention, a large fleet, a source of endless energy, the ambition of stadtholders of dubious constitutional standing: such were some of the constituents of the greatest age the Netherlands has ever known—a combination of elements that no single cause can explain, and no amount of sheer hard work or wishing could hope to produce, or reproduce in another time. Like artists, empires are born of such fleeting combinations of things that coalesce for a moment and then disappear forever.

The Cityscape

AMSTERDAM IS built in the midst of a vast swamp—or mud flat—laced with streams and rivulets and the Amstel River which runs sluggishly to the sea. At the place where the river was dammed in the twelfth century—that is to say, at the Amstel Dam—the city grew up as a crude little fishing village. Its houses sit above the sand and water on a forest of pine pilings; its canals were dug out of the mud and sand and river silt by hand.

By the time Rembrandt arrived in Amsterdam in 1623, the city had become a spiderweb of canals, with the Dam at its center, and around its periphery a brick wall, and a moat, and eighteen sentinel-like windmills. The Amstel spilled over the dam, down a channel called the Damrak, into the Ij (a dialect form of A, the old Dutch word for water), an inlet that led to the Zuider Zee, or southern sea, an enormous pond that opened into the North Sea, the herring schools, and the trade routes of the world.

The odors of Amsterdam were those of fish and salt water, of roses and tulips in the fields at the edge of town, of garbage and raw sewage coming through the canals in the middle of town, of wet wool in the market squares and pipe tobacco in the taverns, of beer and wet dogs, of pancakes and turnips and roast pork with prunes and raisins, of burning peat or beech wood in chilly weather, of wet pine wood and of mold, and above all of other Dutch men and women: for, despite the reputation of the Dutch for keeping their homes and streets immaculate, they rarely bathed.

The colors were dark: clothes of black and grey and brownish yellow; a touch of orange-brown; the brown of coffee, cocoa and chocolate; nut brown, dun brown, and the reddish brown of

the brick warehouses—burnt umber, russet, and raw sienna—
startled occasionally, at different times in the century as fashions changed, by a well-to-do woman in peach-colored silk or
ivory or cerulean blue, a man in a crimson cloak lined in emerald
green, a splash of scarlet-patterned Persian rug, and the green
leaves of linden trees.

The shapes were round and soft: big-bottomed boats, women
under many layers of petticoats and full skirts, men in panta-
loons and round hats, billowing sails, children playing with
hoops, full-bellied pots and tankards and milk jugs and bowls,
kegs and baskets and tureens.

The Ij was filled with ships—the grandest of them the tubby
"bus" that brought in the herring catch and started the Dutch

View Across the IJ from the Diemerdijk. Drawing, about
1650–51

tradition of big ships able to carry big cargoes, and the new, sleeker "flute," which had come into service in 1590 and was especially good for the European trade, and a third, three-masted ship, even newer than the flute, that had several decks and a double forecastle and a complex rigging that was well suited to carry the biggest cargoes on the high seas.

On the square at the Dam, in what was the largest fish market in the world, fish were sold from open stalls, both wholesale and retail, and street peddlers flogged their goods from one side of the Dam to the other; and horses and wagons, sides of beef, bolts of cloth, kegs and casks of beer and wine and gin, bags of grain, uncut diamonds, furs, and barrels of pickles were all trundled across the square at once on their way into Amsterdam homes or shops or back out to sea again on another boat to France, or Brazil, or South Africa.

Nearby, in a building built just six years before Rembrandt got to town, was the Grain Exchange, the biggest grain market in the world, where much of the cereals that fed Europe were traded, where each merchant had a stall to display samples. And on all sides in this neighborhood were the stout, heavily reinforced, Dutch warehouses—Amsterdam's secret weapon—stuffed with all sorts of goods but principally with grain, which the merchants bought cheap in years of bountiful harvests, stored, and then sold in times of scarcity. They dealt with perfect sophistication in commodities futures: they bought whole forests before they were cut, whole harvests of grapes before they were pressed, and they had become masters of the techniques of holding goods back to raise prices and dumping goods to ruin foreign competitors. Famine was widespread in southern and western Europe from the late sixteenth to the mid-seventeenth centuries, and the Dutch profited from it.

The Dutch Exchange Bank, whose office was in the Town Hall on the Dam, had been founded only in 1609—this boom was still new—but its basement vault became quickly famous throughout the world. No one knew how much it contained: The Dutch kept that secret, and let foreigners believe its reserves were as large as they wanted to imagine. Confidence in the bank, and the fact that the government mints struck honest coins, made Amsterdam currency the European standard.

Rembrandt became attached to the look of the town as he first saw it, and his affections never changed: He sketched the buildings, the old squares and churches, as he first saw them. When new buildings went up (as they did with increasing rapidity), he continued to sketch the old ones—although usually he didn't bother sketching buildings at all. For the most part, Rembrandt's drawings throughout his life are not filled with architecture so much as people: beggars in the street, a mother and baby, a nude woman, a frail old man on his deathbed, a crowd listening to and studying a speaker, two old men walking along the street and putting their heads together to talk confidentially, a self-important bugler on horseback, a man bent far forward to drag a heavy load behind him, a man with hands outspread in a gesture of innocence, a fellow on hands and knees scrubbing the pavement.

All this new construction into which Rembrandt stepped was not, of course, financed by individual men working with their meager life's savings. The merchants of Amsterdam had learned early on how they could get real financial power over one commodity or another by pooling their resources, by gathering enough capital in one set of hands to buy a fleet of ships or a cluster of warehouses. In the early days, they met in a street behind the fish market, to make a deal on a cargo of wood or corn or to go into a venture together, and later on the meeting place was at one end of a bridge over the Damrak. When it rained, they went into the Old Church. Then, in 1611, they built the Beurs, a two-story covered gallery around a courtyard that became the center of world trade, a place where merchants could not only buy and sell their stocks of goods but where they could get together to finance huge investments. For the most part, the merchants made their deals in the coffee houses and restaurants in the nearby streets, and only went to the Beurs to sort out questions of insurance and shipping, foreign exchange and legal details, but eventually almost everyone in Amsterdam was drawn into their dealings. The Dutch East India

Company, formed in 1602, was the first joint stock company in history, its organizers the first stock brokers in history, and the people of the Netherlands, whose investment was solicited by a national subscription, were the first stockholders, and profits were such that in one year the dividend paid to shareholders by the East India Company was fifty percent. "Here I am," the French gentleman, and famous philosopher, René Descartes, who had settled in Amsterdam, wrote home to a friend, "in a great town, where everyone, except me, is in business."

The Dutch East India Company transformed the whole nation into a single great speculative enterprise, and those who missed a direct investment in the Far East trade could still profit by the general atmosphere of prosperity by getting into shipbuilding or rope making or sail making, calking or provisioning, or by investing a little something in tar or sugar or tulip bulbs. Even Rembrandt—especially Rembrandt—did not escape the money-making fever. As soon as he got a little money together he, too, began to speculate. He certainly did not fail to notice that some artists got rich; indeed, an artistic talent was one of the best ways there was to get rich quick if you were on your own, without big financial backing.

The spread of wealth was intoxicating, and it buoyed up the textile business, soap making, tobacco curing, beer making, printing, and gave names to whole streets: the shoelace makers' street, pencil makers' street, skull cap makers' street, shuttle makers' lane, razor makers' lane, sieve makers' lane, cork cutters' lane. There was such wealth in Amsterdam that it was said there was more gold there than there were trees, or stones. And the building and furnishing of the houses in these lanes gave work to carpenters and plasterers and stone masons, glass makers, tinkers, and spoon makers. Well-to-do tradesmen had offices on the ground floors of their houses and lived above their shops, and the shops had cast iron signs or carved stones on their facades: a pot for a potter's shop, scissors for a tailor's, uroscopy flask for a doctor. In one sales contract of the time, a house is identified as "the House of the Bell, opposite the Brush, near Ironmongers' Street."

View of Amsterdam. Etching, 1641

Quack Addressing a Crowd at a Fair. Drawing, about
1637

The boom in business was accelerated by the gold and silver found in the New World that flooded back into the European market, a phenomenon that was good for business, good for the prospering capitalist investors, but dreadful for the poor who found the price of food and clothing rising beyond their means. Many of the poor, or the struggling, left wherever it was they were and went to Amsterdam in the hope of joining in the new prosperity.

Almost three-quarters of the population of Amsterdam came from elsewhere, perhaps a third of them from the southern Netherlands, the others from elsewhere in Europe, from Germany, Armenia, Poland, Italy, Scandinavia, Greece. The immigrants gave Amsterdam a rich mix of cultures and religions and styles and made it a very sophisticated city—and a city full of exotic characters for an artist to sketch, people with odd turbans, curious ways of presenting themselves, interesting stories to tell. Most fled the upheavals of the Eighty Years' War. The fall of Antwerp caused an enormous jump in Amsterdam's population. French Huguenots moved north to avoid religious persecution, as did English Dissenters. (The Mayflower sailed from Leiden, not London.) And Jews—Ashkenazim from Germany, but more especially Sephardim from Portugal and Spain, in flight from the Inquisition—poured into Amsterdam and called it the New Jerusalem. The tolerance of the city became famous throughout Europe. It was a town, after all, mostly built not by a settled, rigid aristocracy but by the newly rich, who were very liberal, open to all sorts of deals, and people. As one of Amsterdam's Protestant clergymen said, the town fathers "countenance only Calvinism, but for Trade's sake they Tolerate all others, except the Papists; which is the reason why the treasure and stock of most Nations is transported thither, where there is full Liberty of Conscience: you may be what Devil you will there, so you be but peaceable." (The tradition of tolerance was only that, however, not necessarily more, not necessarily acceptance: The reason the Jews became such specialists in diamond cutting was that the industry was not yet big enough to have a guild to keep newcomers out.) In 1585, the population of Amsterdam had been about 30,000. When

Rembrandt arrived in 1623, the population had exploded to 115,000, and the whole city was a construction site.

At the turn of the seventeenth century, the new houses were not so often built of oak, as they had been. Stone and red brick were in fashion in the new, prosperous century, though, still, because there were no very solid foundations to build on, most houses were only two or three stories tall, and they were narrow—built atop sixteen or twenty pilings driven down into the sand. Inside, the staircases were narrow and twisting, and so each house was built to jut out at the top and to have a block and tackle attached to the peak of the facade so that furniture could be hoisted up the outside of the building and in through its windows. The windows, neatly framed in white stone, were wide, to accommodate the furniture, and to suck in as much light as possible out of the misty sky. No wonder so many of the Dutch landscape painters filled their canvases with clear, bright, blue skies: The Dutch must have had a terrible hunger for such skies.

Close to the Dam were a good many warehouses, shops, small alleyways filled with taverns and brothels frequented by the sailors, a boisterous drunken lot according to the paintings of the time (which no doubt took their own poetic license) with their reveling besotted men sprawling on the floor, iron pots on their heads for a hilarious joke, men leaping onto tables with their boots on in displays of terrific wit, an overturned chair, a spilled keg of beer, a barking dog, an old man grabbing (unsuccessfully) at a barmaid, a chubby, perspiring soldier—a family man no doubt, shy looking, a bit on the vulnerable side— offering a handful of coins to a pretty, slightly tipsy woman, young enough to be his daughter.

As one moved farther out from the center of town, the streets became less noisy and crowded. A vegetable market by a canal, tree shaded, with a boat tied up nearby, could seem almost sylvan in its pleasures as a woman argued with a stallholder over the price of turnips and her maid pretended not to hear the flirtatious remarks of an elegantly dressed young man. Not all these pleasures of daily life were entirely guileless. In one painting of a housewife at a poultry market, the man who runs the

*Three Studies of an Old Man in a Long Coat and a High
Fur Cap, Walking on Crutches.* Drawing, about 1636

stall is offering her not a hen but, with a suggestive expression, a cock, a bird well-known in folklore for its insatiable sexual appetites. (In fact, any bird in a Dutch painting is slightly suspect, since the word *vogel* [bird] and *vogeleren* [to bird] were commonly used to suggest a man's cock and intercourse.) The most somber interpreters of Dutch iconography raise an eyebrow at depictions of oysters or fish, and even suggest that a musical duet, or a game of chess, is likely to have a double meaning. A woman sitting alone at a clavichord may have one meaning; a woman sitting at a clavichord with an unused cello leaning against a nearby wall, presumably about to be picked up by the man for whom she waits, may have another meaning. Men seem often to have been absent from these domestic scenes—away at work, at war, or at sea: the authors of the ubiquitous letters one sees being read by solitary women seated by a window with the sunlight filtering hazily in, with a wallmap in the background suggesting voyages and distance.

From time to time, through a shop door, one caught a glimpse of a tailor at his workbench, his wife sitting nearby nursing a child: a vision of the complete integration of work and homelife, of children raised to take over the family trade, of skills permeating every home, of an economy built on the abilities and willing participation of the whole population (save those who were wandering the streets): a vision of middle-class society in one of its finest hours.

And, in the more well-to-do streets, one might see a well-scrubbed young boy delivering a basket of apples to a gentle housewife—and see through the open door to the sparely furnished, cool, tiled rooms inside the house, brightened more or less, depending on the weather, by the soft light falling through a window. Or one might see even farther through the front room, through another open door, into a room where an open window lets in both soft light and soft air. The Dutch painters were masters at capturing such scenes of this quietly prosperous life, of housewives in their clean, tranquil kitchens, helped by a daughter or a maidservant, peeling apples, or making pancakes, or ironing, or sewing, or spinning, or taking a supply of clean linen from an ornate linen chest—the rituals of domesticity raised to sacrament.

This was the world of Rembrandt—the very heart of middle-class bourgeois European society, the society in which he would spend his life—though never entirely comfortably—alternately trying to rise to its very top, or spurning it, never wanting so much to climb into it as above it.

In the best houses, built extravagantly double the width of their neighbors, with double the number of pilings driven into the sand, a broad, highly polished front door, and four large rooms on the ground floor, one saw well-dressed women sitting at tables beneath pewter or copper chandeliers hanging from the ceiling, a china cupboard filled with painted dishes, a glass of wine, a silver ewer, a lapdog. And inside the elaborately carved linen cupboard—symbol of social position, wealth, and comfort—were to be found the tablecloths and napkins and shirts and bonnets and neckerchiefs so crucial to the appearance of cleanliness. One Amsterdam bookseller of only moderate wealth possessed sixty sheets, thirty tablecloths, and more than three hundred table napkins. And one of the unbathed burgo-masters of Amsterdam possessed 150 shirts, 154 pairs of ruffled cuffs, twenty dressing gowns, sixty hats, ninety-two night caps, and forty pairs of undershorts. So neat were these houses, so meticulously kept, so scrubbed and waxed and polished as to make foreign visitors squirm in discomfort. Sir William Temple, an English diplomat, was made extremely anxious at a dinner party one evening because, every time he turned around and spat on the floor, a servant appeared to wipe it clean.

The homes of the rich were set as far apart from the stink and crowding as they could be—along several of the newest and broadest canals: the Herengracht or gentlemen's canal, the Prinzengracht or princes' canal, and the Keizersgracht or em-peror's canal. Here one found the home of the Trips and the de Geers, who were engaged in mining, manufacturing, and the arms trade. During the Thirty Years War, which dragged desul-torily on through Europe from 1621 to 1650, the warehouses of the de Geer family supplied weapons on all sides—for Sweden, Denmark, France, Christian of Brunswick, and anyone else who had the money. Like any other Amsterdam merchants, these wealthy families advertised the sources of the wealth that had paid for these mansions right out front: The pediments of the Trip house were decorated with handsomely carved stone cannons, and the chimneys were built in the imposing shape of mortars. Nearby, on the Herengracht, another well-to-do family decorated their front door with a pair of Negroes' heads to signify that their money came from the slave trade (an instance of the value of the Netherlands' traditionally big ships able to pack in large cargoes).

These houses of the very rich were recognizable at once, too, for their cosmopolitanism, for the chic new rage for foreign things: for English and French furniture, which was so much lighter in design than the old, solid Dutch tables and chairs, for cups and saucers from China, for Persian and Turkish rugs to cover the tables, and, most especially, for anything Italian—for a new facade topped with a crest or balustrade, for interior floors paved in the Italian manner with marble or colored tiles, for small Venetian mirrors framed in crystal, and, to fill all the new empty walls of their new houses, for paintings—paintings of flowers, paintings of landscapes, paintings of ships at sea, paintings of towns and poultry markets and windmills and ice skaters and country villas, paintings of bowls of fresh fruit and views of churches and clouds, and, above all, paintings of themselves, portraits of the newly rich princes of the world's new ruling order of commerce, whose center in Amsterdam one Dutchman of the time had taken to calling, with cynical affection, the golden swamp.

The Strolling Musicians. Etching, 1634

The Street
of Artists

ACROSS TOWN from the grand canals of the rich, between the old Singel Canal and the town wall, was the artists'
quarter of Amsterdam—a dozen blocks centered on Sint Antoniesbreestraat (St. Anthony's Broad Street), a street beginning at the New Market square and running over a hump-
backed canal bridge on its way to the wall, a street of little
houses of artists, art dealers, immigrants, antique shops, writers,
scholars, publishers, Sephardic Jews, and prostitutes. Here, at
the center of Dutch art, Rembrandt evidently felt, a young man
could see all of the world he needed to see without going any
farther: Here lived a good many of the leading painters of the
day; here, in the dealers' shops, could be seen some of the latest
work not only of Dutch painters but of Italian and German
painters as well, and, in books of engravings, the work of the
leading painters of the past.

Here, in the shops, one could find all the cloaks and old helmets and swords and shields and boots and books, pots, pans,

violins, plaster casts of ancient sculptures and chandeliers that an artist needed as props for his paintings. (The sheer number of *things* people liked to have in their paintings suggests an age of happily abandoned materialism.) Here one could find paints and brushes and panels and canvases and other young artists to drink with in the taverns. Here one could find all the prostitutes one needed for models for nude paintings (and one could engage, too, in another business on the side, since rich patrons would sometimes choose young women from seeing their pictures, and ask the artist to arrange a meeting). Here one could find old Jews to pose for Old Testament paintings and down-and-out soldiers to pose for military pictures and peculiar-looking immigrants to serve as models for paintings of foreign scenes.

Werner van der Valckert was living in this neighborhood at the time, buying and selling paintings and turning out his own meticulously detailed and lucid portraits of the city's leading citizens, such as his group portrait of *Three Regentesses and the Housemistress of the Amsterdam Leper Asylum.* Cornelis van der Voort, a neighbor of van der Valckert's, and probably Amsterdam's leading portrait painter at the time, was painting such well-to-do Amsterdamers as the *Regents of the Old People's Hospital*—a half-dozen men, with every hair of their beards and eyelashes rendered as precisely as if they were seen through a magnifying lens. Yet another neighbor, Adriaen van Nieulandt specialized in exacting still lives or scenes such as his *Kitchen Piece,* in which he painted a market scene so painstakingly as to show every cabbage leaf, every delicate feather of a goose, every hair on the hide of a deer.

It could not be said that van der Valckert and van Nieulandt lived exactly in a backwater of European art. The Netherlands had not produced any world class painters back in the 1500s, when Italy had Leonardo and Michelangelo and Germany had Dürer. Nor in truth did the Netherlands even yet have anyone of the stature of El Greco in Spain or Caravaggio in Italy or Elsheimer in Germany, certainly no one who approached the renown of the Flemish painter Peter Paul Rubens, who was at this time the most famous artist in Europe. But the painters of the

Male Nude Standing. Drawing, about 1646

Netherlands were beginning to rise to the occasion of Dutch imperial influence with such locally renowned painters as Frans Hals in Haarlem, Abraham Bloemaert in Utrecht, and, some years later, Jan Vermeer in Delft.

These Dutch painters were becoming known for their ability to render appearances. Stories circulated in Sint Antoniesbreestraat about such great ancient masters as Zeuxis, who could paint fruit so exactly that the birds came to peck at it, or Parrhasius who fooled even Zeuxis by painting such a perfect veil over a picture that Zeuxis tried to pull it off. Samuel van Hoogstraten (who would be one of Rembrandt's pupils) bragged that his own father painted such a convincing goat that the original model for the painting, when he saw it, butted the canvas to pieces. It can be no surprise to learn that the great Jewish philosopher Baruch Spinoza, who was born in Amsterdam ten years after Rembrandt arrived, made his living as a lens grinder, or that Anton van Leeuwenhoek, born the same year as Spinoza, invented the microscope. Long before Spinoza and Leeuwenhoek, Dutch businessmen had been obsessed with exact and detailed knowledge of the world, with facts and with seeing facts clearly, and Dutch painters had become the masters of descriptive painting.

The market for this Dutch art was astonishingly vigorous on its home ground. Perhaps nothing like it has been seen in any other time but our own. Everyone wanted pictures, pictures of all kinds. Pictures were needed for the decoration of banqueting halls, the rooms of inns, the board rooms of charitable institutions, orphanages, hospitals, leperhouses, homes for the aged, public buildings, guildhalls—all of them hung with portraits of individual philanthropists or boards of directors. Ready-made paintings were sold out of the shops in Sint Antoniesbreestraat, by peddlers on the street, and at outdoor fairs. As one English traveller, John Evelyn, said of an outdoor fair he came across: It was "so furnished with pictures (especially landscips and drolleries [that is, genre paintings], as they call these clownish representations) as I was amaz'd . . . 'tis an ordinary thing to find a common farmer lay out two or three thousand pounds in this commodity, their houses are full of them. . . ." Another

English traveller, Peter Mundy, was struck by the observation that "all in general [strive] to adorn their houses, especially the outer or street room, with costly pieces, butchers and bakers not much inferior in their shops which are fairly set forth, yea many times blacksmiths, cobblers, etc. will have some picture or other by their forge and in their stalls." Amsterdam had, perhaps, a thousand artists turning out landscapes and drolleries and portraits and flower paintings and townscapes and seascapes.

Near the New Market end of Sint Antoniesbreestraat, just under the shadow of the steeple of the Zuiderkerk (south church), lived the master to whom Rembrandt had been sent to study in Amsterdam, Pieter Lastman. Not surprisingly, the man to whom Swanenburg had sent Rembrandt was another painter who had made the journey to Italy—made the journey, as a matter of fact, at the same time Swanenburg had been there. It may be that Lastman was an old friend of Swanenburg's, that they had shared escapades in Italy. He was, in any case, a man who had also been deeply impressed by the Italian masterpieces. Indeed, Lastman had been so impressed by the Italians that he had often taken to signing his paintings not Pieter but Pietro.

As a would-be Italian, Lastman stood completely outside the developing tradition of Dutch descriptive painting. If the Dutch were becoming recognized masters of description, the Italians were already masters of narrative, or, as it was called, history painting—pictures that are not so much about the exact appearances of things as about the stories they tell, biblical and mythological and historical stories. Such a love of Italian narrative painting put Lastman outside the popular mainstream of Dutch descriptive art—but well within a new fad for anything Italian. And he was, in fact, Amsterdam's leading history painter.

Of all the painters who had impressed Lastman in Italy, none had had a more striking impact than the young Caravaggio, who was then startling his peers with the dramatic power of his paintings. Caravaggio astonished people with his technique of chiaroscuro—contrasts of light (clarity) and deep darkness (obscurity) that set up a highly dramatic interplay in a picture—

Naked Woman Seated on a Mound. Etching, 1631

and, by the way, he used ordinary people from the street, not idealized noble types, for his models. This use of real, irregular, odd, scruffy carpenters and stonemasons and street urchins— not prettied up, not transformed into classically proportioned ideals, this chiaroscuro of casting as it were—was shocking and offensive and, to some, exciting in the way it colloquialized history, catapulted it into the present, democratized it, reclaimed it from its upper-class custodians, and, simplest of all, made it more dramatic. Although Lastman did not himself pick up on Caravaggio's technique of chiaroscuro, he can hardly have failed to tell Rembrandt about such new Italian ideas.

Unlike painters of still lifes or portraits or landscapes, who needed special talents within a limited range—so, at least, the champions of narrative painting would argue—history painters needed to be able to do everything: faces and landscapes, water and dry land, clouds and armor, nudes and flowers, still lifes and animals, and genre and architecture. History painting required an artist to master composition, the mythological or biblical or historical sources of his work, and to know how to shape the depiction of an historical event in such a way as to make a comment on contemporary life or events.

Lastman, for example, when Rembrandt arrived at his studio, had just finished painting *The Volscian Women and Children Beseeching Coriolanus Not to Attack Rome*, in which he had to paint more than two dozen figures and faces, both men and women, their historical garments, helmeted soldiers, two horses, armor and spears, red and green and golden cloaks—all disposed in front of a tent, with kneeling women in the foreground, and Coriolanus on a platform above them. The historical, or legendary, event that this painting refers to is that of Coriolanus, who was about to lead his troops in an attack on Rome, being confronted by his mother and his wife and other women and their children, who beg Coriolanus not to attack the city. One scholar suggests that the painting was made because a truce between the Netherlands and Spain had just expired, and the Dutch were debating whether or not to go back to war—and that is very likely an inspiration for the painting, although Lastman, and the Dutch, were not the only ones thinking about Coriolanus, and the possible anti-war moral of his story, just then. (Just across the water, in England, Shakespeare wrote his play about Coriolanus sometime before Lastman painted his picture.)

His painting, however, no matter how well-intentioned, is boring. The conventions he employs no longer ring true today. For all the passion of the event, the figures are patently staged: They symbolize the passions; they don't contain or express them. Their gestures are histrionic, not spontaneous, not motivated. For all the attempt at drama, it is too much without contrasts to be dramatic; it is even too uniformly lit; it could have used some chiaroscuro.

But what Lastman was attempting to do—evidently succeeding by early seventeenth century tastes—was a great challenge, maybe the highest challenge the art of painting offers: to portray events on an operatic scale, drawing on light, color, gesture, composition, character, the whole range of a painter's talents. Unlike the fellows who turned out decorative flower paintings or naval vessels, history painters had at least the pretension— even if their countrymen did not yet entirely recognize their right to it—to consider themselves the equals of playwrights and poets, that is to say, the elite of artists.

And it was for paintings like this one of Coriolanus that Rembrandt now set about preparing wooden panels, grinding colors, priming the panel first with glue, then with a mixture of chalk and glue, and finally with a thin coat of paint, possibly working a little bit here and there on some of the master's paintings, such as the one Lastman did of a horse and wagon and several men by a stream (*The Baptism of the Eunuch*) during the time Rembrandt was with him.

Who else, aside from Caravaggio, did Rembrandt think about as he worked in Lastman's studio? Certainly he thought a good deal about Rubens. Every young painter did. And later on, Rembrandt's paintings would show that he had studied Rubens' compositions carefully—copied them sometimes, and absorbed a good deal of their brilliance and grandeur in his own work. And one of his very first etched self-portraits, looking rather grand in a floppy wide-brimmed hat and a lace collar, was an unmistakable imitation of a self-portrait by Rubens.

He evidently studied, too, the popular prints of Jacques Callot, one of the most prolific printmakers of the day. Callot did scores of prints of ordinary people, farmers, townspeople, beggars, wanderers, old women, extravagantly costumed actors; and Rembrandt not only took up Callot's subjects of daily life but learned a good deal, too, about such technical matters as laying in shaded areas with long vertical lines.

In case there was any doubt about what sort of pictures were worth painting, or which artists had a right to be considered something more than decorators, just down Sint Antoniesbreestraat from Lastman's house the first book about painting ever written in Dutch was published. Probably the most influential book about painting ever published in Dutch, it was certainly the only Dutch language art book in existence in Rembrandt's time, and if Rembrandt read any book about art, he read this one: *Het Schilder-boeck*, the painter's book, by Carel van Mander, the second edition of which appeared just five years before Rembrandt got to Amsterdam, with a new frontispiece designed by Werner van der Valckert and engraved by Pieter Lastman's brother Nicolaes.

The painter's book is divided into six sections: an essay "The Foundations of the Noble Free Art of Painting," a set of biographical sketches of ancient painters, several similar sketches of contemporary Italian painters, another such section on Dutch and German painters, an essay on Ovid's *Metamorphoses* which provided so much of the mythological material that painters used for source material, and an essay on the rendering of mythological figures. Van Mander did not even bother to mention paintings of domestic life or peasant life—genre painting was certainly beneath contempt, nothing to elevate a painter to the level of poet or playwright.

The claims that van Mander made for painting as a great art were based on his observations about the painting of mythology and classical history and allegory. Nothing else to speak of engaged van Mander's admiration. Not even portrait painters had the prestige of history painters; portrait painters had to try to please or flatter their patrons; they had, to a greater or lesser extent, sold their souls; only history painters could give free rein to their imaginations and arrange their compositions to please themselves. Some years later, in 1678, when Rembrandt's pupil van Hoogstraten wrote a new version of van Mander's "foundations," he did not hesitate to divide painting explicitly into three distinct categories. The lowest category included caves and grottoes, flowers, kitchen scenes, and other still lifes ("the humble foot-soldiers in the army of art"); the intermediate category included night scenes, fires, humorous paintings, decorative stuff tricked out with satyrs, wood gods, Thessalonian shepherds, street scenes, barbers' and cobblers' shops, and similar genre scenes; and the highest category of all was history painting, including mythology, classical history, biblical scenes, and scenes from literature.

Of these three grades of painting, then, because of the training of his masters, because of his own sense of comfort with old things, because he had the talent to do all that history painting demanded, and because of the ambition and pride that had apparently been planted in him from earliest childhood, Rembrandt chose the very highest.

To look again at Rembrandt's earliest self-portraits, he does not seem the sort of young man who would shrink from carousing with other young apprentices, or with the sailors and workingmen and drifters who passed through Sint Antoniesbreestraat, from frequenting the neighborhood taverns (as most Dutchmen, and many women, and not a few adolescents and children did), and putting away vast quantities of food and drink. A good many of these taverns had "orchestras" that played from four in the afternoon until nine or ten in the evening. Some had girls lining the walls, available for dancing and sex. On some celebratory days gangs of young men were known to descend on these taverns and down tumblers of gin until, amid the commotion, one of them would draw his knife and try to stick it in the ceiling. The others would join the game, trying to wrest the knife from him, drawing their own knives, and a brawl would break out. According to the only rule of the game, no one was allowed to go for another's eyes. Otherwise, they could slash at each other's faces until the spectators called a halt—and the winner was judged the one with the best technique.

To judge once more from Rembrandt's youthful self-portraits, he does not seem the sort of young man, either, who would throw himself into such carousing without holding something back. There is about some of the self-portraits not only a sensitivity, but a sense of princely bearing, of one who knows he has something to conserve, who holds himself apart from others as the very gifted or very ambitious often do, decidedly charting his own course, knowing that he is playing for higher stakes.

He stayed with Lastman only six months—an uncommonly brief apprenticeship. No one knows why he left Lastman's studio so soon, whether they had a falling out, or, as seems more likely, one or the other of them decided that he had learned all that Lastman had to teach him.

Rembrandt's Earliest Known Painting

REMBRANDT'S EARLIEST known painting is a disappointment to anyone whose vision of a Rembrandt comes from his later work. Indeed, most of his early work is so unlike what is clearly Rembrandtesque that it simply wasn't recognized as Rembrandt's at all in the eighteenth and nineteenth centuries. His very first known painting is a history painting, like one of Pieter Lastman's: *The Stoning of St. Stephen*, based on the story of the first martyrdom in the Christian church (Acts 7:58), in which Stephen, accused of blasphemy, was taken outside the walls of Jerusalem and stoned to death.

In Rembrandt's painting, Stephen is up front, on his knees, his hands raised above his head—to ward off the rocks about to be thrown at him, or in prayer to God. And the rocks that are about to crush his skull are grapefruit-sized boulders. This is a bad moment, and arms and hands and rocks are raised everywhere in a flurry of rage and terror. In a second, this helpless young man, who still has a bit of babyfat in his pink cheeks, will be dead.

It's not a very good painting, but it is an amazing painting for a near beginner. All the figures in the painting are pushed forward into the foreground—the way Caravaggio liked to do. And the whole painting is lit with a very bright light—the way Lastman lit his paintings—except for the left foreground, in which there is a big horse and rider in deep shadow. This use of a big, contrasting area of darkness in the painting may be a Caravaggesque touch.

He has done a good job with Stephen's cloak of red and gold, with the flesh of the half-naked rock throwers, with the white shirt of a man to one side whose back is turned, although he has not done too well with the rocks, which, in truth, look less like rocks than like large potatoes. Bob Haak, who was once a curator at Amsterdam's Rijksmuseum and later director of the Amsterdam Historical Museum, thinks the heads don't quite fit the bodies, and Gary Schwartz thinks the whole thing is an "airless, aggressive" composition in "harsh colors."

But the faces are not bad. Even the older men seem to have a problem with babyfat, but otherwise there are well-done expressions here of viciousness and desperation. And there is an especially nice touch in the depiction of several figures on a hill in the background—older men, wise men, men of authority—who sit back in utter indifference to what is going on under their noses.

Rembrandt has painted his own self-portrait, too, in the background. He is looking straight out at the viewer, underneath a couple of upraised arms, past the scene of incipient carnage, with what can only be called an expression (familiar from those early self-portraits) of glee—another nice, chilling touch.

He has made the moral of his painting good and clear; he has put in nothing extraneous, he has put the central message at the center of his canvas: this is a painting that champions tolerance. As a text for preaching tolerance, the stoning of St. Stephen is ideal. Not only was Stephen the church's first martyr, not only is the event itself a compelling cry for tolerance, but the Bible gives the last tolerant word to Stephen before he dies, when he turns his eyes to heaven and raises his hands to God and cries out: "Lord, lay not this sin to their charge." No doubt Rembrandt was preaching tolerance. But why?

For all the Netherlands' fabled welcoming of the Jews and of foreigners and of other unconventional sorts, relationships were not always easy. Lutheranism had been born in Europe in 1517, when Luther tacked his ninety-five theses on the door of Wittenberg Castle church. Not long after, Calvinism, the Protestant sect that preached an especially austere set of virtues, began in Geneva. Calvinism was spread north by preachers sent out of Geneva and by Huguenots fleeing into France and Belgium, and it reached the Netherlands in the mid- to late 1500s. In Holland, many Dutch welcomed Protestantism. The Dutch were at war with Catholic Spain, and that provided some motivation to become Protestant. Half the Dutch remained Catholic, but the rest became Calvinists, Lutherans, Anabaptists, Mennonites, or followers of other, small splinter groups, and the troubles began.

The religious groups split first along social lines. The liberal Calvinists tended to come from the upper classes. The more severe Calvinists tended to come from among the lower classes. Each side had its theological champion: Jacob Arminius preached the liberal line; Franciscus Gomarus preached the hard line. The liberal Calvinists lined up with Arminius, calling themselves Remonstrants. The hard-line Calvinists lined up with Gomarus, calling themselves Counter-Remonstrants.

Perhaps none of these religious differences would have mattered if they had not become intermingled with politics. A lull had occurred in the war with Spain. But the son of William I, Prince Maurits of Orange, who presided over the court at The Hague, understood that his ambitions to re-take the southern provinces of the old Netherlands could only be served by going back to war with Spain. The merchants of Amsterdam thought the war was bad for their wish to dominate the northern provinces, and for business. Religious leaders took political positions: The hard-line Calvinists declared themselves in favor of the war; liberal Calvinists sided for peace.

Soon enough a liberal man who had been the prince's own

tutor, Johannes Wtenbogaert, found it prudent to flee the country. Hugo de Groot, better known as Grotius, was sent to prison for life (although he escaped in 1621). And Johan van Oldenbarnevelt was beheaded.

It was in this context that Rembrandt painted the stoning of St. Stephen: a protest against the execution of Oldenbarnevelt, a plea for tolerance of religious differences, a cry for peace. It would seem to have been an act of daring and courage to declare himself a Remonstrant and to speak out in opposition to a prince who had just beheaded a man for doing the same thing.

But perhaps it is not so simple. In the first place, no one knows whether Rembrandt was a practicing Remonstrant, or whether he had any other religious faith. His parents were almost certainly Remonstrants, but Rembrandt was apparently indifferent to organized religion. He would paint all sorts of people—Calvinists, Remonstrants, Mennonites, Jews—all with equal sympathy, or, at least, lack of judgment. He seems to have been, not out of intellectual conviction but simply out of temperament, interested more in human than in theological issues.

As for his act of courage, standing up for the persecuted Remonstrants in their hour of need, well, in truth, Rembrandt seems to have painted the picture in the year that the dreadful Prince Maurits died and Maurits' brother Frederik Hendrik had taken over at the Hague. Under the circumstances, it seems less a matter of courage than of seeking favor—with Frederik Hendrik perhaps, or else with those liberal upper-class, patrician Calvinist merchants who had so much money to spend on commissions to artists. Rembrandt was a young man trying to make a success as an artist: He cannot be begrudged his practical motives by those of us who would have him be more pure.

In any case, Rembrandt's choice of subject matter is quintessentially Rembrandtesque. Throughout his life, the Bible would always be the principal material source for his paintings.

As for the sheer artistic qualities of the painting, what can be said here to be Rembrandtesque?

The most obviously characteristic touch of Rembrandt in this painting is a strong sense of drama. In most of Lastman's paintings, the master has chosen a moment of high drama, a key moment, just as history painters were supposed to do. But in *The Stoning of St. Stephen*, Rembrandt seems to have learned better than his master taught: This is not just a key moment, it is the key moment raised to the highest possible intensity; it is the very instant before a rock crushes Stephen's skull. (Rembrandt's pupil, van Hoogstraten, would codify Rembrandt's special intensity in the book he wrote about painting: From the whole historical narrative on which a painting is based, said van Hoogstraten, an artist must choose the "immediate action" or "instantaneous deed" to paint.) And then, unlike Lastman, who often frames his figures in a well-composed setting, Rembrandt shoves the setting aside and thrusts his figures right up to the front. The passions occur right in the face of the viewer. And the figures are not placid, as Lastman's often are; they are filled with rough passion.

Rembrandt had already moved beyond what could best be called narrative painting, beyond even what could be called dramatic narrative; he was painting the decisive moment of the drama and he was already, in the first painting of his that we know, well on his way to becoming the master of the decisive moment. He was, then, not an historian, or a narrative painter, he was a young dramatist.

The Young Failure

IN THE SUMMER of 1623, at the age of seventeen, Rembrandt returned to Leiden, the accomplished pupil of the great Lastman, able to paint faces and figures and landscapes and horses, available for commissions of the largest and most prestigious kind.

His first lesson in Leiden must have been one of humility. To get started on his new career, he set up shop with another young painter, Jan Lievens, who had a studio in his father's house. Lievens had studied with Lastman some years before, and it may be that the old master encouraged his pupils to get together. In any case, they shared studio space and models and ideas and seem to have touched up one another's canvases from time to time, too.

But Rembrandt was definitely the junior partner in this arrangement, completely overshadowed by Lievens. Though Lievens was a year younger than Rembrandt, he was far more advanced in his career. He had been a child prodigy, apprenticed to a Leiden painter when he was only eight years old, and sent to Lastman when he was ten. He stayed with Lastman for two years, and, by the time he was twelve, as Jan Orlers said, he was painting so well "that the connoisseurs were incredulous." When he was fourteen years old, he did a portrait of his mother "so well and skillfully that everyone stood amazed." By the time Rembrandt returned to Leiden, Lievens was an established master, with apprentices in his shop, knocking out commissions at a fast clip, embarked on a career that would soon take him to England, where he would paint the portraits of the king and queen and the prince of Wales.

But Lievens was not just a successful painter; he was a good painter. His and Rembrandt's paintings from this time have been mistaken for one another, and there is good reason for it. When they painted the same subject, using the same models, mimicking one another's compositions, only the most biased partisan can claim to know which was better—or even, for that matter, to be entirely sure that a particular painting was not done by some young apprentice who might have worked in their studio. Dozens of paintings of a few old men were done in Leiden during these years, most or all of them out of the Rembrandt-Lievens studio. One old man with a mustache and goatee was done over and over—he seems to have had plenty of time to pose, and Rembrandt at least seems to have had plenty of time to paint him—in a velvet hat, in a velvet hat with a plume, in a bigger velvet hat with a bigger plume, with a fur collar, with a neckpiece of armor, with a gold chain, with a lace collar, without a lace collar; and the connoisseurs have battled over the poor old fellow ever since trying to sort out whether this painting or that is by Rembrandt or Lievens. In one, the man's skin is too yellow for a Rembrandt, in another his eyes have an uncharacteristic touch of red, in another the handling of the fur is too crude, or the brush stroke is too free, or the pose is too lethargic. But whether this is Lievens whom the critics are faulting, or another young artist in the studio—or, indeed, Rembrandt—is impossible to know for sure.

What is possible to know is that young Lievens was getting one commission after another while Rembrandt, in his late teens and into his early twenties, was mostly idle, or working on his own things for practice, reduced to painting his own self-portrait, or yet another portrait of the old man with the goatee. True enough, he did get a few commissions: *The Stoning of St. Stephen* had been done on commission from a Leidener, and another history painting about Agamemnon and Palamedes had evidently been done on the same commission, to make a similar point (Palamedes was unjustly accused of a crime, tried before Agamemnon, and stoned to death) about the religious contro-versy in the Netherlands. He did a painting of David and Goliath (another painting on the same controversy?). He was trying to be a history painter, to pursue painting's highest calling, and he was working hard; he was turning out drawings and etchings and paintings, and making every effort to improve in all of these dis-ciplines, but his career simply didn't begin. At least, one doesn't hear in these years of incredulous patrons and amazed connois-seurs. Quite the contrary: an out-of-towner from Utrecht, who came through Leiden at about this time and saw some of Rem-brandt's paintings, wrote in his journal: "The son of the Leiden miller is highly praised, but before his time."

He might have seemed a talented enough youngster when he was a boy, but as a young man—compared to Lievens—he was definitely second-rate. If Lievens was too busy with commissions to fill a request, one might order something from Rembrandt; but if Lievens were free, one would hardly prefer something by his associate.

Indeed, with few commissions to speak of, Rembrandt may even have been reduced to painting pictures of his mother and father. At least that seems to be what he did in a painting he made about the biblical character Tobit and his wife. The old man and woman in the biblical painting look very like the old man and the old woman who have been identified as his mother and father. Perhaps filial devotion pays: This, *Tobit Praying for Death*, is Rembrandt's first really good painting.

According to the Book of Tobit, Tobit had gone blind. Be-cause he was unable to work, he and his wife Anna were im-poverished. Anna got a job but made little at it. They both

Rembrandt Bareheaded; Bust, Roughly Etched. Etching,
1629

dressed in old clothes, and Tobit's were in tatters. One day Anna brought home a goat. Tobit at once accused her of having stolen it. She replied that her employer gave it to her as a gift— and that Tobit is more generous to strangers than he is to her. Filled with remorse at having unjustly accused his wife, he breaks down and prays to God to let him die. That is the moment that Rembrandt chose to paint: Tobit, his head thrown back and hands clasped together, prays to God; Anna, astonished, holds the goat in her arms; a little dog, at Tobit's feet, doesn't understand what is happening.

To look at the painting simply as a painting, it seems that Rembrandt has learned something from Lievens: The lighting in this painting is soft and full of warm shadows, altogether unlike the harsh, evenly lit paintings by Lastman; the faces and figures are more detailed, more specific individuals; and the whole piece is subtler and more intimate. The extraordinary swiftness of Rembrandt's development since *The Stoning of St. Stephen* is the first evidence we have that we are dealing here with someone who is exceptional.

Just why Rembrandt chose to paint Tobit and Anna is a puzzle. To be sure, the Book of Tobit was not unknown; it had provided subject matter to a good many other artists—including Lastman. But this was the beginning of a near obsession that Rembrandt had for the story. In the course of his life, Rembrandt would do about fifty-five drawings, etchings, and paintings of the story of Tobit. Apparently none of these were done on commission; they were done because Rembrandt himself chose to do them. No one knows whether or not there was a particularly lively demand for paintings of Tobit. Rembrandt must have wanted to do it for reasons of his own.

He would illustrate the full story: this incident and the remainder of the story, in which Tobit's son Tobias is sent on a journey to a neighboring town to collect a debt for his father; God sends the angel Raphael to accompany the son; along the way Raphael directs Tobias to a cure for blindness; in the neighboring town Tobias gets married but, always remembering his father's errand, sets out again to return home. At last when

Raphael and Tobias arrive home, the first thing Tobias does is to cure his father's blindness.

What is Rembrandt's fascination with this story? Julius S. Held, a scholar long devoted to Rembrandt, published a monograph a few years back in which he addressed this question. First of all, Held pointed out, it is a story of God's compassion, a theme that Rembrandt seems especially to have liked, or at least to have painted often. Then it is a story of the intervention of the angel Raphael—and the sudden intervention of the supernatural was another theme that would often engage Rembrandt. Thirdly, the story contains a set of Mennonite morals—the stressing of familial ties, strict honesty, piety, charity, patience—and Held thinks Rembrandt might well have been a Mennonite.

Then there is the matter of the dog. Rembrandt loved to put dogs in his paintings—"small, shaggy, undignified, and lovable. The perfect companions of the common people who make up the cast of Rembrandt's characters, they help the master to achieve the air of simple domesticity that is basic to his art." (As another of Rembrandt's admirers once wrote, Rembrandt would always have a preference for "the humble, the rough, the decayed, the awkward, and the heavy.")

And there is the theme of the abiding love of father and son, another theme that would recur often in Rembrandt's paintings, in particular in paintings he would do over and over again of the prodigal son.

Finally, there is the matter of Tobit's blindness, and blindness, too, is a theme that would preoccupy Rembrandt all his life. He would paint the blind Tobit over and over again, and a painting of the aged Jacob (nearly blind) blessing the sons of Joseph, and the blind poet Homer, and, of course, Christ healing a blind man.

Freud, says Held, spoke of the connection of the eyes with sexual interests, of "the lust of the eye," that the punishment of "peeping Tom" of Coventry was blinding, the appropriate retribution for a forbidden use of his eyes. In classical literature, Oedipus is most famous for blinding himself as a symbolic act of self-castration. But Tiresias blinded himself, too, according to one version of his story, for having seen Minerva bathing in the fountain of Hippocrene. Was Rembrandt preoccupied with blindness because of guilt at being, as a painter, a professional voyeur? Or is this just a little bit far-fetched?

If we turn to the portrait of the old man inscribed "Harman Gerrits vande Rijn," we will notice something uncommonly arresting: The old man, his head lowered, his brow furrowed, his hands folded idly in his lap, appears to be blind. If this is Rembrandt's father, that would certainly explain the son's obsession with blindness and sight; it would lead us to understand Rembrandt's identification with Tobias and his longing to restore his father's sight. And it would help explain why Rembrandt's paintings would be so famous forever for being clouded, their figures emerging from, or buried deep in darkness, why the very surfaces of the canvas would be so rough and coarse and scumbled, as though to insist that the surface of things was not important—as though to force the viewer to look beyond the merely visible world to what is invisible, as though he saw with his father's eyes.

Christ at Emmaus

A<small>T ABOUT</small> the same time that he was painting the picture of Tobit and Anna, Rembrandt was also doing a little experimenting with the way he lit his paintings. He had softened the light considerably in the Tobit painting, but he was experimenting, too, with much more dramatic light, in particular with chiaroscuro. And what seems to have begun as a technical experiment ended by going way beyond technique to the very heart of what he might do as a painter.

The painting that took him to this new place—or was the result of it—was a painting of Christ; and it is completely unlike anything he had ever done before. The whole painting is thrown into complete darkness, with only a pool of light to pick out the principal characters. It is chiaroscuro with a vengeance.

The subject of the painting is taken from the Gospel of Luke (24:13–31). Luke tells how the body of Christ disappeared from the tomb after His death, of the bewilderment, when disciples came to the tomb, about what could have happened to the body, and of two disciples who happened to go out of Jerusalem to a small village called Emmaus, where they stopped at an inn to eat. Along the way they had met a stranger and there, at Emmaus, where they stopped at the inn with the stranger to eat, they realized to their astonishment that it was Christ who broke bread with them, that Christ had risen from the dead.

Out of the whole story, Rembrandt has chosen to show that instant when the disciples recognize Christ: They are seated at a table, with food in front of them. But one of the disciples has drawn back in such surprise that he has knocked a dish from the table; the other has drawn back so suddenly as to knock over his chair and fall, kneeling, before Christ.

There is a candle or oil lamp on the table, but the body of Christ, who is closest to us, facing sideways, hides the lamp entirely, so that the whole scene is in darkness except for the strange light of the lamp at its center. The kneeling disciple is lost in darkness. We see Christ only as a great, dark looming shadow of a profile; and we see, across the table, an amazed disciple's face, lit only in the eerie glow of the lamp. It could be a case of mistaken identity. It could be a trick. It could be an hallucination. It is, in short, a miracle. Can the disciple believe it? We see in his face: this is the very moment that he does.

The subject of the painting, then, is the surprising revelation of the divine in human form, and the shock of recognizing it. This, certainly, whether Rembrandt got to it by stumbling on it or by thinking his way to it, was a theme worth painting. In fact, it was a theme worth painting over and over again in all sorts of variations, a theme an artist might even think worth spending a lifetime painting—not just the revelation of Christ in human form, but all sorts of manifestations of the spirit behind the flesh.

It is the sort of theme that an artist can even begin to imagine is, after all, the essence of art: an act of revelation, an act of making the invisible visible, an act of painting the invisible—in short, the act of making miracles. It is the sort of thing that, once you've done it, makes everything else not quite as satisfying. One can easily imagine Rembrandt, as he tried to make his way in his career, establishing himself in his own right, scrounging commissions for portraits and history paintings, consumed with the vision he captured in his painting of Christ at Emmaus, and hoping to find a patron who might appreciate something miraculous.

Almost a Career

In 1629, when Rembrandt was twenty-three years old, his name appeared in a manuscript of a memoir written by Constantijn Huygens, the private secretary to Prince Frederik Hendrik, the stadtholder of Holland. Here, in the manuscript, Huygens refers to Rembrandt of Leiden as a prodigy. Here, it seems, is the beginning of an extraordinary career: Rembrandt is recognized outside his home town; he is known at the court of The Hague; he is about to become painter to the stadtholder. Indeed, soon enough he will be asked to paint a portrait of Amalia van Solms, the stadtholder's wife. He is on his way to world renown.

The Hague was a city of diplomacy, not of vulgar commerce, a city of ambassadorial residences, not home weaving shops, a city with only a few canals, and those filled with fresh, clean water, and no barges moving through them. It had a feeling of French elegance about it, a feeling of lace, of display, of palaces

decorated with cupids, naked women, and scenes of battle, a
city filled with rich patrons of the arts.

Just how Rembrandt managed to be known at The Hague is
not clear. It seems that he and Lievens visited a fellow artist
named Jacques de Gheyn III who was a good friend of Huygens.
Huygens himself was the son of Christiaen Huygens, who had
spent his life as a courtier at The Hague and left his son well set
up to succeed him as secretary to the stadtholder. Constantijn
had been given the education of a young aristocrat: He was
schooled in horseback riding and dancing as well as literature
and mathematics. He was a bright, smooth, talented young man
who knew astronomy, theology, physics, and the arts, and
wrote poetry in Latin and Greek as well as in a number of
modern languages. And now his job was to look bright in the
court of Frederik Hendrik, and to make the court look brilliant.

Among other things, Huygens took an interest in the microscope and turned it on all sorts of curiosities. When inexperi-
enced people first look through a microscope, said Huygens,
they can see nothing, "but soon they cry out that they perceive
marvelous objects with their eyes. For in fact this concerns a
new theatre of nature, another world. . . ." Huygens tried to
get de Gheyn to use the microscope to draw all sorts of objects
and insects that he would then compile into a book to be called
The New World, and when de Gheyn showed less than a full
commitment to the project, Huygens began to complain about
his laziness and lack of ambition. Obviously, to have caught the
attention of Huygens was to have caught the attention of a very
important man, indeed the most important arbiter of taste in
art in all the Netherlands; but it was a mixed blessing, since
Huygens had a lot of his own ideas about just what a painter
should paint, and how he should go about painting it.

As it happened, both Frederik Hendrik and Huygens were
militarists—able to see considerable advantage to the House of
Orange if the war against Spain were continued—and Rembrandt, who may have established himself as a pacifist with his
painting of the stoning of St. Stephen, now quickly turned his
hand to a few things to show that he could as easily paint mili-

Rembrandt with Long Bushy Hair. Etching, 1631

tarist pictures. He did a self-portrait, for instance, that showed him an honest, square-jawed, forthright young man with a firm and steady gaze, wearing an armor neck-piece, very much the young man you would want standing next to you in battle—or to do your military portrait. Did Huygens want a painting of Samson—a forthright statement about war and strong men, reminding everyone how Delilah had deprived Samson of his manliness, warning against making peace with Spain? Rembrandt turned one out.

Did Huygens want something that looked like a Rubens? Rembrandt was ready to turn out a Rubens—though he didn't get a chance right away. Rubens was "one of the wonders of the world," according to Huygens, "a painter experienced in all the sciences . . . I have always been convinced that no one exists outside the Netherlands, nor shall soon appear, who merits comparison with him, whether in richness of invention, in daring or in grace of form, or in complete versatility in all genres of painting." Rubens had done portraits of real kings and queens, and in the seventeenth century an artist was judged by his patrons: Everyone wanted his portrait done by a painter who was fashionable at some court or other. To be painted by a portraitist who had done kings and queens put one on the same plane, or so one could think. One hardly wanted one's portrait done by an artist who painted common people. Huygens and Frederik Hendrik wanted nothing more than to get Rubens to come and paint at their court. Unfortunately, Rubens was not only a painter, he was also a working diplomat, working, as it happened, for the King of Spain.

Unable to have Rubens, Huygens evidently decided to make his own Rubens, and he saw the raw material in Lievens and Rembrandt. He loved the fact that this "noble pair of Leiden youths" came from lowly parentage (a rich miller was still a miller, after all): "no stronger argument can be given against nobility being a matter of blood" (Huygens himself had no noble blood). And the fact of their birth made the two young men so much more claylike, so much more likely to be shaped by a skillful hand.

"When I look at the teachers these boys had, I discover that these men are barely above the good repute of common people. They were the sort that were available for a low fee; namely within the slender means of their parents."

Rembrandt, declared Huygens, "is superior to Lievens in judgment and in the liveliness of emotion. Lievens surpasses him in inventiveness and the loftiness of his daring themes and forms. From his youthful spirit Lievens breathes forth nothing except what is great and magnificent and he is inclined to paint things not life-size but larger than life. Rembrandt, completely wrapped up in his activity, loves to work on a small canvas and present an effect by condensation." On historical subjects, said Huygens, Lievens "will not easily attain the vivid invention of Rembrandt." Both young men, he thought, had the makings of truly great artists.

Unhappily for Huygens, neither Lievens nor Rembrandt much wanted to be shaped and molded. One fault of Lievens, said Huygens, needed to be pointed out: "he either flatly rejected every criticism or took it once admitted with a bad spirit because of a certain rigidity based on too much confidence in himself. This is a vice quite harmful to a person any age but is truly pernicious in youth. . . ." And Rembrandt was the same sort.

Above all, Huygens thought the two young men needed to make a tour of Italy to see the great Raphaels and Michelangelos, to steep themselves in the masters of history painting, that they might become "Italians to their own Holland," the equals, even superiors, of Rubens. But neither Lievens nor Rembrandt wanted to go to Italy. Rembrandt may have felt he had already passed the Italian narrative artists up as he moved on to become a dramatist. As malleable as Rembrandt may have been about imitating Rubens or painting the stadtholder's wife, he drew the line at being asked to swallow the Italians whole. He was beginning to become his own man.

They are "carelessly content with themselves," Huygens said in astonishment and disgust, "and till now"—if one can imagine such a thing—"have not thought Italy of such great importance. . . ." (From Huygens' report, one can almost hear the defensiveness of the young artists' replies to the overbearing patron, the cavalier dismissal of the great masters of Italy.) What could be done with such arrogant youths? What could be made of them?

A sudden loss of interest in Rembrandt overtook the court at The Hague. As for the noble youth's commission to paint the stadtholder's wife, evidently the portrait was meant to be a companion piece to a portrait of the prince that had already been painted by another artist, and it was meant to hang in a picture gallery in the place of honor next to the prince. A few years after Rembrandt had delivered the portrait, however, an inventory of the prince's works of art was taken, and the portrait of Amalia van Solms was found to have been hung by itself not in a prominent place but in a little room off the gallery, very much the "wrong" room. Evidently, in his effort to become court painter, Rembrandt had failed.

10

The Picture Business

ODAY, ON 20 June 1631, appeared before me, Geerloff Jellisz Selden, public notary . . . Henrick Ulenburch, art dealer, and confirmed that he owes Rembrant Harmensz, a resident of Leiden . . . 1000 guilders lent to the aforementioned Henrick Ulenburch by the above-mentioned Rembrant. . . .

So, in June of 1631, Rembrandt loaned one thousand guilders to Hendrick Uylenburgh—an Amsterdam beguiler, charmer, con man, in short, an art dealer. Why would Rembrandt want to do that?

Uylenburgh had appeared in the town of Leiden as early as March of 1628—or perhaps earlier; but we have documents to prove he was there in 1628. He had relatives living in Leiden, and he appeared there in 1628 to give testimony to help settle the estate of his dead brother's wife and children. It may be that he took the opportunity to poke around town then, looking for new work to take back to Amsterdam to sell, and met Rembrandt for the first time.

Whenever Uylenburgh met Rembrandt, he must have sensed that Rembrandt was just his sort of painter: not an artist of the first rank such as Lievens, but, what was more important for Uylenburgh's purposes, a good second-rater, one who was tremendously facile, able to paint anything—just the sort of person Uylenburgh needed as master painter and designer for his art factory back in Amsterdam. At the factory (or the "Academy" as it was called, with an eye toward image), Uylenburgh and his assistants bought and sold old and new paintings and other art works, imported great numbers of works of art from elsewhere in Europe, especially Italy, made oil or etched reproductions of works in stock (or of famous paintings or etchings), painted portraits to order, made multiple copies of etchings and bought and sold etching plates, gave art appraisals for use in court, did cleaning and varnishing, and gave art lessons to interested amateurs. It may even be that Uylenburgh spotted Rembrandt for a potentially first-rate artist, one Uylenburgh would be lucky to get to oversee the art factory and one who, in 1631, could be gotten because of his disillusionment over his failure to get a career going in partnership with Lievens as a history painter, or as a court portraitist, or even as much of a painter in his own home town.

Uylenburgh may have offered to make Rembrandt famous; he must at least have offered to make Rembrandt rich, because only a few months earlier Rembrandt had bought a little plot of ground just outside Leiden, where he may have had some thought of settling down. When the prospect of joining Uylenburgh presented itself, however, Rembrandt left Leiden without a moment's hesitation.

Where Rembrandt got the thousand guilders to go into business is not clear. More than one historian has suggested that he contributed a thousand guilders' worth of paintings, not cash, to the enterprise. But it would not seem characteristic of Uylenburgh to settle for anything less than hard cash. Rembrandt's father had died in April of 1630, and though there are no documents to suggest it, perhaps Rembrandt's mother, or his brothers, felt it was his due to be given this stake to get started on his career.

At this same time, in 1631, an abrupt change comes over Rembrandt's self-portraits: He is wearing a new collar. No more neck pieces of armor, no loosely wrapped scarf, no open-necked look, no simple linen; rather, all of a sudden, in a drawing, two etchings, and an oil self-portrait, Rembrandt is sporting a broad stiffly starched, white ruff collar. These self-portraits show him for the first time in such a collar—and they will be the last.

He is, in fact, all decked out in the very latest fashion of the well-to-do merchant class of Amsterdam. He has spruced up his hair, too, which no longer seems so wildly struck by lightning. It is still long, but it is coiffed. And he has neatened up his whiskers; he has the most delicate little mustache and whisper of beard beneath his lower lip. He wears a dashing, wide-brimmed felt hat that is decorated with a gold chain, and beneath his sparkling white collar he has on a fine black quilted doublet with golden buttons down the front. He is ready to go to the city. Whether Uylenburgh told him to do this, or he came up with the idea all on his own, it would seem he has done a few self-portraits to present himself in the right light to potential Amsterdam patrons.

We tend to look at Rembrandt's self-portraits as though they were all more or less the same, as though they were all trying to serve the same purpose, but the purpose of the self-portraits was continually shifting. Some of the earliest ones were meant to serve as practice, or as a young man's trying on of different attitudes, others were meant as probing self-analyses or meditations on who he had become or was in his deepest self, some were simply self-advertisements, self-promotions, calling cards: Here is Rembrandt, Harmen's son from Leiden, able to paint portraits of merchants with white ruff collars, indeed, even able to pass for one. Here is Rembrandt from Leiden, not a tough young military man from The Hague but rather an honest man with an open countenance, a dependable sort of fellow, altogether the sort you would want to do business with. Look on this face, and commission your own portrait.

Rembrandt went straight to Amsterdam, back to Sint Antoniesbreestraat, and there he took up residence in a building Uylenburgh had bought to serve as house, workshop, and emporium, a dozen doors down and across a little bridge from Lastman. Uylenburgh, though he was Dutch, had grown up in Cracow. His father (or perhaps his grandfather; the records are not clear) had been a cabinetmaker to the king of Poland; a brother had been a painter to the king; and he himself had been trained as a painter. His family had all been Mennonites, a milder branch of the relatively radical Anabaptists whose most famous local leader was Jan van Leyden, who claimed to be the Messiah and practiced polygamy. The Mennonites refused to baptize their babies, swear oaths, hold public office, or take up arms to defend themselves—a group, certainly, to test the tolerance of the Dutch. These were the eccentric libertines among whom Rembrandt had come to live.

Nowadays, an art dealer takes a generous percentage of his artists' earnings. Uylenburgh had an even better idea: He not only took a share of the earnings from his establishment, he made artists pay to get into the operation at all. In addition to Rembrandt, Uylenburgh took "loans" from eight other painters to get in on the action. For their entry fees, they were entitled, among other things, to make copies of any paintings the Academy turned out: here, in this arrangement, is the foundation of much of the confusion over attributions for centuries to come— not just whether a painting ought to be attributed to Rembrandt or the "school of Rembrandt," but whether any given painting is an original of a member of the school or a copy of a lost Rembrandt, or a copy by one member of another member's original. All of the Academy members, as it happens, might better be considered members of the school of Uylenburgh than the school of Rembrandt.

But Uylenburgh did not take money only from his painters. He also took it from his friends, his next-door neighbors, his relatives, and fellow Mennonites—sometimes individually, sometimes in a group. And, when he brought in a new investor, he would always give the fellow some very solid security on his loan—the most solid there was: his stock of valuable paintings. Indeed, so effective was this promise of putting up his stock of paintings that he could not resist making it over and over again; he secured nineteen separate loans with the very same collateral promised to all: his *entire* stock of paintings "including those to be acquired in the future." Certainly the entire stock of paintings was worth incalculable amounts more than any of the loans creditors put up; it was an offer few could refuse.

Nor was Uylenburgh finished with his investors once he got their money. Some of the investors were of double use to Uylenburgh; they were well-to-do Amsterdamers with good connections to other well-to-do Amsterdamers, and their financial stake in the Academy gave them reason to commend its artists to their acquaintances to have their portraits done. The investors, then, could be counted on to promote the Academy among that very group of people who had money to spend on paintings. Uylenburgh had invented a perfectly Amsterdamish money machine.

There was big money to be made in the portrait business and in paintings done for town halls and hospitals: paintings such as these were done on commission, often with money up front, and a fairly sure guarantee of being paid at the end—and this was the part of the business that Uylenburgh's investors helped to secure. But there was another market to be had, too. It was a riskier market—the open market, and it required an artist and his dealer to make accurate calculations about what the traffic would bear for paintings of flowers, say, or holy families, or landscapes—but it was a volume market; and Uylenburgh was interested in that as well.

Extremely few artists made a living in the Netherlands. At one raffle that was held in the mid-seventeenth century, a painting by Abraham van Beyeren went for a mere twelve guilders, Jan de Bont's paintings of fish went for fifteen to seventy guilders, and Benjamin Cuyp got fifty guilders for his big biblical scenes and cavalry battles—although Jan Weenix did fairly well; his painting of dogs fetched 136 guilders. This was at a time when a municipal physician got about 1500 guilders a year, a ship's carpenter might make as much as five hundred guilders a year, and even a minister who lived rent-free got more than three hundred guilders for living expenses.

Sometimes even the best painters had to take other jobs. Jan

Steen, the son of a brewer, ran an inn. Jan Vermeer took over his father's tavern, dealt in pictures on the side, and died broke and in debt to his baker. Jan van Goyen dealt in real estate, pictures, and tulip bulbs—and died broke. Karel van der Pluym was appointed municipal plumber in Leiden. Frans Hals, Jacob van Ruysdael, and Meindert Hobbema all ended up sooner or later in charitable institutions. Ferdinand Bol married a rich widow and promptly quit painting.

For those very few who made the right connections, however, the money could be superb. Municipal commissions were usually worth big money. Jan van Goyen, for instance, who never got more than fifty guilders for one of his landscapes, was given 650 guilders by the town council for his *View of The Hague.* For those who became stars, the rewards could be very good indeed; although flower paintings were generally cheap, Ambrosius Bosschaert got one thousand guilders for the last flower painting he did. The Leiden "fine painters," who did those exquisitely detailed works, were among the best paid: six hundred to a thousand guilders a picture for the top painters—but these paintings took a long time to turn out. Portraitists could work at a faster clip (the fastest of all may have been Michiel van Mierevelt, who seems to have churned them out at the rate of three a week for his entire life, presumably with pupils doing the clothes and background and Mierevelt putting the face and hands in the empty spaces). Portraits were priced by size. So much for a head, so much more for a half-length, so much for a full figure or a three-quarter length. To have your head done by a good painter cost fifty guilders. A group portrait cost one hundred guilders per person. A life-size, full-length portrait went for five hundred guilders (with the result that few people commissioned them).

In addition to portraits, Uylenburgh's establishment did a brisk traffic in histories, mythologies, religious subjects, exotic characters (both faces and full figures), Catholic subjects for Catholic buyers, and a torrent of cheap prints. Rembrandt turned out all these things: the rape of Europa, the rape of Proserpina, Bathsheba being groomed for King David, naked Susanna surprised by the elders, and then the more chaste Holy Family

The Ship of Fortune. Etching, 1633

(looking very cozily and domestically Dutch), Christ in the storm on the sea of Galilee (a nice mixture of Dutch interest in nautical subjects and religious topics), scholars with their finely printed books, a half-dozen different paintings of men in Oriental costumes—the sort of exotic foreigners a great imperial power is always getting to know (or are these native Dutchmen in their colonial costumes?).

Rembrandt is best known today as a painter, but in his own time he was widely known as an etcher, too, and, as gradually became clear, he was the best of his time. The two principal ways of making prints were engraving and etching. For an engraving, an artist uses a burin to cut deeply into a copper plate. For an etching, an artist uses a needle to scratch a wax layer from a copper plate and then puts the copper plate in an acid bath to let the acid eat into the plate. An engraving will give about three hundred good prints and another three hundred reasonably good ones; an etching will give only fifty good prints and another two hundred reasonably good ones. But it is easier and faster to do an etching, so etchings were wonderful things to put the Academy to work on—with the master sketching the picture in wax, and the assistants handling the acid baths and cranking out the prints.

Rembrandt was definitely an artist with a common touch, a love of vulgarity, a democratizing artist, an artist with a Shakespearean love of the texture of daily life as well as grand themes and passions, an artist who loved to inject a bit of present-day colloquialism into scenes of ancient history to create chiaroscuro shocks of surprise and recognition, to invade the past with the present and the present with the past. He made etchings of the ship of fortune, with a nude woman standing at the mast; Joseph and Potiphar's wife, with Potiphar's wife sprawled naked across the bed; a nude woman who was a slap in the face to all prettified, high-class, court-painted nudes—a nude woman who was a plain, common Dutch woman, a slack-bellied, big-hipped, smiling sack of flesh. He did a cavalry fight, a turbaned soldier on horseback, a Persian with a plumed hat, and a Polander with a plumed hat. He did an etched version of his painting of the stoning of St. Stephen that is even more alarming than the original painting, because Stephen looks as though he has already been hit by a rock, the life is already seeping out of him, and he is about to be hit again. He did a streetcorner seller of trinkets, a Turk, a woman making and selling pancakes on the street (with a baby trying to keep its pancake from being eaten by a dog). He did a rat killer, going from door to door looking for homemakers to hire him; a man stopping to urinate; a woman squatting to urinate. He did a blind fiddler, a couple of respectable-looking tramps (an old married couple?) making their way through the countryside, a surly tramp in rags who has turned to snarl at the intruder, a Polish beggar with knee patches on his trousers, a couple of scruffy itinerant musicians accompanied by a near-dead dog stopping at an open door where a mother and father hold up their small child to hear the music. He did a beggar with a wooden leg, a pair of beggars emerging from behind a sand-bank, a beggar with his dog, a beggar with a walking stick, a beggar with his hands behind him, a beggar with a slashed coat, a dumb beggar.

One can well imagine life in an artist's studio at the time—but one doesn't have to; it has been painted over and over again: The master, seen in profile, sits in front of his easel. He holds the maulstick and palette in his left hand, brush in his right. He rests his forearm on the maulstick as he touches the brush to the canvas. Next to him are his brushes, paints, varnishes. Elsewhere around the room are a clutter of props—a plaster cast, a violin, a globe, a skull, a pile of armor. There are canvases stacked against the wall and there are picture books containing reproductions of famous masterpieces, assistants grinding colors and making copies of finished works.

What is remarkable in this scene in Uylenburgh's studio, what is unlike most of the other studios in Sint Antoniesbreestraat, is that one man, Rembrandt, is able to do everything; he is extraordinarily facile, and extraordinarily productive. He can turn his talent to whatever the market requires and produce portraits or pictures of the Holy Family or a few hundred prints of nude women without a hitch.

But what is equally remarkable, to us, who have access, as the market did not, to his private drawings—the place where an art-

A Man Making Water.
Etching, 1631

A Woman Making Water.
Etching, 1631

ist usually keeps his heart—is that all the time he was knocking off dozens of different subjects for the Academy, he only did one sort of thing in his sketches. Every single one of his surviving drawings from this period takes for its subject what was still an artist's highest calling, a history painting.

Society Portraits

THE FIRST commission Rembrandt got in Amsterdam for a portrait was for one of Nicholaes Ruts, a merchant who was on his way into insolvency—not the most solid, respectable sort of person, but then, insolvency was not an unheard of disgrace in a society whose ships kept sinking. Ruts was about to be destroyed by the continuing European war that would cut off his trade with Russia.

The least prosperous merchants were likely to order portraits that showed only their heads, or their heads and chests without their hands. Those with more money to spend ordered half-lengths or three-quarter lengths with their hands. The richest ordered full lengths. Nicholaes Ruts, perhaps because his business was in such shaky condition and he felt the need to put up a good front, commissioned not a mere head but a whole three-quarter length portrait that showed both hands, in one of which he holds a piece of paper that might be a bill of sale or other voucher that would seem to indicate business is brisk and going well. (He stopped prudently short of commissioning a full-length portrait, which might have made him seem too easy with his money.)

Ruts was engaged in the fur trade with Russia, as his father had been, and Rembrandt painted him in a fur hat and a very prosperous-looking fur coat. He is wearing a handsomely starched white ruff collar and an expression of probity, gravity, dependability, and solvency. He has a neatly trimmed greying beard and mustache that give his face an impression of patriarchal firmness and reminds you that this fur business goes back a generation—far enough to constitute a tradition in Amsterdam society. To give the face even more strength and force of character, Rembrandt used the butt end of his brush to score the wet paint of Ruts' mustache, so that the whiskers bristle. His cheeks are a bit ruddy (those cold Moscow nights). He has an open expression, one you can trust. He is a man with nothing to hide. This man is as solid as a bank, and almost as rich.

To be sure, there is an individual somewhere in this portrait; and it may even be that the suggestion of warmth and understanding and compassion is really part of Ruts and not just part of the impression Ruts hopes to convey. But the point of the portrait is not solely—and perhaps not at all—to paint an individual so much as to paint a (prosperous) merchant, to show that an individual is filling a social role, and filling it well. Certainly Rembrandt has not been commissioned to reveal the pain and doubt of a particular man but rather precisely to hide any pain and doubt behind a fully satisfying type. Indeed, such was generally the rule of portraiture in Rembrandt's Holland, where men who had arrived wanted to be shown, and flattered, in their new roles, not exposed as fallible and vulnerable ex-fishermen. It may be for this reason that portraiture was held in such low esteem among the painters of the day, why van Mierevelt could put faces and hands into backgrounds painted by his assistants at the rate of three a week—and why the criticism that was made of Rembrandt in his own day, that he was not very good at actually capturing an individual's likeness, counted for so little. It is even possible that Rembrandt's ability to transform Ruts into the image of a successful merchant was the best possi-

ble introduction that Rembrandt might have to Amsterdam society: If he could make Ruts look good, imagine what he could
do with a man who was not nearly broke.

In fact, what he did with Marten Looten, whose parents were
in the garment business and who rose, himself, to become a
partner in a trading company, was to make a nouveau riche
merchant look like a nobleman. Looten stands with one hand on
his chest, the other holding a piece of correspondence. (Many have
tried to decipher this scrawled letter. It is clearly dated 17 January 1632, clearly addressed to Looten, and clearly signed RHL,
for Rembrandt Harmenszoon Leidensis. One scholar has made
out the message, "I was lonesome in Amsterdam/ your company, friendship, first brought me unforgettable/ respite . . ./
caused by infinite respect. . . ." And most scholars consider
that decipherment complete rubbish.) Looten was a Mennonite—
like Uylenburgh, like the parents of Ruts, like most of Rembrandt's early subjects who were lined up by Uylenburgh—and
he wore the strictly austere costume of the sect: black cloak,
black full-brimmed hat, and simple white collar without elabo-
rate ruff. In Rembrandt's hands, this austerity has been elevated
to an esthetic of complete elegance. These portraits may not look
like the people portrayed, they may not probe a person's spiritual and psychological depths, but they are very knowing in the
way they boost people up the social ladder, transforming mere
humans into aristocrats. More than that, for all the cynicism of
this transaction between patron and artist, something unusual is
happening here. Through all this facade of social type and social
climbing, distinct individuals do peer out. Simply as paintings
these portraits are wonderful. Rembrandt is trying to make a
living. He is also trying to do work of uncommon, even unprecedented, quality.

Nonetheless, Rembrandt did not yet get to paint the top people. In his early portraits, some of the subjects were even a bit
unsavory. Antonis Coopal, for example, despite his delicate lace
collar and his breezy mustache and his appearance of high-born
poetic fragility, was nothing more than a spy. In the 1640s he
would offer Frederik Hendrik a plan to conquer Antwerp without an army. He claimed he had a way of getting to the com-

Johannes Wtenbogaert, Remonstrant Preacher. Etching, 1635

mander of the garrison at Antwerp and, by giving the commander and certain other people 300,000 guilders, Antonis was able to assure Frederik that he could walk in and take Antwerp without a fight. For his own part, he told Frederik, *he* would require 400,000(!) guilders for his services along with the assurance that he and his heirs should ever after have the hereditary marquisate of Antwerp and also some other good offices and the privilege to grant additional offices to loyal friends and followers and so forth and so on. Frederik, desperate to get his hands on Antwerp, bought the scheme and signed an agreement with Coopal, and although Coopal failed, he did not hesitate thereafter to affect the title marquis of Antwerp.

And then Rembrandt painted the subversive Johannes Wtenbogaert, the Remonstrant leader who had been driven out of the country by Prince Maurits in 1618. Wtenbogaert had returned in 1626, to be welcomed, almost venerated, by his fellow Remonstrants. Although his moment of fame and great influence had passed, and the market for portraits of him was small, the demand in that market was avid and Wtenbogaert was eager for publicity for himself and his cause. That he asked Rembrandt to paint his portrait probably indicates that he recognized in Rembrandt a kindred spirit, a humane, tolerant soul, or at least a man attracted to trouble-makers. If Rembrandt was not a follower of Wtenbogaert's, as his parents were, he was very likely a sympathizer.

In fact, Rembrandt did two portraits of Wtenbogaert, and the portraits could be of two entirely different men. First he did an oil, an extravagant three-quarter length. In black cloak and white ruff collar Wtenbogaert looks like an old, watery-eyed, frail man, worn down by exile and suffering and the burden of wisdom. He is wistful. He holds one hand weakly on his chest. He looks directly at the viewer but as though through a haze. He may even be dying. He is a sad, tragic figure.

The other portrait is an etching—meant to be distributed in many copies among Wtenbogaert's devout followers, and as a broadside among his enemies, because it carries an inscription beneath it, speaking of how Wtenbogaert was censured by the establishment clergy and driven from his home and now returns triumphantly to Holland. The etching, made two years after the painting, is of a younger man, seated at his desk, broad-shouldered and hardy, with a head as strong as a boulder, a firm jaw and jutting beard, a powerful, direct, and piercing gaze. He has a broader forehead than the old man, more widely spaced and differently shaped eyes, a shorter nose. His head and shoulders incline slightly forward, as though he might rise energetically from his chair at any moment and lead a new movement. Which of these is the true Wtenbogaert?

Having painted Wtenbogaert, it cannot have been difficult for Rembrandt to obtain the commission to paint one of Wtenbogaert's followers, Dirck Janszoon Pesser—a Rotterdam brewer, and a companion portrait of his wife, who looks like a large piece of fruit. By now it is clear that Rembrandt has begun to move in the circles of big business. He did Albert Cuyper, a gunpowder manufacturer, and a companion portrait of his wife (her father owned the gunpowder factory). It may not seem to have been good for Rembrandt's career to have painted the portrait of Jan Hermanszoon Krul, a Catholic and a poet, and—what was even worse—a theatrical producer, the impresario of a "music chamber," which produced musicals that he and others wrote. But it may be that the men behind Krul were worth impressing. The music chamber was backed by a group of businessmen who were on the board of governors of a philanthropic old folks' home, and they used the music chamber as a fundraising device for their favorite charity. All profits from the theater went to the old folks' home, and it may be that the businessmen commissioned Rembrandt to do a portrait of Krul as a publicity picture to promote the enterprise. If so, Rembrandt has found just the right touch for the portrait; Krul looks good but not too good. He looks not quite refined.

But there could be no doubt that Rembrandt was moving in the right circles when he did his double, three-quarter length portrait of Jan Rijksen and his wife together. Jan was, at the time, the master shipbuilder of the Dutch East India Company, a very important man indeed, and this painting mixes in a little suggestion of narrative painting along with portraiture. It may be that some of the urge to do history painting that Rembrandt was suppressing was finding its way into his portraits, and that that is one of the things that gives them their energy. Jan is sitting at his desk, with the drawing of a ship in front of him and a compass in his hand. And his wife has just rushed into the room to hand him a slip of paper. Could one of his ships be sinking? Or, more likely, just have returned successfully from a voyage? This gesture of delivering a note or letter was not new; other portraitists had used the convention before in a polite, anecdotal sort of way, but Rembrandt, characteristically, took a polite convention and quickened it into a dramatic moment.

Whether his earliest patrons were strict Mennonites, or not-so-strict Mennonites, or Calvinists, or Catholics, they were all fairly austere in their black and white clothes. But when Rembrandt came to paint Maerten Soolmans and a companion portrait of his wife, austerity vanished and foppishness took over. This young couple is filthy rich and not inhibited about showing it. They are festooned in lace. Lace collars cover their shoulders and their wrists, and lace flowers decorate their waists; the young man wears knee breeches with a gob of lace at each knee, and on his shoes, atop his shoe buckles, are two more garlands of lace. You can't walk down to the dock in this sort of outfit; with clothes like these you can only travel by carriage and step lightly onto clean, tiled floors. You cannot sell fish; you would not even really want to lift a pen for fear of getting ink on those white lace cuffs. All one can really do in clothes like these is issue instructions. This is the dress of the leisure class, of men and women who have been living for some time off their capital, the ideal sorts of people for an artist. Rembrandt had finally not only penetrated the higher reaches of Amsterdam society, but that portion of society that was not embarrassed to spend money on itself. Soolmans went all the way and bought full-length, life-sized portraits, two of them, presumably at the going rate of five hundred guilders each, one thousand guilders the pair, double the annual income of a ship's carpenter.

Rembrandt himself in these years, according to his self-portraits, was a prosperous, smooth, well-fed, handsomely groomed, confident, young, upwardly mobile man about town, the very image of the young careerist in his twenties who has discovered that he can get on well on his own. In two of his self-portraits of 1633 he has given himself a large, expensive-looking, and elegant gold chain to wear at his well-tailored shoulder. His hair is a mass of thick, luxuriant curls. His mustache has a jaunty, upturned twist at the ends. And his gaze, as one of Rembrandt's nineteenth century admirers wrote, is marked by "fire, steadiness, insolence, and contentment."

The very idea of social class had made great strides since the turn of the century. Before 1600, there had not been enough money to make very many social distinctions worth the trouble: There had been nobles, and there had been working people among whom there were not great disparities in wealth. With the boom in commerce, however, all sorts of distinctions, snobberies, and differences in who exploited whom, became possible. Big merchants became as rich as noblemen, or richer; small tradesmen scrambled up into the ranks of wealthy merchants. By the middle of the century, a petty bourgeoisie of shopkeepers found themselves surrounded by an upper middle class and a nobility on one side, and a mass of poor and ignorant tradesmen and farmers on the other, all eager for some recognition of their dignity. The upper classes, having access to no greater wealth than the great merchants, erected barriers of etiquette around themselves. Correct speech and manners became the sign of the aristocrat.

Titles were imported from the French. Members of the States-General became "most mighty *seigneurs*." Officials of the Admiralty became "noble and austere *seigneurs*." A burgomaster was addressed as *monseigneur*; a lawyer or surgeon was *maitre*. Thus high society surrounded itself with a formidable wall of privileged status, while slightly beneath these dizzying heights, the pervasive importance of commerce was recognized. As one Frenchman at the University of Amsterdam was quick to notice, "a man named de Vries, trading in edible fats, would be addressed as '*seigneur* de Vries in oil.'" Small artisans had to make do with *monsieur*.

The Netherlands, sopping wet and sandy, did not have the rich lands on which to base a wealthy landed nobility or gentry. Anyone who wanted money was forced into trade. The court at

The Hague was nothing compared to the courts of England or France. The stadtholder, whose income came only from his own estate and from money voted to him by the States-General to conduct war, hadn't enough funds to support a first-class group of hangers-on, and none of the members of the House of Orange had the sort of personalities that might have attracted a dazzling court society. Huygens tried to repair this defect—bringing in artists and musicians and theatrical producers to give the court a world-class appearance, to make it impressive to foreigners and to induce respect among the skeptical or hostile merchants of Amsterdam—but his efforts remained forever labored. By 1620 there were only thirty-five noble families remaining in the province of Holland, some of them barely able to scrape by, some of them moving seasonally back and forth between manor and town house, devoting themselves to agriculture, hunting, literature, mathematics, and service to the state, "exiles," it has been said, "in the heart of a nation of traders and merchants."

The top people in the Netherlands were those whose families had formerly been in trade and who had accumulated enough capital to become financiers. These were the people who received their incomes from state bonds, shares in corporations, recent investments in (mostly urban) real estate, and the lucrative shipping and import-export businesses. These were the people, the patricians, who were known as "regents" because they tended so often to serve on the boards of governors or regents of old people's homes, hospitals, orphanages, poorhouses. These were the people who managed to have their candidates for burgomasters and representatives to the States-General chosen for office time after time. These were the people of a pragmatic liberal bent in their politics opposed to Frederik Hendrik in general and to his war-making ambitions in particular, who maintained a discrete, quiet, understated set of manners and appearances, favoring a style of austerity and simplicity in all things. Sir William Temple observed that Johan De Witt, one of the most powerful regents in the country, lived in the manner of a middle-level bureaucrat. He dressed with good taste but without the extravagant display of a Soolmans. When he went out on the town, he travelled by foot, keeping his carriage only for special occasions. The food at his table was neither more nor less than one might expect in any burgher's house in Amsterdam. Although, because of a public office he held, the state provided him with several servants, in private he customarily helped with domestic chores.

Just a cut below these patricians were a few very rich merchants, families such as the de Geers and the Trips, who had gotten rich quick in metals and munitions; but the majority of the merchants—the brewers and grain traders and textile dealers, the backbone of this commercial society—lived not so much in luxury as in solid comfort. In a world of daily risk, they necessarily valued dependability, predictability, thrift, calculation, tenacity, and other boring qualities, but they were not a dim or guileless lot. Given the rapid shifts in fortune, the sudden appearance or disintegration of opportunity, the rapacity of those who had just begun in business, the dishonesty of one's competitors, and the uncertainty of weather on the high seas, these were men, like most businessmen of any age, who had to stay alert at all times, and who had little time for anything other than business.

And just below these big merchants were a lot of small tradesmen: dressmakers, butchers, bakers, apothecaries, greengrocers, pewter founders, ironmongers, knife grinders, flower sellers, and artists. This was the class into which most artists were born, and in which most artists stayed. Some rose out of it. Some made good money in the painting market, invested wisely, and lived like merchants. Gerrit van Honthorst, official court painter to Frederik Hendrik (the position Rembrandt had only recently been trying to get), was able to earn enough to afford even the ultimate symbol of success and wealth, a carriage. But very few were ever regarded as much worthier than stonemasons. And of these artists, their fellow artists regarded portraitists with pity or contempt. Once, it is said, Nicolaes Maes visited Jacob Jordaens at his studio in Antwerp, and Maes introduced himself as a portrait painter. "Brother, I pity you!" Jordaens said. "Are you one of those martyrs?" And some years later, when Gerard de Lairesse wrote his book about painting, he said of portraiture:

"It has often seemed strange to me that someone can abandon his freedom to make himself a slave."

Far better, it might have seemed to Rembrandt, to be a merchant than to paint one. And, indeed, in a document drawn up in 1634, in which Rembrandt gives power of attorney to another man to handle a little piece of personal business, we find that he is in fact trying to pass for something that he isn't. Having appeared before a notary public, he has identified himself as "Mr. Rembrandt van Rijn, a merchant . . .", as though he were as well established as the subject of one of his own portraits.

An Anatomy of
The Anatomy Lesson,
Rembrandt's
First Great Painting

R EMBRANDT'S FIRST great painting—the first painting
that takes your breath away—was a portrait, in fact a group
portrait, in which Dr. Nicolaas Tulp, forceps in hand, surrounded
by fellow members of the Guild of Surgeons of Amsterdam, dissects the stiff, pale corpse of a criminal.

The Anatomy Lesson of Dr. Nicolaas Tulp was commissioned
to be not only a group portrait but also to serve as a commemo-
ration of the Guild of Surgeons' annual public anatomy, which
was always held in midwinter—in this case in January of 1632—
as a scientific demonstration, as a sort of Christmas party for
the surgeons (followed by a banquet and a parade), and as a
public entertainment.

The human anatomy had been lost for a thousand years after
the fall of Rome; the church had been more interested in the
soul than the body—or interested in the body as the vessel of
the soul—and medieval physicians, so far as anyone knows,
performed no dissections. For a thousand years, anatomists

relied on the classic Greek texts of Galen (without pictures) for their information about the body, and even Galen had probably never dissected a human body but rather based his information on cutting up monkeys and pigs. Then, at about the time of the Black Death, a sudden resurgence of interest in the inner workings of the body occurred—whether as a coincidental accompaniment or a result of the new fact of death on a massive scale—and even popes took an interest in autopsies.

When the Black Death struck Padua in the 1340s, the Public Health Department there insisted that autopsies be performed on anyone who had died of mysterious causes. But, still as late as 1345, when Guido da Vigevano put out an illustrated handbook of anatomy, dissections of actual bodies were rare, and Guido evidently based a lot of his illustrations on the works of artists rather than actual dissections. Science, such as it was, had to make progress in the back rooms and basements of hospitals, where two or three physicians would gather from time to time to perform a postmortem anatomy—or even less regularly, at the hands of such amateurs as Leonardo da Vinci, who took part in opening thirty corpses.

Anatomies held in public, however, did not occur often until the early 1500s. Then, once they had begun, they caught on with astonishing speed. In 1543, Andreas Vesalius of Brussels published *De Humanis Corporis Fabrica,* his great, beautifully illustrated work, based on his own dissections of bodies, and it created a sensation throughout Europe. By the early 1600s, public anatomies were being held regularly in Bologna and Padua and Paris and nearly every other medical center in Europe. They were held usually in the winter, since the cold weather helped to preserve the dead bodies, and they went on over the course of three, four, or five days. In time they attracted not just a few physicians, or artists, or medical students, but also other intellectuals, doctors of philosophy, writers, businessmen, women of the leisure class, tradesmen, idlers, travellers, dogs—even children if they could sneak in.

While the private performance of postmortem dissections continued to advance medical knowledge, the Christmastime anatomy—as entertainment, as theater, as spectacle—had obviously taken on an importance that no longer had anything to do with science. Special anatomical theaters were built; indeed, such theaters are apparently older than the oldest Renaissance theater for strictly dramatic presentations. Tickets were sold; theatrical producers apparently got the idea of selling tickets from this business of selling tickets to anatomies. The circular design of Shakespeare's Globe Theater, in fact, with its tiers of box seats, looks like a great anatomical theater.

Since the profits from these Christmas anatomies paid for the surgeons' banquet, the food and the hiring of the cook, the wine and tobacco, and the lanterns for the torchlight parade that followed—and sometimes for extra surgical instruments, for fumigators and candles and sponges—the producers of the anatomy always tried to come up with crowd pleasers, just as Shakespeare did across the water in London. To judge by ticket sales, one of the best sellers was always the dissection of a female corpse. The frontispiece of Vesalius' *Fabrica* shows a woman having her womb cut open: She lies naked, big-breasted, on a table amid a crowd of men (and two or three women, a dog, a monkey, a goat), her feet to the front, her arms useless at her sides, her belly a large, gaping hole, into which Vesalius has delicately placed his fingers as he turns to address the audience. As Vesalius himself always liked to say, "Galen never saw a uterus—not even in a dream."

"With a very sharp razor," Vesalius advised his pupils as he demonstrated this procedure, "make a circular incision around the umbilicus, deep enough to penetrate the skin, then from the middle of the pectoral bone make a straight, lengthwise incision to the umbilicus, and from the lower region of the umbilicus . . . as far as the region of the pubic bone between the little mounds of the vulva. . . ." There is a stronger appetite for pain here than even first meets the eye: It was commonly believed in the 1600s, though the physicians knew better, that the body was capable of sensation even after death.

This was a certain crowd pleaser, this ritual of sex and violence, of science, of the arousal and sating of curiosity, of the particular, cool, meticulous, thorough violation of the human body, of the repeated cutting into every last recess of the flesh, of the exhaustive annihilation of mystery. And the ritual was given a certain solemnity and gravity in the way it was staged. As Jan Orlers said of the anatomies performed in Leiden, "they were prepared with circumspection and carried out with great decorum," and the ordinances governing their performance stated that audiences must not laugh or talk, and that anyone who tried to take a souvenir, such as one of the organs that was passed around for inspection, would be fined.

Of course, not all anatomies were performed on women. The bodies chosen for these anatomies were invariably those of executed criminals, most often men, as is the case in Rembrandt's painting, handed over by the state to the surgeons of the Guild. And so, in a very real, and intentional way, these anatomies were spectacular, baroque epics of retribution—retribution played out on three grand public stages in three different extravagant acts. Act 1 was the public execution. Act 2 was the anatomy (admissions fees also went toward paying the hangman). And Act 3 was the celebratory banquet and parade.

That there is something primitive going on here, as well as something baroque and sophisticated, there can be no doubt. This is not simply the notion of an eye for an eye. Here is retribution beyond capital punishment, retribution beyond the grave. Here, too, is the remains of an ancient, primal fear that evil lives on after death, that the body of an evildoer must be carved up and scattered to destroy the root of evil power. Little wonder, after such passions had been aroused, that a public anatomy was commonly accompanied by a moralizing speech about how the dissection revealed the glory of God, whose wisdom could be seen in the arrangement of even the smallest vessel of the human body. Surely some soothing speech must have been necessary.

By Rembrandt's time, the anatomy had taken on yet another aspect, too. It was the official, public affirmation of the knowledge and power of science, of physicians, of the university, of intellectuals—as the mass was the manifestation of the power of the priest and the levee was the display of the grandeur of the king. And even beyond that, the anatomy had become a way of thinking, a form of discourse, a fashion. Everybody did anatomies. It is commonly said that the publication of Sir Francis Bacon's *The Proficience and Advancement of Learning* in 1605 defined the scientific method and inaugurated the modern age of science. It was his intention, said Bacon, to cut through appearances, to reveal all the myriad facts from which a conclusion may be reached, to do no less than to conduct "an anatomy of the world." And his fellow Englishmen were not slow to join Bacon in this endeavor. Indeed, a good many of them were even a step ahead of the great man. Anything, after all, could be anatomized—just as, in the twentieth century, anything could be psychoanalyzed. John Lyly had written *The Anatomy of Wyt* as early as 1578. Robert Greene did *The Anatomy of Lovers' Flatteries* in 1584. Thomas Nashe published *The Anatomie of Absurditie* in 1589. Robert Burton finally weighed in with his vast *Anatomy of Melancholy*, the fashionable disorder of the age, in 1621.

Knowledge, in the 1600s, was no longer simply knowledge; it had become "bodies" of knowledge, which could be dissected. The medieval world of the spiritual and the abstract had been replaced by the physical, sensible, visible, tactile world—in short, the material world: This was, after all, the dawn of the age of materialism, the age of belief that the truth lay not in the realm of the spirit but in the facts of the world, and the idea of the anatomy held the promise that one could penetrate to the heart of the matter.

In Rembrandt's painting of this extraordinary piece of theater, Dr. Nicolaas Tulp, the leading actor, stands to our right in somber black clothes and is surrounded by the other members of the guild, with the naked corpse at center. Tulp is the only one here who wears a hat, a wide, floppy-brimmed black hat. If this were a realistic painting of an anatomy, everyone would be wearing hats, since it is January, and cold in this building, and the Dutch always wore their hats inside during cold weather. But this is theater, and Tulp is the star. The hat picks him out. (It also hides the fact that Tulp had an inordinately small head and might have looked silly without a hat.)

There are seven other men here, crowded intently around the corpse with Tulp. Although all of them are members of the Surgeons' Guild, none of them are doctors. They are prominent members of Amsterdam society. Two of them have sons who would become doctors. Some of them would serve, at one time or another, as administrators of the Surgeons' Guild, in the way that administrators or boards of directors serve hospitals today—as treasurer, or chief administrator, or chief of examinations. These then, are some of the principal patrons of the Surgeons' Guild, along with their star doctor.

Nicolaas Tulp, at age thirty-nine, was one of Amsterdam's most distinguished physicians, and citizens. Tulp was not a family name; it is the Dutch word for tulip, and the name Tulp was apparently taken from the name of the doctor's parents' house, which may have served at some earlier time as an auction house for tulips. Tulp was the first physician in Holland to diagnose a case of beriberi, which came in from the East aboard a Dutch ship, the first to describe the *ileocecal* valve of the large intestine, which became known as the *valvula Tulpii*—discoveries that made Tulp a physician of international reputation. He was a curator of the Latin school and a curator of the university, and a member of the *Muiderkring*, an informal club of the country's most distinguished Latin-writing poets and thinkers. He was a connoisseur of scientific illustrations. He was the first to write a description of the Chinese tea ceremony; he wrote an apothecary book containing sixty prescriptions that set the standard for the handling of prescriptions by apothecary shops throughout the Netherlands; and he wrote a collection of clinical case studies, his *Observationes*, which went quickly into several editions. He served as magistrate and as city councillor, and he served eight terms as city treasurer and four terms as Burgomaster of Amsterdam. He was unquestionably first among the fifty-eight physicians and apothecaries accredited in Amsterdam, conservative in his use of drugs, known for a large practice among artists and their relatives, and known, too, for his warmth and for the personal interest he took in the lives of his patients. And he was not without some sense of his own importance: Unique among the physicians of Amsterdam, who customarily went out to visit their patients on foot, Tulp always went out in his carriage. That Tulp, by riding around in his carriage, was trying to rise above his social station, would have made him a kindred spirit of Rembrandt's.

One can understand why Rembrandt treated Tulp and his confreres with such respect—although, in truth, not many painters of Rembrandt's time would stoop to treating a doctor or a surgeon with anything but contempt. In the 1600s, surgeons were commonly reckoned no better than barbers. General practitioners were considered worth more respect, but not much: In most paintings and plays of the period doctors (like dentists and lawyers) were mocked viciously as brutal butchers or quacks.

The audience at Rembrandt's anatomy of Dr. Tulp—though Rembrandt does not show them in his painting—would have included the usual contingent of idlers and students and doctors of philosophy, women and children and dogs, and it probably would also have included two extremely prominent men: the world-famous philosopher René Descartes, who was himself an anatomist, and who instructed the reader of his *Discourse* "to take the trouble, before reading this, to have cut open in front of them the heart of some large animal that has lungs, because it is, in all of them, similar enough to that of man" and to reach into the cavity and touch the vital organs there, to confirm the presence of "the heat which one can feel there with one's fingers . . ."—and Caspar Barleus, a local poet and intellectual and neurotic with an odd relationship to his own body, a man who was afraid to sit down because he might shatter his buttocks, which he said were made of glass.

We, the viewers, have the vantage point of privilege; we are up close to the dissecting table, close enough to reach out and touch the corpse's toe, a position that, according to the ordinances, was reserved for guild members and for physicians over the age of fifty. We are lucky to be here.

The place itself is a room in an upper floor of the fortified south tower of a building that is still standing in Amsterdam's New Market. It is a dark, cavernous, chilly room. We see nothing of the traditional trappings of these anatomical theaters:

the recesses exhibiting skeletons, pickled serpents, dragon's bellies, specimens of human skins, and the occasional cadaver.

The light here is not the light of the sun. These anatomies usually took place after nightfall, and they were probably lit with a chandelier of a dozen or fourteen candles hanging directly above the corpse, casting a flickering light over the body of the dead man and the faces of the guild members, and leaving the rest of the room in fitful darkness. Chiaroscuro flutters over the painting, spotlighting the center of the piece, giving a warmth to the features of the guild members, even in this cold place, and a dead coldness to the corpse.

The corpse is not comfortable. He lies on a narrow, wooden table, no more accommodating than a kitchen counter. His broken neck slumps down toward the table, and so his chest thrusts unnaturally up. His mouth is open. Rigor mortis has set in, and so his muscles bulge. One of the guild members is leaning forward to get a better view, and his face casts a shadow over the eyes of the corpse.

Who is this poor fellow? His name is Adriaan Adriaansz, also known as Aris Kindt. He was a quiver maker, unemployed, from Leiden. He was evidently not an easy man to get along with. He had been in and out of jail. He had once tried to escape from a jail in Utrecht by an attempt to murder one of the guards. More recently, in Amsterdam, he and another criminal had tried to take the cloak off a man's back, had gotten into a scuffle with the man and had been arrested for assault and battery. On the day preceding the anatomy, he had been hanged for that petty crime.

This is not a sexual drama, then. This is a drama of retribution—or perhaps of retribution and pathos and something else religious: for if this corpse, with a white cloth chastely covering its loins, is reminiscent of anyone, it is of Christ.

All of this—the evocation of Christ, the dramatic light, the uncomfortable corpse thrust right into our faces, the atmosphere of the room, the intimacy of our relationship to the corpse and the men in the painting—is surprising in the tradition of paintings of public anatomies. There is no precedent for all these innovations on Rembrandt's part—not in the history of anatomy paintings, not in the history of group portraiture, and not in the history of Rembrandt's own work. It is as though the painting has dropped down from Mars. He has done something entirely unprecedented here—he has slashed across one genre and mixed it with another. This is the chiaroscuro of staging; he has applied the principles of history painting to the making of a group portrait; he has not rendered a collection of faces; rather he has staged a dramatic event, peopled with its leading actors.

In previous paintings of anatomies, artists had placed the corpse horizontally across the picture, at a reassuring distance from the viewer, and almost always kept it discretely, at least partially, hidden behind the figures of anatomists standing around the table. In a painting done by Aert Pieterszoon early in the century, the artist has grouped the anatomists in three rows, like a picture of a school sports team, with the corpse hidden in the midst of the group. In a painting that the hyperactive Mierevelt did a dozen years before Rembrandt, the anatomists are gathered around the corpse and all are turned to the front, posing for their portraits, so that any drama the scene might have had is thrown away by the mugging of the participants. The light in both these paintings is sunnily even; the atmosphere of the room is bland. These are group portraits that only happen to be occasioned by an anatomy.

William Heckscher, once the director of the Iconological Institute of the University of Utrecht, who wrote the definitive book on *The Anatomy Lesson* back in the 1950s, searched for someplace Rembrandt might have found an inspiration for his painting, and he came upon one precedent that seems at least plausible: old scenes of martyrdoms, paintings of flayings, dismemberments, and other tortures. In these paintings, like Rembrandt's, there is no group of men posing for their portraits; rather, there is a group of men savaging a body, pulling off its skin, hacking at its guts, ripping off its limbs. The blood and guts are shown; the relationship to the viewer is fierce; the whole picture is meant to make you shudder. More recently, another Dutch scholar has suggested that Rembrandt took his inspiration directly from a painting by Rubens called *The Trib-*

ute Money. Here we seem to have got to the heart of things, a source with double significance for Rembrandt—a suggestion of Christ and what was possibly even more important, an echo of Rubens.

It could be that Rembrandt's composition was even better originally than it is now. As it is now, the painting is a tight, dramatic scene: the corpse at center, Tulp to the right, and a cluster of seven confreres to the left, all bent intently forward or craning their necks for a better view, startled by what they see, or looking up and out at us—as though at another anatomist at the table—as though to communicate some thought that has occurred to them as they watch the proceedings, all as tense in their own way as the corpse is. But if you look at the painting in the flesh, and not in a reproduction, you see at once that something is wrong. The man at the very top of the painting, and the man at the far left, don't quite fit in. They have been painted in slightly different tones than the others in the picture. For a time scholars even thought another painter had added them to the group at a later date. The most recent research, however, suggests that they asked to be included in the picture after Rembrandt had begun work, and that Rembrandt himself added them at some point after he had already worked out his original composition. And, if you imagine them gone, then the painting is even more intimate, hushed, even more an intensely private act being performed in public, an embarrassing invasion of another man's private parts, then it is clear that Rembrandt has turned the dramatic screws as far as possible.

The stomach was the place where all dissections began, because the guts decay first. "When these incisions have been made," Vesalius said of the first vertical and horizontal cuts across the abdomen, and when "the upper right angle of the four right angles of the skin facing the umbilicus has been lifted with a hook or with the tips of the fingers of the left hand, then, putting aside the hook, little by little separate the skin from the fat at the breast and as far as the back by the transverse incisions made very close to the skin. . . . If you desire, the fleshy membrane may be separated . . . with the fingers, from the underlying bodies, so that the whole abdomen with a large part of the thorax may be laid bare of the skin, fat and fleshy membrane at one time." So, at least, this was how Vesalius began his dissections, although he did say that, if one preferred, one could explore the skin and fat and fleshy membrane less systematically, "as butchers do without any concerted method."

"*Qui vivi nocuere*," Caspar Barleus moralized on the theme of Tulp at the anatomical table, "*mali, post funera prosunt . . . dum secat artifici lurida membra manu. . . .*" (Evildoers, who did wrong while they lived, can do good when they are dead. The art of medicine wrests advantage even from death. Dumb skins instruct us. And, here, the learned Tulp speaks to us with eloquence, while with nimble hand he dissects the pale yellow limbs.) In another Latin poem "*In mensam Anatomicam*" (On the Anatomical Table) Barleus wrote, he spoke of a man spread out on a table, offering the spectacle of his pitiful state to all the world, exposing his naked limbs without shame, since this state had come to pass because of the wages of sin.

No doubt this moralizing helped to distract attention from the business at hand, or perhaps to redirect attention to the constant preoccupation with death that seemed to stalk Europe in the wake of the plague. (Could this be one reason there was so much interest, commencing with the Renaissance, in the themes of birth and rebirth—and even one reason why Vesalius exposed the generative organs of a woman at the front of his book?) Though the Black Death had done its most dramatic damage in the fourteenth century, reducing whole cities by a half or two-thirds of their populations, bubonic plague and other epidemics still regularly struck the continent, and Amsterdam, sunk amid its own open sewers, was not immune to sudden, inexplicable visitations of death. Yet, all the while Barleus moralized about death and God and sin, in truth *The Anatomy Lesson* marks that extraordinary moment in the history of the Western world when people turned from the belief that death was the result of the wages of sin, to a new belief that death was the result of natural causes.

But, as a matter of fact, this anatomy does not begin with the guts. Contrary to all absolutely universal practice, this anatomy has begun with the arm and hand of the corpse. His stomach is intact; his arm has been flayed; and Dr. Tulp, with his forceps, has taken hold of a muscle in the forearm to show to his fellow anatomists. This is odd.

This arm and hand have caused scholars real consternation over the years. Some have looked long and hard at the painting and decided that Rembrandt not only didn't know how an anatomy started but that he got the arm wrong as well. What Tulp seems to be explaining in the painting is the working of the *"musculi digitos moventes"* that traverse the lower left arm and the palm of the hand, the muscles that move the fingers. But what Tulp has got hold of with his forceps, according to some of the scholars, are the *extensores digitorum*, the tendons that are on the back of the hand. What does this mean? That Rembrandt went to the anatomy to get some sense of the general setting but then worked on the arm and hand out of an anatomy book—and worked from the wrong page?

The anatomists who have studied the painting most recently have concluded that Rembrandt was right after all: The small, yellowish-white line at the origin of the flexors of the lower arm is the tendon of the *biceps brachii;* so the arm is correctly positioned for Tulp to have got hold of the muscles that cross the palm to move the fingers. Most likely, however, Rembrandt did not try to capture this detail when he watched the anatomy; he probably worked on the details back in his studio, using a detached arm for his model. Apparently he was no stranger to body parts as studio models: An acquaintance of Rembrandt's mentioned that he had visited the artist in his studio a week before Rembrandt died, and that he had seen in the studio four dissected arms and legs.

Still, why would Rembrandt have had *The Anatomy Lesson* begin with the dissection of an arm when he certainly knew better? The only possible explanation is dramatic license: Here, the hand of the artist paints the hand of the surgeon as it dissects the hand of a criminal. Here, all the themes of the painting are brought together at once, in a single gesture: Here is the hand, instrument of creation and destruction, of theft, of retribution, and of redemption. Here, too, it may be, in this exorcism of a pathetic, sociopathic, homeless man, is the long arm of the law, and the hand of God.

All this is concentrated not only in the hand, but in a single instant of reaction on the part of all the anatomists. If we look at the eyes of Tulp's confreres, we see that their glances are all darting off in different directions. They look at Tulp, or at his hand, or at a book propped up at the feet of the corpse, or at us, but each glance is riveting and riveted. What has just happened here?

Look at Tulp's hands. With his right hand he holds the forceps that hold the muscles leading to the fingers of the corpse. And with his left hand he flexes his fingers—exactly as the fingers of the corpse must have flexed an instant before. *Quod erat demonstrandum.* The connection between the muscle and the finger, the anatomy and the functioning body, the anatomist and the criminal, the living and the dead. One of the anatomists darts a look at the book illustrating these muscles; two of the others are transfixed by Tulp's own fingers; another shoots a look at us. Rembrandt captures this split second.

Rembrandt's Signature

DID REMBRANDT know how good he was? Modesty had never been his strong suit, but when he came to sign his first paintings, such as *The Stoning of St. Stephen* which he did just after leaving Pieter Lastman's studio, he signed them very modestly and inconspicuously with the single initial "R." Occasionally, in these earliest paintings of 1626, he would add "f." for the Latin *fecit* ("he made it"), as though he was simply distinguishing his work from the other paintings that were done in the small world of Lastman's apprentices.

Once he had gotten settled back in Leiden, however, he began to make a slightly larger claim on the world. He signed one painting after another "RH," "RH," "RH," for Rembrandt Harmenszoon, Rembrandt, Harmen's son, no longer a student, but a local boy made good. This, for example, is how he signed his painting of *Tobit and Anna*.

Then, sometime in 1627, as he began to move out into an even larger world beyond his neighborhood and his home town, he began to identify himself as "RL," for Rembrandt of Leiden. This is how he signed his paintings when he began to hope for work from The Hague.

But then, perhaps as a reaction to his failure to catch on in The Hague, or in a nostalgic return to identifying himself as his father's son, late in 1629 he began to sign his paintings "RHL," or Rembrandt Harmenszoon of Leiden.

He took this signature with him to Amsterdam, and he signed his first portraits there—his portrait of Nicholaes Ruts and his portrait of Marten Looten and his portrait of a young clerk at his desk—"RHL," the new boy in town from Leiden.

But by early 1632, this monogram may have seemed too small town to Rembrandt. In any case, he toyed briefly with a slightly more grand signature that laid claim to an identity beyond being his father's son, and beyond being a son of Leiden, an identity derived from a river that ran through a great swath of Europe. He began to sign his paintings "RHL van Rijn," RHL from the Rhine.

But then, in 1632, with *The Anatomy Lesson of Dr. Nicolaas Tulp*, a new signature appears for the first time—the signature he would use for the rest of his life—his unusual first name alone: "Rembrandt." This was an extraordinary signature in Holland; no Dutch artist signed his work with his first name. The Dutch painters customarily signed their works with their last names, sometimes preceded by a first name or initial. Where did Rembrandt get the idea? The only painters anywhere who signed their paintings with their first names were the great, world-famous Italian masters such as Michelangelo and Leonardo. And so, with the signature "Rembrandt," with his painting of *The Anatomy Lesson*, Rembrandt staked his claim on all of Europe. It was the most immodest claim he could think of making.

The Woman He Loved

SASKIA, LIKE Rembrandt, came from out of town. She was a young country woman, from the town of Leeuwarden, up north in Friesland, where the farmers raised sheep and cattle and cut peat from the bogs. But she was a well-born young woman as such things were measured in the Netherlands: Her father had been a burgomaster of Leeuwarden, one of the most important men in the province of Friesland, and even, at one time, attorney general of the whole Dutch republic. His sons were all lawyers, and his daughters all married well—one to a lawyer, one to a Zeeland patrician, one to a professor of theology. Rembrandt had been the ninth of ten children; Saskia was the youngest of eight. When Saskia was six years old, her mother died; when she was twelve, her father died—and she became the ward of her sister Hiskia and Hiskia's husband Gerrit van Loo, the lawyer.

From time to time, it seems, she traveled to stay with her other sisters, and occasionally she was allowed to go to Amsterdam to visit with her cousin Aaltje, and Aaltje's husband Johannes Corneliszoon Sylvius, who was minister of the Groote Kerk in Amsterdam. One can only imagine how it would have been for a girl to be a guest in the household of a Calvinist minister, even, as Sylvius apparently was, a moderate one. Fortunately for Saskia, she had another relative in Amsterdam: Hendrick Uylenburgh, over in the artists' quarter. And she spent some time, too, visiting her cousin Hendrick at his house, where she met Rembrandt.

On June 8, 1633, Rembrandt drew a beautiful portrait of Saskia in silverpoint on a piece of vellum prepared with chalk—not a casual technique of portraiture, not a sketch, rather a technique that requires forethought and care since no false line could be corrected. She was twenty years old at the time, a pretty young woman with a round face and delicate hands. She wears a large straw hat and a loose-fitting summer blouse, the sort of thing she might wear for a walk in the country. She holds a flower in one hand, and there is a string of flowers around the crown of her hat. She is sitting at a table, outdoors it would seem, her head leaning lightly on one hand, and the angle of the sunlight suggests the late afternoon. There is a feeling of intimacy, gentleness, and dreaminess about her.

Beneath the drawing, Rembrandt wrote this inscription: "This is drawn after my wife as she was 21 years old [in fact, only 20] the third day after we were married on 8 June, 1633." It is odd that Rembrandt should have referred to Saskia as his wife, although they were not married until June 10, 1634—though perhaps not so odd. The word translated as wife (*huys-vrou* in Rembrandt's original) was often taken to mean fiancee, and the word translated as married (*getroudt*) was often used to mean engaged. So perhaps the inscription ought to be translated "my fiancee," on "the third day after we were betrothed," which would make chronological sense. But, to look at the drawing above this inscription, it is at least possible that what Rembrandt really meant was the third day after they first made love. If that is the case, they must have made love in a meadow, where all the flowers in Saskia's hat came from, in the middle of a sunny summer afternoon. (In the years to come, Rembrandt would draw a beautiful, quiet landscape from time to time, with nearly invisible lovers nestled in a hollow of a meadow or hillside. This sort of thing was not unheard of.)

Rembrandt almost never painted flowers, except in pictures of Saskia, where he did them repeatedly, portraying Saskia as Flora, the goddess of love, and (how could her family have felt about this?) goddess of prostitutes. Rembrandt did two paintings of Saskia as Flora. In the first one, she is innocent and apple-cheeked, holding a phallic staff in one hand and a bunch of flowers in the other, and her dress is full enough to suggest pregnancy months earlier than her family might have been happy to expect. In the second painting, an X-ray analysis has revealed that Rembrandt originally painted her bare-breasted, as Judith, holding the bloody, decapitated head of Holofernes in her lap.

In another painting, Rembrandt has rendered Saskia as Bellona, goddess of war—but, in Rembrandt's version, she is a fat, dumpy goddess of war. She wears a plumed helmet and is covered with armor over her shoulders, breast, and torso. She holds a massive shield in one hand, with a shrieking head of Medusa sculpted on it, and a sword dangles uselessly from her other hand. The painting is shabbily done; the goddess of war looks a bit dim-witted and silly in all of her appurtenances of defense. Can this be a genuine Rembrandt? It is. But maybe it's not entirely serious? One scholar once claimed to see in an X-ray analysis of the painting that underneath all this armor Rembrandt's future wife is in the nude. And even if the scholar is seeing things, a certain suspicion remains that the armor is a joke.

That sweet, wistful young girl in the straw hat with the flower in her hand seems to be something of a bawdy, bold, dirty-minded, fun-loving, adventurous young woman, more than ready to leap into the midst of a Bohemian life in Sint Antoniesbreestraat with the painters and musicians and theater people and vagabonds, and try on different costumes for her artist-lover and possibly even pose nude. This can hardly be what her family had in mind when they let her go to Amsterdam, and they can hardly have been happy with Hendrick Uylenburgh for allowing it to happen. No doubt they suspected Rembrandt of wanting to marry up, and of wanting to get his hands on Saskia's inheritance.

Nonetheless, Saskia and Rembrandt were married in a little village church outside Leeuwarden on June 10, 1634. Just after their marriage, they stayed at Hendrick Uylenburgh's house, but within a year they moved out on their own, some blocks away from Sint Antoniesbreestraat, on the edge of town, overlooking the Amstel River, where they rented rooms in the home of a rich widow with two daughters. Although one suspects that Saskia's relatives were right to think that Rembrandt wanted to marry up—he was still an aspiring young man—there was clearly much more to the marriage than that, and, if the evidence of Rembrandt's paintings can be trusted, he and Saskia had a wonderful time.

About a year after their marriage, Rembrandt painted a picture of himself with Saskia—both of them dressed up extravagantly, seated at a table in a tavern, looking back over their shoulders at the viewer, Rembrandt holding a *pas-glas* of beer high over his head in salutation, Saskia perched on his knee. Here they are, just as her family feared: the wastrel artist and his slumming, low-life courtesan—flaunting it.

On the table in front of them is a peacock pie, symbol of pride and sensual pleasure—as are the peacock feathers in Rembrandt's hat, and the expression on his face, and the sweet, near-smile on Saskia's face, and the luxurious clothes they both wear. The sword at Rembrandt's waist is a bragging, swashbuckling touch. In fact, he looks a little drunk.

This painting comes from a long line of tavern scenes and variations on the theme of the prodigal son, who wasted his life in riotous living and was reduced to the condition of a swineherd before he returned to his father to seek forgiveness. Some historians insist that this painting has little to do with the life Rembrandt and Saskia were living, but that Rembrandt is here virtuously turning out a painting with a strict moral lesson about the evils of a wasted life. Certainly that's possible.

Such moralizing paintings on the theme of the prodigal son were especially popular in the first several decades of the 1600s.

Portrait of Saskia in a Straw Hat. Drawing, 1633

The Anabaptists were deeply offended by extravagant dress, conspicuous consumption, idleness, drink, sensual indulgence, vanity, and smoking tobacco; and painters dutifully turned out pictures of drunks lounging in taverns, rakes putting their hands on the breasts of tipsy young women, and couples flirting: There was a brisk market for paintings of tavern and brothel scenes. But it is not always possible to tell just where these painters leave off their moralizing and begin to revel in tavern life out of sheer pleasure. Most of these paintings recall the prayer of Saint Augustine, to be led away from temptation, though not yet.

But Rembrandt did not paint Saskia only as a prostitute or to make a ribald joke. Right before they were married, he did a straightforward portrait of her, in a simple but elegant dress, with a single strand of pearls. She is very much the well-born lady in this picture; she is also a very self-possessed, direct, clear-eyed woman. And, of all his paintings of Saskia, the one Rembrandt kept with him and didn't sell for twenty years was a picture of her dressed in her most elegant costume of all— quite likely a costume borrowed from one of their theatrical friends. There is nothing Calvinist black and white about this painting, but nothing lascivious either. Saskia wears feathers, fur, velvet and lace, gold and pearls, a necklace, earrings, and a dozen bracelets. She is seen in profile, a woman of regal bearing and dignity, a fit companion to Rembrandt's monarchical self-portraits.

And he did casual sketches of her, too—in particular, during the year 1635, some sketches of her in bed, not romantic pictures, but pictures of a woman in discomfort, and bored, attended in one instance by a nurse at the foot of the bed. She wears a nightcap and layers and layers of bedclothes. This is daily life without any touching up, but with a good deal of sympathy. Most likely, Saskia is pregnant and confined to bed: Their first child, a son, named Rombertus after her father, would be born on December fifteenth.

Several months after he had drawn these sketches, Rembrandt painted his first full-length, life-sized nude—of Danae, and it looks like Saskia was his model. According to legend, King

Acrisius of Argos was warned by an oracle that he would one day be killed by his grandson. To thwart that forecast, he locked up his only child, his daughter Danae, in solitary confinement—so that she could not possibly have a child. But Zeus found his way to her, in the form of a golden shower.

Is there any sense of humor here, in Rembrandt immodestly casting himself as Zeus? No, the romance here is too serious. In Rembrandt's painting, he comes to her not as a golden shower, but as golden sunlight. She lies on her side, just rising up, eager to meet her lover, putting one hand out into the sunlight. She is a dairy-fed Dutch woman, smooth and round, not skinny. Her breasts are not large, but she has a nice big round fertile belly, the size almost of a basketball. The painting, this unembarrassed, naked affirmation of love and desire and fertility, was done in 1636; it must have been not long after their child died at the age of two months.

15

Independence

JUST AFTER he married Saskia, Rembrandt suddenly slacked off in his painting. The drop in productivity was dramatic. When he had first arrived in Amsterdam, he had turned out a blizzard of paintings: sixty paintings in two years (save a few that scholars may finally decide are not reliably by Rembrandt), more than one entire painting every two weeks, as well as etchings of the Good Samaritan and the Flight into Egypt and the Rat Poison Peddler and others. But by 1636 he was down to a half-dozen paintings a year, and fewer etchings.

What happened? Was he spending all his time making love? Was he luxuriating in domestic happiness? Had he had a falling out with Uylenburgh because of the marriage, and had Uylenburgh stopped representing him? Or had he decided, like Ferdinand Bol, and as Saskia's relatives had feared, to retire on his wife's money?

To look more closely at his output: What he had painted in those first two years in Amsterdam were portraits, almost all portraits. Of the sixty paintings from those two years, fifty-four are portraits. The clients had become increasingly august; the lace collars, the clothes, the poses had become very high-toned. Rembrandt was a success. He was painting the very rich. He was making a great deal of money, and he was probably the envy of a good many of his fellow artists.

Could it be that Rembrandt, the successful careerist, had come to feel a surfeit, even some sense of revulsion at flattering all these new rich society people, at getting so rich himself at what his fellow painters considered one of the meanest occupations of all for an artist, and that he felt some compulsion to get back to the history painting that he had considered his true calling? Indeed, in 1634, of twenty paintings (more or less) that he did, six are history paintings. And, in 1635, out of fifteen pictures, five are histories. He was maintaining a nearly consistent rate of producing history paintings, it would seem, but gradually he was letting portraiture fall by the wayside.

It seems odd that Rembrandt, who is most deeply admired these days for his portraits, should have really preferred doing something else—but it is not unusual for artists and writers to become famous for things they thought they only tossed off for money or entertainment. Rembrandt's fellow countryman Erasmus became famous in his own lifetime and is remembered today for having written *The Praise of Folly*, which he turned out in a few days and considered his most trivial work. What he considered important—his *Adagia*, for instance, or his *Enchiridion*—are almost impossible to find any more in a bookstore.

Just a few days before Rembrandt and Saskia had been married, Rembrandt and Uylenburgh had apparently been sitting in the studio together when a traveller from Weimar named Burchard Grossman came by to look at paintings and other art objects for sale. Grossman had a little album that he kept with him in which he collected autographs or little favorite sayings or sketches from the famous people he met on his journeys, and he asked Uylenburgh and Rembrandt to write something in his album. One can imagine the three men sitting around a table, Rembrandt taking the book, turning it sideways,

Sketch of Uylenburgh and Inscription in Burchard Gross-
mann's Album, 1634

and doing a quick pen sketch of an old man with a white beard, his head cocked slightly to one side, as though engrossed in conversation—this might be Grossman, but more probably is Uylenburgh, because beneath the sketch Rembrandt added a common saying that seems to speak to the art dealer. "A pious mind," says the inscription, "places honor above wealth," as much as to say, it is better to do history painting than get rich doing portraits. Presumably Rembrandt passed the book then to Uylenburgh, and, as they carried on their conversation with Grossman, they conducted a private exchange in the album. "In restraint," wrote Uylenburgh, "lies strength," as much as to say, hold off, don't be impulsive, don't jump into things, make money first, you have a wife to think of now.

But self-restraint was not one of Rembrandt's talents. Perhaps he thought now he was a famous enough artist in Amsterdam that he could do what he liked. Perhaps he thought, after his marriage to Saskia, and with her money, that he could afford to drop the lucrative portrait trade—or at least to take the gamble on making a living from history painting alone. Perhaps his marriage caused him to think again about what he was doing with his life and made him anxious about frittering it away doing society portraits. Or perhaps marriage simply gave him a feeling of exhilaration. Certainly, if his paintings can be relied on to give us any sense of his life with Saskia, he was enjoying an extraordinary feeling of confidence, even exuberance. Maybe Saskia encouraged him to take the risk. In any case, in 1636, he stopped painting portraits altogether. So much for success at something other than your true calling, no matter how good at it you are. For the next three years, he painted not one single portrait—not even a portrait of Saskia, not even a self-portrait. After establishing himself as the leading portrait painter of Amsterdam, he dropped portraiture entirely. It was no small gamble for an artist who could look around and see so many of his fellow painters headed for the poorhouse.

Soon after his marriage to Saskia, Rembrandt dropped Cousin Uylenburgh, too, which must have left some strained relations. He and Saskia not only moved out into rooms in the nearby home of the widow, but Rembrandt stopped using Uylenburgh altogether as his dealer. Indeed, Rembrandt set up as an art dealer on his own. In 1635, he made a few purchases, collectively worth eighteen guilders, at art auctions. By 1637 his purchases totalled 130 guilders; by 1638, 224 guilders. He was becoming his own man, completely independent. And he was having it both ways, or hoping to; he painted only histories; and he had become a merchant. Nothing beats the bohemian life of an artist if he has the income of a merchant.

Having set up on his own, then, he painted all sorts of things—as long as they fell within the artist's highest calling of history painting. Immediately he turned out three paintings based on compositions of his old master Pieter Lastman, who died in 1633. (Perhaps the death of Lastman had been another motivation for Rembrandt to return to history painting— whether by inspiration, or as a reminder of what he had originally set out to do, or as an opportunity to fill a vacancy in the ranks of Amsterdam history painters.) The three compositions included one of the angel stopping Abraham from sacrificing his son Isaac, another of the flight of the Holy Family into Egypt, and another of Susanna surprised by the elders as she bathes naked. He also painted a vast canvas of the goddess Diana and nineteen other nudes bathing. It would be pleasing to be able to find personal meanings in all these paintings—something about fathers and sons, say, or a newfound interest in nudes because Rembrandt's marriage had led him to be preoccupied with sex. But there is not enough evidence to corroborate any such guesses. And it may well be that a patron asked for a painting of the naked Susanna, or that Susannas were selling briskly in the market, or even that Rembrandt was just taking up a few commissions that Lastman had left unfinished at his death.

In any case, Rembrandt still had his taste for vigorous drama, and melodrama. In this new, exuberant burst of energy, he tried his hand at landscapes for the first time, too, and painted scenes of the Dutch countryside that have nothing whatever to do with the Netherlands. In their dramatic lighting, mountainous dunes and cliffs, giant gnarled trees and raging rivers, they are pure dramatic fantasy.

Susanna at the Bath, and the Two Elders. Drawing, about
1637–38

He painted Abraham's sacrifice of Isaac in two versions, if both paintings are authentic. Both paintings, in any case, capture the very millisecond before Abraham, at God's command, is about to slash his son's neck. One of the father's massive hands covers his son's face, the other has been raised with the knife; the boy's head is thrust back and pinned to the ground by his father's hand; the boy's arms are tied behind his back. He is the size of a young man, ready to begin his grownup life, but he is a child, too, still with a child's slight pudginess. In Rembrandt's first version of the scene, the angel appears just in front of Abraham and reaches out to stay Abraham's hand that holds the knife. In the second version, the angel appears suddenly from behind—and so catches Abraham completely by surprise. Abraham's upraised wrist has been seized by the angel; and the dagger drops from Abraham's hand—Rembrandt has caught it in mid-air—as the man's head whirls around in bewilderment and anguish, love and dumb belief.

He painted the moment of the blinding of Samson, a moment even more dramatic, or melodramatic, than that of Abraham's sacrifice of Isaac. In the Samson painting, Delilah is fleeing from the scene with a pair of shears in one hand and a hank of hair in the other while Samson is pinned to the ground by four burly fellows in armor. One has him in a choke-hold; another hauls back on one of his arms with a length of chain; a third threatens him with upraised sword; and the fourth—here is the goriest version ever painted of this subject—drives a dagger right into Samson's eyeball, and the juice spurts out. The real question is: Who would want such a painting on the parlor wall?

Then, too, Rembrandt was still interested in painting miracles. Having painted Tobit back in 1626, and having done nothing about the story since, in 1636 he went back to it. And this time he shows Tobit's son Tobias, having returned from his journey, attended by the angel Raphael, curing his father of blindness. According to the biblical story, Tobias laid the gall of a fish on his father's eyes, because Raphael had told him this would cure blindness. In Rembrandt's painting, Tobias, holding a needle in his hand, is leaning intently over his father, performing an operation on one of his father's eyes. According to Dr. Richard Greef, Tobias is performing a medically perfect removal of a cataract. Perhaps Rembrandt had watched such an operation? It is known that Dr. Job Janszoon van Meekren, a pupil of Dr. Tulp, had specialized in eye operations since 1635, the year before Rembrandt painted this picture. The event as Rembrandt painted it is a miracle of human making.

At some point in the 1630s, Rembrandt got to know some members of the Jewish community, or at least became acquainted with a young Jewish scholar and rabbi named Menasseh ben Israel who lived just a few doors down from Uylenburgh in Sint Antoniesbreestraat. Menasseh was uncommonly bright. Among other things he had written a comprehensive Hebrew grammar when he was only seventeen. By the time Rembrandt met him, when he was thirty, he knew ten languages, and he ran the leading Jewish press in northern Europe. He also had some radical ideas—that the coming of the Messiah was at hand, for example, a notion that must have intrigued Rembrandt, who always liked to show the past breaking in on the present. Such ideas put Menasseh outside the circles of the orthodox members of the Jewish community, and made him congenial to Rembrandt, who was doubtless upsetting some of his orthodox Christian neighbors by insisting on painting Jesus as a Jew.

In some instances, it is possible to see Menasseh's direct influence on Rembrandt. Menasseh wrote a book called *The Glorious Stone, or Nebuchadnezzar's Dream* (Menasseh considered the dream of Nebuchadnezzar in the Book of Daniel proof that the Messiah was at hand), and Rembrandt made four etchings to illustrate the book. Rembrandt also did a spectacular picture of Belshazzar's Feast, at which Belshazzar, Nebuchadnezzar's son, suddenly rises from the table (wine goblets knocked over, the other guests drawing back in astonishment) to see the handwriting on the wall: *"Mene, mene, tekel upharsin. . . ."* (God hath numbered thy kingdom and finished it. . . . Thou art weighed in the balance and found want-

The Synagogue. Etching, 1648

ing. . . . Thy kingdom is divided. . . .) And, according to Menasseh, who probably told Rembrandt how to do the script for the handwriting, the Messiah was about to appear.

What more general influence Menasseh and other of the Jews in the Breestraat had on Rembrandt is hard to know, although some sense of closeness might be deduced from the fact that no other Amsterdam painter did as many portraits of Jews as Rembrandt. One scholar has guessed that about a fifth of Rembrandt's portraits of men are of Jews—this at a time when the Jews represented perhaps one percent of the population of Amsterdam. This would fit with the general impression that Rembrandt gives of a temperament moved more by personal warmth than by ideology.

With nearly everything he did, Rembrandt stirred things up. First, and most astonishingly to his contemporaries, he mixed his categories—doing portraits as though they were history paintings and history paintings as though they were genre paintings of everyday life. Just as he did the group portrait of Dr. Tulp as though it were a dramatic painting rather than a group portrait, so he would put low life into high drama. He would slip a bit of lewd sex into a scene that was meant to be prim, a few swilling drunks into a solemn biblical story. He would put real emotions and recognizable people into the past, something of the exotic into the familiar and something of the familiar into the exotic. His biblical heroes and heroines often looked not so much like noble and ideal people as one's next door neighbors—or worse, people you might see in a tavern. He brought things down-to-earth. He tossed in gore and modern surgery. He brought things home. He held nothing back. As he used chiaroscuro, so he jarred his paintings with sudden—some would say vulgar, certainly irreverent—juxtapositions. He was not above bad taste. He was unpopular for this, and popular, too. No one else did this as he did. He brought a thrill to painting. He was a great democratizer. It may be that the greatest gift art has to give us is to set us free of old limits of perception, thought and feeling; certainly that is what Rembrandt does above all in painting after painting after painting.

His friends were definitely in bad taste. Beginning in 1635,

Rembrandt began to do all sorts of sketches of disreputable performers who appeared in theatrical works reckoned lewd by the authorities, pieces that had to be closed down by the burgomasters from time to time, pieces insulting to the Calvinist church or to the police or simply to society in general. Rembrandt sketched character after character from theatrical performances—the theater, after all, was his natural home. He befriended the low-life types from the theater and, no doubt, other marginal types who passed through the artists' quarter as well. Joachim von Sandrart, a German artist and writer and a bit of a dandy who worked in Amsterdam in the late 1630s and early 1640s, noted in a book he wrote that Rembrandt, who was then among the most famous artists in Amsterdam, "although he was no wastrel . . . did not at all manage to consider his own station, but always associated only with lowly people. . . ."

And when he came to paint a picture of St. John preaching, he filled the picture with lowly people listening to the saint—or, rather, he showed some people listening in rapt attention, a couple of others walking idly away in gossip, another dozing off, another sitting there just to rest his feet, a mother trying to calm a restless child, a whole gaggle of humanity behaving in just the way it tends to during great historic moments. There is no pretension here, no inflated moment, no otherworldly saint. There is nothing properly Calvinist going on here, nothing upper class. Here is divinity set firmly on earth—still divine, but thoroughly humanized.

This painting of St. John bothered one of Rembrandt's students, Samuel van Hoogstraten, desperately. Van Hoogstraten studied with Rembrandt in the early 1640s, and he never forgot this painting of St. John. It stayed in his mind for years, nagging him, because, it seemed to him, it betrayed his great master's "lack of intellectual sophistication." Although some might say that what the painting showed was "normal and natural," van Hoogstraten said, he himself considered one marginal event depicted in the lower lefthand corner of the composition "an execrable impropriety in a History," one that rendered the whole painting no better than "ludicrous."

What was it in the lower lefthand corner that roused such a reaction in van Hoogstraten, and, very likely, in so many others who saw this painting of Rembrandt's and others like it? In the offending lower lefthand corner of the picture—a *biblical* picture, not a picture of daily life or of the present day but a picture of an important and somber historical event, a picture of a saint preaching the word of God—is a dog, defecating.

How to Handle
a Patron

F

EBRUARY 1636
My Lord
My noble Lord
Huygens, Councillor and Secretary to His
Excellency
Postage [paid] The Hague

My Lord, my gracious Lord Huygens, I hope your lordship will be so kind as to advise His Excellency [Frederik Hendrik] that I am diligently engaged in completing as quickly as possible the three Passion pictures which His Excellency has personally commissioned me to do. . . .

This can hardly be a surprise: Having set out on his own to do history paintings, having had a little time to reflect on the precariousness of his income, having had a chance to canvas

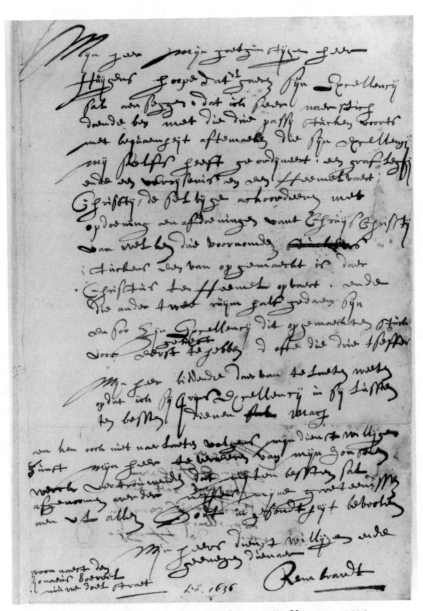

Letter to Constantijn Huygens, 1636

prospective clients in Amsterdam, Rembrandt is now scrambling for patrons. And his first thought is to send off a letter to Constantijn Huygens, a classic letter to a patron, full of flattering obeisances to the purse holder, assurances about his own diligence and sense of responsibility, and anxious reminders of past commitments in case anyone has forgotten ("which His Excellency has *personally* commissioned me to do . . .").

Whether Huygens will believe it is another matter. Apparently, before Rembrandt had arrived in Amsterdam, Huygens had gotten him a commission to do a series of paintings of the crucifixion, entombment, and resurrection of Christ. Rembrandt had done two paintings out of a series of five—the elevation of Christ on the Cross, and Christ being taken down from the cross—which he finished up after he had arrived in Amsterdam and delivered in 1632 and 1633. Then, for some reason, he dropped the commission. Perhaps he had become too busy with portrait commissions and no longer needed the work from The Hague. Or perhaps he had never meant to do a series of paintings to begin with. These first two paintings don't really go together: The *Elevation* is painted on canvas; the *Descent* is painted on wood panel. It is just barely conceivable that these were two old paintings that Rembrandt simply had around his studio, and that he had pawned them off on Huygens with some fast talk about a series of works on the Passion.

In any event, here he was—three years later—talking about how he was finishing up his commission as quickly as possible. Of course, he claimed to Huygens, he was taking such great care with the paintings that only one more was finished, and two others were only "half finished" (one wonders if brush had yet touched canvas on these two). "Please, sir, let me know whether it would please His Excellency to have the finished piece first, or all three together, so that I may best serve His Excellency the Prince, according to his desires." Then, just to sweeten the old relationship, Rembrandt put in a few prints that he had done—for Huygens to keep as a gift.

The hypocrisy of an artist is a terrible thing, but, then, this business of fund raising took its toll. Rembrandt's countryman

Desiderius Erasmus of Rotterdam wrote a lot of grant-seeking letters to patrons, and it always put him in a bad humor. Just a hundred years before Rembrandt's letter to Huygens, Erasmus had written a potential patron, Lady Anne of Veere, a letter of such outrageous insincerity that he could not get it out of his system until he wrote a letter to his friend James Batt ("may I die if I ever in my life wrote anything with so much repugnance, as the nonsense . . . which I have written for the Lady . . .").

For Huygens' part, whether he sniffed any hypocrisy in all this or not, he was probably content to put aside his suspicions: The first two paintings had been extremely good. *The Elevation of the Cross* shows the crucifix at the moment it is being swung up to a vertical position, as though Christ were being cast up into the sky as a sacrifice, and *The Descent from the Cross* is an equally powerful picture of five men lowering a sack of broken, limp flesh to the ground.

Presumably Huygens replied to Rembrandt's letter—as far as we know Rembrandt didn't save the letter, he was never good at filing—expressing pleasure at hearing of Rembrandt's progress, thanking Rembrandt for his gift of the etchings, and asking that Rembrandt send the first painting along at once. Rembrandt dispatched the painting immediately, and then evidently got another letter from Huygens, this one expressing displeasure.

This third painting went with the first two even less than the second had gone with the first. The first two were dark, moody pictures, full of a feeling of tragedy and lament. The third picture, of the Ascension, was naturally more triumphant, but it also lacked a certain depth of feeling. It was filled with little cherubs accompanying the ascending Christ, and people back on the ground reeling in astonishment. Altogether it was on the conventional side; certainly it was not up to Rembrandt's own standard of high drama and surprising new touches. Huygens evidently asked Rembrandt to come to The Hague and look at the three paintings together to see whether he could do anything to make them look more like a set. Meanwhile, he asked Rembrandt how much he expected to be paid.

My Lord
My Lord Huygens
Secretary to His Excellency the Prince
The postage is paid.
My dear Sir, first let me offer my kind regards. I agree
that I should come soon to see how the picture accords
with the rest.

So Rembrandt did not get into any unseemly fight over how well the three paintings went together. He promised, possibly with the thought that Huygens would forget the promise anyway, to come and take a look—a promise he never kept so far as we know. And, as for the price, he had been paid six hundred guilders each for the first two paintings. What could he possibly do, given the fact that he was several years behind schedule, and that his latest painting was not entirely liked, but to ask for twice as much for this one? "I certainly deserve 1200 guilders for it," he wrote Huygens—though he added, with a politic sense of handling patrons, "I shall be content with whatever His Excellency pays me."

How much Huygens paid for this third painting, we don't know. Probably not a bit more than six hundred guilders. As for Rembrandt, having gotten his money, he dropped the commission again.

The Dealer

Today, 17 December 1637, appeared before me, Benedict Baddel, notary public . . . in person, as follows, Outger Maertsz Groot, about twenty years old . . . and Dirck Hendricksz, about sixteen years old . . . who, at the request of Samuel d'Orta, a Portuguese painter . . . [now] attest, testify, and declare that yesterday . . . in the evening, they were present, heard, and observed that the plaintiff complained at his house to a certain Reijnbrand van Rhijn, a fellow painter . . . that he, van Rhijn, had not treated him properly as regards a certain print . . . of which the aforementioned van Rhijn had sold him the plate. . . .

Justice was swift in Amsterdam. A neighborhood row breaks out one evening; the next day the squabblers are on their way through the judicial process; by afternoon, the dispute is solved, the records are filed, and life resumes. Such dispatch, such effi-

ciency, such availability, such ease: It left a trail of legal documents in many people's lives, but the courts were not permitted
to bog down. This was a town of merchants who wanted to settle their disputes and get on with business while their oppor-
tunities were still hot.

What Rembrandt had done was to sell an etching plate of one
of his etchings to Samuel d'Orta. Artists almost never sold their
plates: They kept them to make more prints and sell the prints.
In this case, evidently, d'Orta wanted to buy a plate so that he
could make and sell Rembrandt prints. And Rembrandt let him
have this one—an etching of Abraham and Hagar—a good deal
for Rembrandt since, in truth, it was not one of his better etchings. Rembrandt sold it to d'Orta with the promise that he,
Rembrandt, had not kept any prints from the plate himself except for two or three that he would use only as reference and that
"he would not sell them to anyone."

"The aforementioned Reijnbrant van Rijn did clearly and repeatedly agree and admit that he had promised not to sell any
prints and had promised not to sell the three or four [already
it's more than two or three] of the same which he still had in
his possession (so he said)."

So Rembrandt had been selling these prints—or d'Orta had
good reason to believe he was about to. Maybe there had been
rumors in Sint Antoniesbreestraat. Maybe one of d'Orta's
friends told him he was a fool to trust Rembrandt. Evidently
the argument in front of Rembrandt's house drew a crowd—the
two young men who appeared as witnesses before the notary
were in the crowd. Even in the midst of that public uproar,
d'Orta thought Rembrandt was trying to cling shrewdly to a
technicality, saying specifically that he would not sell *the three
or four prints* in his possession. Did he have no more than three
or four prints in his possession? *"So he said."* But d'Orta had
Rembrandt anyway: In front of witnesses, Rembrandt had distinctly said he had agreed not to sell *any* prints. The statement
was recorded before a notary. Now no more prints had better
appear on the market than the ones d'Orta made, or he would
have a clear basis for a lawsuit. (How, d'Orta must have won-

Abraham Casting Out Hagar and Ishmael. Etching, 1637

dered, could he keep Rembrandt from selling prints surrepti-
tiously, through friends, to buyers perhaps in foreign countries?
Total peace of mind could be assured to no man, not even by
Amsterdam's legal system.)

It may be that d'Orta libeled Rembrandt with this accusation
of sharp practice, but it is not likely. Art dealers, throughout
history, have never been held up to children as models to emulate, and Rembrandt had been trained, after all, by Hendrick
Uylenburgh. According to Sandrart, Rembrandt also tried to
manipulate the market in his own work—buying back his prints
"all over Europe, wherever he could find them, at any price"
in order to keep or drive prices up. "Among others he bought
one for 50 scudi at a sale by auction in Amsterdam, which was
a *Raising of Lazarus*, and this he did while himself possessing
the copper-plate engraved by his own hand." There is no archi-
val evidence to back up Sandrart's story, but the idea does not
seem out of character for Rembrandt, or any dealer.

But Rembrandt was not only shrewd; he was too shrewd by
half. This effort to inflate the prices of his own prints, if he
made it, was doomed to fail, and to be monstrously expensive:
The market was already too big for Rembrandt to control in
this way. And otherwise, in the course of his career as a businessman, he was a pathetic amateur. He tended to buy high and
sell low. The archives contain a few records of good trades that
he made. In 1637, for example, he bought a Rubens for 424
guilders, and seven years later he sold it for 530 guilders. But
more often he paid too much for things and had to sell them at
a loss, if he could sell them at all. He seemed to get carried
away at auctions—jumping in at the beginning with a high bid
that scared other buyers out, or getting caught up in the auction and winning with a bid that was much too high. One of
his students said he once saw Rembrandt at an auction pay 1400
guilders for fourteen prints by Lucas van Leyden—an extravagant one hundred guilders a print, twice as much as it would
cost to commission an original oil portrait.

It may be that Rembrandt was simply moved by the greatness
of others, and unable to restrain his impulses when he saw some

wonderful drawing or painting or antique sculpture come up on the auction block. Or it may be that he liked to be seen as a big spender, a man who didn't have to count his money carefully. His friends grilled him about his reckless spending, and he finally gave them an explanation that sounds plausible, knowing his terrible sense of pride, his sense of being not quite the equal of the Amsterdam merchant society. He paid high prices for art, one of the artists in Sint Antoniesbreestraat quoted him as saying, "in order to emphasize the prestige of his profession."

18

The Teacher

S OMETIMES, depressed by my master's teaching, I would cry, and, going without food or drink, I would not leave my work until I had amended the fault . . .

So Samuel van Hoogstraten recalled studying with Rembrandt. No doubt van Hoogstraten was overly sensitive, but Rembrandt suffered no nonsense either. Students were a money-making proposition taken in to support Rembrandt in his own career, not brought in to coddle. Not only did Rembrandt demand the steep sum of one hundred guilders per student per year for his instruction (which meant that a lot of his pupils were the children of the rich), but, like all masters, if Rembrandt approved of something one of his students did, he signed his name to it and sold it and kept the money himself. According to Sandrart, Rembrandt sometimes had as many as twenty-five pupils at a time, which brought him 2500 guilders a year from fees alone. To be sure, he had some expenses; by 1637, he had so many students he had to rent an entire stout little warehouse across town on the Bloemgracht to have room for them all—and some of the prints he bought at auction were meant to be taken back to his school to be used for students to copy—but profits were terrific.

In effect, Rembrandt now had his own art factory, just as Uylenburgh had had his. In addition to his students, Rembrandt had several full-fledged assistants over the years who were of considerably higher standing in the pecking order. But in one respect at least they were all equal: They all tried to copy what the master did as exactly as they could; so that, if he liked it, Rembrandt signed the work of his assistants as well as his pupils—or retouched it a bit and then signed it—and so created even more confusion for future scholars over which paintings were authentic Rembrandts.

Among other things, Rembrandt apparently sat his pupils down with pen and paper in front of a mirror to practice on their own self-portraits, and so there are, in prints and drawing collections here and there around the world, a number of self-studies of earnest young faces: Heyman Dullaert, a musing, quizzical young fellow with long blond hair and a jaunty, feathered hat, was a poet as well as a painter; Nicolaes Maes (if it is he), a scant fourteen years old, well-scrubbed, with delicate slender hands, and a grownup frown of concentration; Aert de Gelder, a round-faced young man in a frilly shirt and floppy hat, who would always remain faithful to the master's commitment to biblical and mythological scenes; Willem Drost, in a wide-brimmed, stovepipe hat, head slightly cocked, a smile on his lips, a pupil who would study Rembrandt's way of etching with particular care.

Even more famous than these four were van Hoogstraten, from whom we have already heard, who painted nearly everything, and wrote poetry and plays as well; Ferdinand Bol, who joined Rembrandt in 1636, first as pupil and then as assistant, and became one of Amsterdam's best portraitists; Gerbrand van den Eeckhout, the son of a goldsmith, who joined Rembrandt about 1635 and who would do very Rembrandtesque biblical scenes in later years; and Govert Flinck, who came to Rembrandt in 1633, having already served an apprenticeship in Leeuwarden and possibly, too, with Uylenburgh in Amsterdam. Flinck worked as an assistant to Rembrandt until 1636, when he left to become chief portraitist in the rival firm of . . . Uylenburgh! One would like to think that Rembrandt handed his talented assistant back over to Uylenburgh to help out an old business partner, especially since Rembrandt was moving out of the portrait business, but the more likely interpretation is that, in the competitive spirit of the Amsterdam art market, Uylenburgh stole Flinck from Rembrandt.

Rembrandt's studio looked almost like a museum, filled as it was with the treasures he had bought at auction: a wooden trumpet, costumes for an Indian man and woman, swords, halberds, Indian fans, seashells, silver trays, busts of Roman emperors, terrestrial globes, specimens of land and sea creatures, iron helmets, African spears, crossbows, powder horns, suits of armor, pistols, a small cannon, gourds, walking sticks, Venetian glass, baskets, animal skins, robes, anatomical plaster casts, nude statues, friezes, a harp, bamboo wind instruments, baskets, stags' horns, portfolios and scrapbooks of prints and drawings (including works by Adam Elsheimer, Lucas van Leyden, Albrecht Dürer, and Caravaggio). According to Sandrart, he was "a great lover of art in its various forms . . . of which he possessed a great number, displaying a great keenness about such matters. This was the reason why many people thought very highly of him and praised him." To have such a collection was useful as a source of studio props, but what was perhaps even more important for Rembrandt: Collections such as these were the mark of a gentleman.

In the loft where his students worked, he had put up partitions of paper or canvas to give each student a private cubicle to work in; but, to judge from the sketches that some of his pupils left behind, a group of students would often cluster around a model, to draw from life, and the master would go from student to student, making comments, or, sometimes, with a pen or brush, making corrections on the student's work. Sometimes, to illustrate a point, the master himself would dash off a

Rembrandt's Studio with Pupils Drawing from the Nude.
Drawing, 1650–60

The Artist Drawing from a Model: Unfinished Plate. Etching, 1639

sketch; some of these sketches survive, some of them copied exactly.

The master did his own self-portrait, too, as he must have looked at the center of this scene: In his narrow-brimmed stove-pipe hat, a sleeved, belted smock that goes all the way down to his shins, soft slippers, his hands on his hips, he looks as solid as a warehouse.

A drawing by one of Rembrandt's students shows what went on in class. A naked model reclines on a couch. The master is drawing on paper. An old man (not all of Rembrandt's students were necessarily young, some were aging amateurs) has paused in his drawing to study the model. A young man, who squats on the floor to one side, is studying his own drawing. Another young man, leaning against the wall at the left, is drawing in a small sketchbook. And two young men stand in the background, with drawing materials in their hands. One of them leans over to get a good look at what the old man is doing. These two are not drawing at all but only watching. Their turn will come later, after they see how the master does it.

The course of learning was firmly set. Working on a grainy white paper with a flexible swan's quill or goose pen or with a brittle reed pen, with brush and ink and red, black, and colored chalk (corrections with white chalk, shading with a smudged finger), the students first copied prints and drawings. Once they had mastered these, they moved on to plaster models, and finally to live models. One of Rembrandt's etchings of an artist drawing from a model may itself be a lesson in how to draw. The etching is, perhaps purposely, "unfinished," that is to say, the figure of the artist is very roughly sketched in; the model is more precisely drawn; and the background of the studio, with its props of draperies and plaster busts, is completely finished. As a whole, then, the etching shows three stages in making a finished drawing—and, as usual, Rembrandt has begun to work out the details starting in the background and moving forward.

Occasionally, a whole clutch of drawings has survived: an etching by Rembrandt, for example, of a seated male nude, his hands clasped before him, his head turned to one side; followed by a student's drawing of the same subject, with a slightly different feeling, with the head cast languidly to one side, as though the model were tired of posing; or a Rembrandt etching of a standing male nude, daydreaming; followed by a student's copy of the same model, where the daydreaming looks rather like discouragement, or another where the daydreaming looks like annoyance, or another where the model looks like a sneering aesthete.

In a few rare instances, a student's drawing survives with the master's firm, bold corrections in India ink. On a student's drawing of the Annunciation, for example, where a modest, sweet-tempered angel speaks to a timid Mary, Rembrandt has moved in to ink an angel a couple of feet taller than the student's version—to bring a real supernatural presence into the room. In a drawing of Job lamenting with his wife and a friend standing nearby, Rembrandt has cast in a whole new figure standing in front of Job with his arms raised to heaven, and he has turned Job to face directly front, and raised one of his arms to heaven, too, to give the whole scene a sense of anguish. In a drawing of Christ on the Cross, Rembrandt took a stiff reed brush and penned in some emphatic strokes to keep Christ and Mary and John clearly in focus. In a drawing of Jacob saying farewell to his son Benjamin, who is about to depart for Egypt, Rembrandt has made sure that the donkey being loaded in the background is seen distinctly—so that we notice right away that the scene is about a departure. At the bottom of another drawing—either done by Rembrandt to illustrate a point, or done by a pupil under the master's guidance—Rembrandt wrote, "This should be amplified with many neighbors who watch this highborn bride depart." In almost every case, what Rembrandt's corrections call for are a greater clarity in the figures, a re-arrangement of the composition—always with a view to sharpening the dramatic focus of the picture.

What other tips did Rembrandt have for his students? Van Hoogstraten codified some of the rules—some, perhaps, no more than general precepts of the time, others with a slant that seems Rembrandtesque: "One must not neglect, right from the beginning, to look at the shadows," van Hoogstraten notes, which sounds like the master's obsessive interest in dramatic lighting.

"Be content," van Hoogstraten quotes Rembrandt as saying, when the pupil was pestering him with too many questions, trying to think too far ahead of what he was doing at the time, "to put into your work the things you already know, and you will soon enough discover the secrets that you ask of now."

Some of Rembrandt's lessons are apparent not from what documents we have but from what documents we don't have. Nowhere among the surviving students' drawings are there any anatomical studies of muscles. The pupils must have done some, but the master was not interested in merely realistic representations of the human anatomy. What his students saved from his classes were drawings of the human form showing light and shadow, movement and mood—drawings that captured the moment.

Above all, said Sandrart, "he alleged that one should be guided only by Nature and by no other rules." What Rembrandt meant by this was what Caravaggio and Lastman had meant— to avoid those ideal, beautiful bodies of the classical Italian tradition, paintings deduced from ideas of perfect proportion and the correct depiction of noble virtues; to look to the everyday world, especially for plain, gawky, awkward models, not for the sake of accurate, "realistic" depiction but rather for the sake of democratizing the event and bringing it home, for the sake of removing a sense of false nobility, for the sake of emotional and dramatic impact for the sake of opening up his sense of pleasure to take in more of the world around him.

Rembrandt's liking for homely models was not always shared (or, perhaps, even understood) by his students, who may have been hoping for pretty young women to draw. "I certainly regret," said van Hoogstraten, who seems not to have had a good time studying with Rembrandt, "when I look at my old Academie drawings, that our youthfulness was so spared in the teaching: it being no more work to depict a graceful model than an unpleasing and loathsome one." Van Hoogstraten seems to have been a man who bore a grudge; he passed this judgment on Rembrandt down to his own pupil, Arnold Houbraken, who wrote almost ninety years later, "His nude women . . . the most wonderful subject of the brush, upon which all celebrated masters from time immemorial spent all their industry, are (as the saying goes) too pitiful for one to make a song about. For these are invariably figures before which one feels repugnance, so that one can only wonder that a man of such talent and spirit was so self-willed in the choice of his models. . . ."

But this is not all the students said behind the great man's back. Another bit of gossip, or invention, was that Rembrandt was so greedy for money that his students one day, to play a joke on him, painted a coin on the floor and all waited around to see the master bend down and try to pick it up. (Or it may be that this is just another variation on the sort of story that begins, 'He captured a likeness so perfectly that if he painted a coin on the floor . . .'.)

Another piece of gossip that came down from his students, whether true or false, may contain a kernel of Rembrandt's feeling, by this time, about painting society portraits. According to the story, Rembrandt had a pet monkey. The master was working on a group portrait of a man and his wife and children, so the story goes, when the monkey happened to die. "As he had no other canvas available at the moment," said Houbraken, "he portrayed the dead ape in the aforesaid picture." Naturally, the family whose portrait now included "a disgusting dead ape" in the middle of it was not pleased at the way the commission was turning out and asked Rembrandt to remove the dead ape. But Rembrandt refused and, rather than finish the commission and get his money, kept the picture in his studio, and used it as a dividing wall for one of the students' cubicles.

On Top of the World

B Y THE LATE 1630s, Rembrandt was on top of the world. He was rich, famous, happily married, flourishing at the work he wanted to do, living in a city he sketched with pleasure, surrounded by art he loved. Exactly which paintings and sculptures and household furnishings surrounded him in the late 1630s are hard to pin down; they were something more than those he had for the use of his pupils, and not yet all that would be listed in an inventory of his household possessions in 1656. But he was on his way to the vast collection he would have in 1656. Among many other things he had a little painting of a pastry cook by Adriaen Brouwer, a still life of food by Brouwer, a candlelight scene by Lievens, a moonlight scene by Lievens, a raising of Lazarus by Lievens, a hermit by Lievens, a plaster cast of two naked children, a landscape by Hercules Seghers, some small houses by Seghers, a wooded landscape by Seghers, a Tobias by Pieter Lastman, a small ox by Lastman, a portrait head by the great Raphael of Urbino, a mirror in an ebony frame, a marble wine-cooling bucket, a walnut table, a copper kettle, an embroidered tablecloth, an oak stand, some rare Venetian glass, a Chinese bowl filled with minerals, a small backgammon board, a large lump of white coral, an East Indian basket, a bird of paradise, a marble ink stand, a bin filled with thirty-three antique hand weapons and wind instruments, a bin of sixty Indian hand weapons, arrows, javelins and bows, a bin of thirteen bamboo wind instruments, a harp, a Turkish bow, seventeen hands and arms cast from life, a collection of antlers, four crossbows and footbows, five antique helmets and shields, a satyr's head with horns, a large sea plant, seven stringed instruments, a giant's head (a giant's head?), skins of both a lion and a lioness, a painting by Giorgione, another painting by Raphael, a book of prints by Lucas van Leyden, "the precious book" by Andrea Mantegna, a book of prints by the elder Brueghel, a book of prints by Raphael, a book of prints by Tempesta, a book of prints by Cranach, a book with almost all the work of Titian, a book of portraits by Rubens and others, a book full of the work of Michelangelo, a book of erotica by Raphael and others, a book of Roman architecture, baskets full of prints by Rubens, Jacob Jordaens and Titian, a book of woodcuts by Albrecht Dürer, a painting by Frans Hals, a pistol, an ornamented iron shield, a cabinet full of medals, a Turkish powder horn, a collection of shells, another of coral, forty-seven specimens of land and sea animals, a Moor's head cast from life, an East Indian sewing box, several walking sticks. . . .

Some neighbors noticed, as we know from another scrap of a document, that he and Saskia also had a diamond ring, two diamond pendants, two pear-shaped pearls, two strings of pearls, six silver spoons, a set of gold buttons with pearls, a pair of gold and enamel bracelets, a prayerbook with gold fittings, two large silver platters, a silver plate, a silver decanter, and many pewter, copper and iron utensils.

By the standards of Louis de Geer, perhaps Rembrandt and Saskia were not so wealthy, but for an artist and his wife, they were doing extraordinarily well. Their life at home together, if one can tell anything from Rembrandt's sketchbook, must have

Rembrandt with Raised Saber. Etching, 1634

been both cozy and marked by frequent sorrow. Their family was small, unlike the families they had both grown up in. Their first three children died soon after birth. Their fourth, named Titus, who was not born until 1641, was the only one to survive to adulthood. (That just one out of four of their children survived meant that Rembrandt's and Saskia's family corresponded to the statistical average, but there is no reason to think they accepted those statistics without feeling.) Saskia, then, was often pregnant, and Rembrandt sketched her frequently in bed, waiting.

It may be, too, that Saskia was frail as well as frequently pregnant. In addition to losing three children in six years, she may have inherited, as some scholars have suggested, a predisposition to tuberculosis. Then, too, it was the custom for Dutch women to fast after the seventh month of pregnancy, perhaps with the thought of keeping the baby small, but with the effect of weakening both mother and child. Childbirth itself was fraught with complications; among other things neither doctors nor midwives washed their hands. Small infections could be fatal. Typhoid fever, smallpox, and even occasional outbreaks of bubonic plague were common. There is some reason to believe that, with each year of their marriage, Saskia grew weaker and weaker, and that Rembrandt's affectionate drawings of her—done sometimes as she slept, and he sat by her bedside—were documenting a woman slipping into ever-increasing infirmity.

Even so, their life together must have had its pleasures. In any case, Saskia's relatives put it about town that the young couple had *too many* pleasures; indeed, Saskia's relatives said that Saskia had "squandered her parents' legacy by ostentatious display, vanity, and braggadocio." Evidently Saskia's relatives had had enough of rumors about the young couple's high-living ways in the artists' quarter. Rembrandt sued for libel: Not that he denied the vanity and display; but he did deny that Saskia had squandered her inheritance on their pleasures.

What could Saskia and Rembrandt have been doing? They did not live in one of the most expensive neighborhoods of Amsterdam. They didn't occupy a large and lavish house. They had not bought a country house, or even a little garden plot out of town, as so many other well-to-do Dutch burghers did. Surely the relatives would not have been upset if they had heard, for example, that Saskia and Rembrandt were employing a housekeeper, as so many other Dutch people did. As far as we know, they lived a typical burgher's life: the master of the house, bundled up in his dressing gown, throwing open the shutters at daybreak, stepping out the front door to check the weather, exchanging a few words with the neighbors, seeing the milkman and the baker come down the street hawking milk and rolls, standing by as the servant took the chamber pot from under the bed and emptied it in the canal; eating breakfast silently (the master of the house with his hat on his head) at a bare wooden table—with pewter pots and earthenware plates, with fingers and the assistance of a knife (forks appeared about 1650, but they were not common until 1700)—the faint sunlight coming in through colored glass, a good deal of butter, cheese and, later in the day, salted meat, meat broth, a great deal of fish, bread, the ever-recurring *hutsepot* (of chopped beef or mutton, green vegetables, parsnips or prunes, lemon or orange juice, boiled with fat and ginger), fresh vegetables (the Dutch were the biggest consumers of vegetables in all Europe), beer (for breakfast, lunch, and dinner); an end of business hours by late afternoon, and back home to cap and dressing gown, sitting for a while on the bench in front of the house, gossiping, watching the children play, then a simple supper of bread and butter and cheese, parlor games and singing—so that, by ten o'clock at night, the streets were deserted except for the town criers, who whirled their rattles and announced every hour on the hour through the night.

None of this suggests ostentatious display. Ostentatious display suggests, rather, that the fancy clothes and jewelry in which Rembrandt had been painting Saskia were not just studio costumes for the sake of a portrait but were actually the clothes she wore around town. It suggests parties—not just quiet dinner parties but large, loud, boisterous parties that became the gossip, even the scandal, of the town. It suggests that the young couple were seen often at theatrical entertainments of a not entirely respectable sort. It suggests that Rembrandt and Saskia were spending time in some of the more expensive parlors in town, that the artist and his wife were feted by some of his well-to-do patrons and their friends.

The case appeared before the court in Friesland in July of 1638. (Another instance of swift justice in the Netherlands: Rembrandt's relatives made their charge on July fifth; the case was in court and settled on July sixteenth.) Rembrandt's attorney—speaking for Rembrandt as the guardian of Saskia—stated that, far from squandering Saskia's parents' legacy, Rembrandt and Saskia were fortunately, for the world's information, "quite well off and were favored with a superabundance of earthly possessions (for which they can never express sufficient gratitude to the good Lord). . . ." They were not poor, they were not struggling. They had no need to dip into Saskia's inheritance to support the manner of living that had come to the attention of Saskia's relatives. "And because this charge is (praise God) entirely contrary to the truth," and because, after all, Saskia and Rembrandt had their pride, being, among other things, figures of enormous respect and standing in the artists' community in Amsterdam, "the plaintiff [Rembrandt] cannot let this pass." Thus Rembrandt, an aggrieved man of high social standing, was suing Saskia's relatives for libel—for a formal retraction, and for stiff, punitive damages of sixty-four guilders for Rembrandt and sixty-four guilders for Saskia, 128 guilders total.

The defendants replied to this. In the first place, they denied everything—that is to say, they denied committing an offense. They had not used the words they were accused of using "with the intention to offend." They had done no wrong. Nonetheless, if the court should conclude that they had slandered or libeled Saskia and Rembrandt, and in some way damaged their reputation, then the defendants asked the court to keep in mind, in assessing damages, what that reputation was worth—which was, in truth, not much, since the plaintiffs were "a mere painter and his wife." And so the defendants thought suitable damages might amount, at the most, to, say, eight guilders. Rembrandt lost the suit; he and Saskia got nothing.

To have lost was bad; to have been called "a mere painter" must have been worse. Here was a phrase to stick in the craw of Rembrandt after all those years of trying to pass for a merchant, marrying a burgomaster's daughter, becoming Amsterdam's most famous portraitist and then giving it up for a higher artistic calling.

Was it for this reason that, within six months, Rembrandt and Saskia bought one of the biggest houses in Amsterdam, a near palace of a house, a house fit for one of Amsterdam's leading merchant princes, a house of unimpeachable status and respectability right on a prime block of Sint Antoniesbreestraat, for the staggering sum of 13,000 guilders?

For this kind of money in Amsterdam, one got real grandeur. The house was, first of all, a double house, four windows wide—almost twice as wide as most of the houses in Amsterdam—and five stories high counting the semi-basement. Casement shutters swung back away from the windows, which were quite large on the first floor (eighty shining little panes of glass set in lead) and successively smaller on the upper floors. The front door was of heavy oak, waxed and polished to a glistening sheen, set in an arched frame of crisp white stone with a small classical pediment on top. Built of brick, stone, wood, and glass as most other houses in Amsterdam were, it was made grand not by the materials but by the dimensions.

It had a dozen rooms, beginning with the *voorhuis* or entrance hall, the successor to the traditional front room which served as shop or workshop for small tradesmen. Traditionally, shopkeepers would work at their benches in this room and leave the front door open and display their merchandise just outside. In Rembrandt's house, the *voorhuis* had become an elegant, well-appointed entrance hall, where the host and hostess could greet their guests, or where students or other callers could wait to see the master. It would be furnished (eventually, though not at once) with a half-dozen chairs (one of them on a raised platform near the window, to give a good view of the street), and it had white, plastered walls, where Rembrandt (the keeper of a shop dealing in paintings) put four of Brouwer's paintings, a Seghers, several Lievenses, and fourteen of his own paintings, which, as the clients waiting there no doubt observed, could easily bear comparison with the others.

To the left of the *voorhuis* was the *sael*, or best room. Families did not often use this room: They kept it for entertaining company. The same three pieces of furniture—table, chairs, and cupboard—were to be found in most rooms of the house; but the best table, chairs, and cupboard were put in the *sael*. In Rembrandt's house were seven Spanish chairs in the latest style (that is to say, with velvet upholstery, in this case green) and a good walnut table with a fine worsted tablecloth from Tournai, Belgium. The windows of the *sael* were commonly fitted with colored glass to give a subdued light to the room during the day—and the walls were hung with small mirrors to reflect and augment this subtle daylight and the candlelight at night. The floor here was tiled, and there was a fireplace in the room—and footwarmers, too (metal boxes with a cake of slow-burning peat inside), since Dutch houses were barely heated. Here, too, were some more paintings: This is where Rembrandt hung an early painting he had done of the raising of Lazarus from the dead (along with his old partner Lievens' painting of the same subject, done at the same time), and Lastman's painting of Tobias, some more Brouwers, a Lucas van Leyden, a couple of Rembrandt's own landscapes, and—crowding the wall up to the ceiling—several dozen other paintings.

Just behind the *sael* was the family room, the heart of the house, the *binnenhaert*—furnished with a plain oak table (possibly painted pink), four plain chairs with seat cushions, a copper kettle, pewter and iron utensils hung along the walls—where the mistress of the house was to be found with her servant, sewing, knitting, cooking. There was a cupboard here containing the crockery, the table linen, the sauce boats. The floor was tiled, a window opened out onto the small back yard. A big fireplace dominated one wall of the room. Foreigners, especially French travellers, could hardly believe so much space and care was devoted to the kitchen in a Dutch household, since the cuisine was so unimpressive. "They would prefer to die of hunger," said the Abbé Pierre Sartre, who passed through Hol-

Study of the Interior of a House. Drawing, about 1632–33

land about this time, "surrounded by their shining cauldrons and sparkling crockery rather than prepare any dish which might conceivably disarrange this perfect symmetry." Even here, in this combination kitchen-family room, the walls were covered with two dozen paintings. Raphael's painting of the Virgin (not a genuine Raphael) rated a place here.

Just off the *binnenhaert* was a set of steep, narrow, twisting stairs up to the bedrooms, tiny little rooms with the beds built into the walls like wall cupboards—so short that everyone slept half-sitting up on a big down bag of a mattress and piles of soft down pillows, covered by another big down bag. This is where Rembrandt made all those sketches of Saskia in bed.

There were several bedrooms here, enough for five or six children without any crowding, especially since the smallest children slept in drawers underneath the cupboard beds; and, no doubt, without those children, the house felt empty.

When the children did not appear—or survive—one of these bedrooms was eventually let slip, carelessly it seems, into a storeroom, where Rembrandt put ten of his paintings and a bedstead.

Upstairs on the next floor was Rembrandt's domain: a small studio filled with all sorts of weapons and plaster casts and musical instruments, a large studio with more weapons and some pictures, another small room filled with pictures, and then the main Art Chamber, containing 149 inventory items, including the books of prints, shelves full of weapons and powder horns and coral branches, busts of Roman emperors, paintings and drawings, along with jars of pigments, palettes, brushes, easels, mirrors, chairs and stools and benches for the assistants and students and models. The Art Chamber stretched across the front of the house, and all four windows let in the north light.

Of course, Rembrandt couldn't afford the house. He put down 1200 guilders, with another 1200 guilders due in eleven months, and the whole sum of 13,000 guilders due within six years. In order to pay for the house, Rembrandt had to go back to portrait painting—and, it seems, back to dealing through Uylenburgh to get portrait commissions.

However he felt about having to return to money grubbing,

Portrait of Maria Trip, Preliminary Study. Drawing, 1639

he threw himself into it with enormous energy. He did a dashing full-length portrait (the top price size) of the aristocratic Andries de Graeff with one glove on the ground at his feet. Just why de Graeff had thrown down the gauntlet is not clear, but he looks like the sort of man who would make you think twice before you picked it up. And Rembrandt did a modest head (and one hand) of Alijdt, the elderly widow of the wealthy Elias Trip, and then a half-length of Alijdt's daughter Maria Trip, who was on the marriage market at the time, and Rembrandt made her look lovely. (There is another surviving portrait of Maria, perhaps by Ferdinand Bol, in which she looks like a large boulder. Whether Bol was inept at capturing her likeness, or Rembrandt better understood what sort of flattery was called for, is unknowable, though one could guess.) In short, Rembrandt proved he could still get commissions, and turn out the same desirable portraits he always had.

Nonetheless, even with returning to portraiture, even with the income from his students, even with Saskia's inheritance, he did not have enough to pay for the house in the next six years. The purchase of that grand house on Sint Antoniesbreestraat, the symbol of Rembrandt's having arrived at last to a secure and respectable position in Amsterdam society—the symptom, too, of that extravagance of character that so often led him to break new ground in his art—was to prove his crucial error.

Letters to Huygens

NINE DAYS after he signed the contract to buy the house, Rembrandt wrote a letter to Constantijn Huygens. Three years had passed since Rembrandt had last been in touch with Huygens, three years since the artist had told the patron that he had two paintings ready to send to The Hague at almost any moment. How was he to explain what was taking him so long this time?

My lord,
Because of the great zeal and devotion—

So that was to be it: he had been working so hard on these paintings—day and night, one supposes—because nothing less than perfection would do for the noble and discriminating Huygens, that it had taken him *three years* to finish them. But now:

these same two pictures have been completed as a result of my diligence, and I am now ready to deliver
them and so to afford pleasure to His Highness, for in
these two pictures—

Here Rembrandt gave the only statement he ever gave in his
own words of what he was trying to achieve as an artist:

the deepest and most lifelike emotion has been ex-
pressed, and that is the reason they have taken so long
to execute.

"The deepest and most lifelike emotion": because it is the only
phrase Rembrandt ever used to describe his art, the scholars
have been over the phrase again and again to plumb its meaning. Traditionally, the phrase (*naetuereelste beweechgelickheijt*,
in the original) was translated as "natural motion," referring
presumably to Rembrandt's ability to capture and freeze a
moment of action and have it appear altogether natural. Then,
in the 1940s, the Rembrandt scholar H. E. van Gelder pointed
out that seventeenth century Dutch usage of the word *beweechgelickheijt* argued for a translation of "emotion" rather than
"motion." Van Gelder noted, too, that these paintings for Huygens were not so much about a captured action as they were
about a captured emotion, about capturing the emotional reaction of all the characters in the picture to the event being portrayed.

This seemed to settle the matter to most scholars' satisfaction
until John Gage, another Rembrandt scholar, raised the issue
again in the 1960s. He agreed with van Gelder's translation of
"emotion"; but he argued that the word referred not to the
emotions of the people in the picture but to the overall emotional impact that the artist put into the picture, and so the
emotional impact that the viewer took away from it. Gage
pointed out a relevant passage in Franciscus Junius' book *The
Painting of the Ancients*, which was in Huygens' library, and
so something Huygens might have mentioned to Rembrandt.

Junius spoke of a great artist as one who expresses in his works "the inward motion of his most forward mind"—which is to say, one who expresses in his work an emotion that *he* feels.

Many other scholars have been over the words to tease out one nuance or another, but none of them seem entirely convincing. Indeed, the most likely sense of what is going on here was conveyed in a book on painting written before Rembrandt's time, way back in 1435, *Della Pittura* by the Florentine Leon Battista Alberti. Rembrandt would not have known the book first-hand, but ideas from it might have been passed down to him as "folk wisdom" by Lastman or Swanenburg. Alberti said that Giotto had been highly praised for a picture he painted in Rome of Christ walking across the water toward his disciples in a boat. Why? "Eleven disciples are all moved by fear at seeing one of their companions passing over the water. Each one expresses with his face and gesture a clear indication of a disturbed soul in such a way that there are different movements and positions in each one. . . . Some movements of the soul are called affections, such as grief, joy, and fear, desire and other similar ones." In other words, outward movement mirrored the innermost "movements of the soul." The accomplished painter found gestures and expressions that exactly corresponded to the deepest stirrings of the soul. And that sounds like Rembrandt.

Still, for all the accomplishment of Rembrandt's paintings for Huygens, they were several years late in getting done, and Rembrandt cast about for something more to charm Huygens after the long silence. (No one is more transparent than an artist who needs money.) What could Rembrandt give him? Evidently Rembrandt had some reason to believe that Huygens had a taste for violent pictures. And Rembrandt had that gory old painting of Samson having his eye gouged out with a spear. Apparently no one else wanted it, and Rembrandt hadn't been able to get it off his hands. So:

> And because you have been troubled in these matters
> for the second time, I shall send along, as a token of
> gratitude, a painting measuring ten feet in length and

The Descent from the Cross: Second Large Plate. Etching, 1633

eight feet in height which you will prize in your house. Wishing you all happiness and the blessing of salvation. Amen.

Your obliging and devoted servant
Rembrandt

Huygens wrote back within forty-eight hours to acknowledge Rembrandt's letter, to thank him for completing the two paintings, and, above all, to tell him not to send that large painting. Maybe Huygens was worried about where he could put an eight foot by ten foot painting; maybe he was even more worried about seeming, as the purchasing agent for Frederik Hendrik, to accept a blatant bribe. Whatever Huygens said, Rembrandt didn't reply for thirteen days. What was Rembrandt doing? Painting the paintings? By the twenty-seventh he was ready to reply:

My noble lord,
I have read your pleasant letter of the 14th with singular pleasure. I discern your kind inclination and affection which I feel deeply obliged to requite you with service and friendship. Because of my inclination to do this, and in spite of your wish, I am sending you along with this letter a canvas, hoping you will accept it, because it is the first memento I offer you.

So there was no stopping the gift of the Samson, however big, however gory, however obvious a bribe. It was sent to The Hague. Whether Huygens kept it or not, it did not show up in an inventory of his possessions later on. He might have sent it back to Rembrandt; or he might have sloughed it off as a gift to someone else. The farthest back the ownership of the painting can be traced today is to the collection of the prince-bishop of Würzburg in 1746; how it got to him is anybody's guess.

In any case, as Rembrandt wrote Huygens, while the painter was packing up the two commissioned pictures for shipment to Huygens, the prince's local tax collector—who was Johannes Wtenbogaert, a young relative of the famous Remonstrant preacher of the same name, whose portrait Rembrandt had painted—happened to drop by (Had he really? What for? Or isn't it more likely that Rembrandt had gone to his house?). Remarkably enough, young Wtenbogaert said he would love to see the paintings. As he admired them, Wtenbogaert mentioned, incidentally, that he could pay Rembrandt for them out of the prince's Amsterdam office if that was agreeable to Huygens. (Rembrandt's sense of urgency about all this would suggest that he was trying to scrape up the first 1200 guilders down payment on his house.)

Meanwhile, Rembrandt finished packing up the pictures and sent them on to Huygens. But Rembrandt must have knocked these paintings out and packed them up in terrific haste, possibly even packed them before the paint was dry—at least this is Gary Schwartz's conjecture—because the topmost layer of paint never properly adhered to the layers beneath. Whether or not they were damaged before they reached Huygens, the painting of the *Entombment of Christ* eventually lost most of the bright pastel tones of the top layer with which Rembrandt finished it, and the other picture, the *Resurrection of Christ*, fared even worse. In 1755, as Schwartz says, the *Resurrection* was restored, and the restorer himself felt he had had to do such an extensive job that when he finished his work he appended this inscription: "*Rimbrand creavit me. P.H. Brinckmann resuscitavit me 1755*"—that is, Rembrandt created me, P. H. Brinckmann brought me back to life 1755.

As the paintings are now, it is hard to imagine how they first appeared to Huygens. As usual, Rembrandt has caught a dramatic moment: in the one case, the moment that Christ's lifeless body, cradled in a sheet, is lowered into a cold stone sarcophagus, and in the other case, the instant that he sits up, zombielike, about to rise again. But what is really best about both paintings is a wonderful ghostly quality in the light, a sort of terrible pallor—which may be due less to Rembrandt's inspiration than to Brinckmann's, or to the fact that the surface paint came off.

In view of the delays, and the condition of the last two paintings he sent to The Hague, a lesser man than Rembrandt might have felt sheepish about presenting Huygens with a steep bill for these paintings. But this was no time for a failure of nerve. Rembrandt enclosed an invoice in the package containing the paintings: The paintings were of "such high quality," Rembrandt noted on the invoice, that he thought he should be paid "not less than 1000 guilders each." (That seemed a plausible sum: less than the 1200 guilders he had asked for the last time, more than the six hundred guilders he had gotten.)

Once again, Huygens' reply to Rembrandt is lost, but clearly Huygens held the line again firmly at six hundred guilders. And Rembrandt had no time to haggle. He had only done the paintings in the first place because he needed the money desperately. Presumably in reply to a letter from Huygens refusing to pay one thousand guilders, Rembrandt wrote at once:

> if His Highness cannot in all decency be moved to a higher price, though they are obviously worth it, I shall be satisfied with 600 guilders each, provided I am also credited for my outlay on the 2 ebony frames and the crate, which is 44 guilders in all. So I would kindly request of my lord that I may now receive my payments here in Amsterdam as soon as possible. . . .

And then Huygens behaved as all patrons, who seem always to have a steady income, or several sources of income, and never to understand the needs of those who have an unsteady income, always behave: He let his paymaster dawdle over authorizing the payment for more than six weeks. Rembrandt's first payment on the house was coming due May first. In April he wrote Huygens once more. Huygens' paymaster had been claiming that there was no money in the account from which Rembrandt was to be paid, that he was waiting for certain deposits to be made before he could draw on the account. But Rembrandt knew better; he had his own sources of information; young Wtenbogaert told Rembrandt that the paymaster was lying. Rembrandt relayed this gossip to Huygens and begged him to pry loose the "well-earned" 1244 guilders. And so, soon enough, Rembrandt got his money.

Presumably, everyone was more or less content with the way

this commission had at last turned out, or at least they decided not to argue about it. Huygens got his paintings, whether or not Rembrandt ever went to The Hague to try to adjust the first three paintings as Huygens had asked him to do and whatever condition the last two paintings may have been in; Rembrandt produced at least two good paintings, and paid for his house. And yet, everyone could not have been entirely satisfied. Once again, and this time for a period of seven years, Rembrandt and Huygens did no more business together.

The Self-Portrait
of 1640

O_N APRIL NINTH, 1639, Rembrandt was sitting in an auction in the home of Lucas van Uffelen, who had died the year before. Van Uffelen's home was an elegant one on the grand Emperor's Canal, and he had an art collection equal to the house. The auction had attracted a good crowd. Rembrandt was there—though only to look, not to buy (he was still waiting for that 1244 guilders from Huygens). Joachim van Sandrart was there, and so was Alphonso Lopez, a man of intense interest to an artist, since Lopez was in Amsterdam buying art for Cardinal Richelieu and the French crown. A painter would naturally watch Lopez closely in this auction to see if he could figure out Lopez's tastes.

Lopez was a Portuguese Jew who had converted to Christianity. Some years before he had moved to Paris where he set up as a dealer in textiles. On the side he also employed one of the best diamond cutters in Europe. In time he became an agent for Richelieu, dealing in ships, arms and other war material; Indian

Portrait of Baldassare Castiglione, After Raphael. Drawing, 1639

and other Oriental curios; art, and precious jewels. He had lived in Amsterdam briefly in 1628, and he had returned in 1636 to stay until 1641, to deal in arms for the Cardinal. Lopez had a grand house himself, with his own extensive art collection, and he was a man who could afford the best taste.

During the auction at van Uffelen's a painting by Raphael came up on the block, a supposed portrait of Baldassare Castiglione, who had lived from 1478 to 1529. Castiglione was an Italian diplomat who had lived at the court of Guidobaldo Montefeltro, the Duke of Urbino. It was Castiglione who had written *The Courtier*, a book about courtly life that defined exactly how a modern gentleman ought to look, dress, act, speak, play, and think. To have a portrait by Raphael was a fine thing; to have a portrait of Castiglione by Raphael was to have a unique treasure. Both Sandrart and Lopez were in the bidding, and stayed in the bidding until the end, when, finally, Sandrart dropped out and let Lopez have it for 3500 guilders—3500 guilders!

Rembrandt took out pen and paper and made a quick sketch of the portrait—a distinguished gentleman with a calm expression, in well-cut clothes, with a floppy velvet hat on his head (which Rembrandt put at a more rakish angle in his sketch). Next to the sketch, Rembrandt wrote "sold for 3500 guilders."

Perhaps Rembrandt had been in Lopez's house and seen his collection and knew that, in addition to this Raphael portrait of Castiglione, Lopez was especially fond of another portrait that he owned, a portrait by Titian of Ludovico Ariosto, the Italian diplomat and poet who had written *Orlando Furioso*. In Titian's portrait, Ariosto is turned sideways, with his head turned back to look directly at us. His arm, in a gorgeous silk sleeve, resting jauntily on a balustrade, seems to be sticking right out of the picture frame.

Rembrandt set to work at once on a self-portrait that took the pose of Ariosto, the hat of Castiglione, and the rich clothes of his own making—fur and lace and velvet and silk—and he did himself up as an Italian poet-diplomat-virtuoso–titled aristocrat with an expression of lofty, exquisite, and proud sensibility that makes Castiglione look like a country bumpkin. It is a great,

Rembrandt Leaning on a Stone Sill. Etching, 1639

commanding portrait, a stunning piece of work. This is Rembrandt looking his very best.

It may be that Rembrandt painted the portrait only because he had admired the Raphael and the Titian and wanted to do one like theirs. Or it may be that Rembrandt did the picture because he wanted to think of himself in this new, grand way now that he was the owner of a substantial new home. Or it may be that his competitive instincts had been aroused—that he wanted to prove he, an Amsterdam painter, could do as well as an Italian master—even better if he chose to, and this self-portrait proved it.

Or it may be that he looked on this portrait as a way to get Lopez's attention. Certainly here was a portrait to send to Cardinal Richelieu if he was looking for painters for the French court, if Lopez wanted something sensational to send back to Paris, if Richelieu wanted someone who could knock Titian off the wall, if the King wanted a portrait done by a great painter. This was Rembrandt once again trying to break in as a court painter, as a painter even above those who worked at the court of The Hague, as a painter for the French court that the Dutch aristocrats tried so hard to emulate.

But, of course, Rembrandt never did paint Richelieu or the King of France or anyone else at the French court. What happened to this self-portrait we don't know. It doesn't appear that Lopez bought it, or that it ever got to France. After all, Rembrandt wasn't Ariosto or Castiglione; he was only a painter from the Netherlands, a person of no interest at the French court, and, in his manner of painting, not nearly refined enough for Richelieu—or what was perhaps even worse, a man who refused to honor the distinction between king and commoner, rather a man who insisted in self-portrait after self-portrait that he could make of himself whatever he wanted.

His Melting Bones

A DISTINGUISHED painter, for some time harassed with black bile, was under the delusion that all the bones of his body had softened to such a flexibility that they might easily buckle like wax if he put the slightest weight on them.

This was the report of a case study that Dr. Tulp published in his *Observationes*. "A distinguished painter" (*Insignis Pictor*) and "in his own art accomplished and second to hardly any" (*in arte sua abunde sagax, & vix ulli secundus*), a painter Tulp knew and treated: In short, though it is far from certain, this might be Rembrandt. Between December 1640 and September 1641, there is a gap in Rembrandt's work—a period which would correspond to the time Tulp's patient was languishing in bed.

> He kept to his bed for a whole winter; for if he were to get out of it [he feared] something disastrous would assuredly come to pass, and that with even more certainty than the decomposition of his bones that he had feared hitherto—nay, rather the total collapse of his body.

Tulp diagnosed melancholia, a state of mind that was, as it happens, quite fashionable in the seventeenth century, especially among people of talent and sensibility, although not everyone agreed on just what melancholia was. The physicians followed along behind, trying to shape the fad into a defined illness. According to one authority it was "a long, persistent delirium without fever, during which the sufferer is obsessed by only one thought." According to another it was "a madness without fever or frenzy, accompanied by fear and sadness." As anyone of learning and deep thought knew, learning and thinking bring one to a realization of the futility of learning and thought and of the inevitability of death, which makes melancholia almost required of any serious, thinking person.

Many of the greatest scholars of the seventeenth century tended to feign melancholia if they didn't feel it spontaneously; paintings of melancholy scholars and astronomers were popular; in England, of course, Robert Burton wrote his *Anatomy of Melancholy*, a work that was surely as characteristic of his time as Freud's *Interpretation of Dreams* was of his. For an artist who already had fame, fortune, and his own home, all he still really needed was melancholia.

Whatever melancholia was, the proximate cause of Rembrandt's case—if it was Rembrandt whom Tulp treated—was very likely the purchase of that big, expensive house, and the realization that, after several years of trying to break out of portraiture and into history painting, he had condemned himself once again to portraiture, to an endless scrambling for money, to a perpetual sensation of being behind, to an interminable scurrying for commissions to paint people he didn't like and a ceaseless avoiding of people to whom he owed money. That might be enough to send anyone to bed for a few months. His sedentary style of living, his lack of recreation, his constant, obsessive work, would have concerned any physician. The death of three infants could not have helped. As absurd as this stylish melancholia was, it could nonetheless be underlaid with real anguish.

> Once I had comprehended this dread [of a collapsing body, wrote Tulp], I did not want to antagonize him; I wanted to take a roundabout rather than direct measures to undermine the fancy that he had conjured up. Granting, then, that this species of softening was no new story to the medical profession . . . I said that, just as softened wax is rehardened [just the right sort of metaphor for an artist], so the art of medicine can work upon the bones. . . .

Melancholics were hard to treat, Tulp noted in his case study. Sometimes one had to resort to outlandish measures to cure them. The ancient physician Philodotus, said Tulp, once cured a melancholic who thought his head had been cut off, by fashioning a leaden headgear that he placed on the fellow's skull. Feeling the weight, the man knew his head had been restored.

Tulp decided to try the lie direct. Within three days, Tulp told the artist, his bones would be restored to their former rigidity. Within an additional three days, the artist would be able to walk again. Meanwhile, the artist was not under any circumstances to get out of bed on his own, or Tulp would not be held responsible for the consequences. Tulp would say when it was time to walk. If the artist followed Tulp's instructions precisely, Tulp would himself "give him leave to walk anywhere."

Meanwhile, Tulp prescribed enemas to get rid of the black bile that was causing the difficulty. (Medicine was a contemptibly primitive affair in the seventeenth century, although one must admit that Tulp worked a lot faster than a Freudian analyst.) Enemas, like melancholia, were extremely popular in the seventeenth century. In one year, 215 enemas were administered to

Louis XIII. "The seventeenth century," as William Heckscher has written, "might be called the age of the enema."

The patient, filled with a dread of his disability, dutifully submitted to all of Tulp's prescriptions, and Tulp kept up the enemas steadily. Then,

> with the approach of the second three-day period I made an outright demonstration of the truth of my promise by suffering him not only to walk about his bedroom, but also to show himself in public and to perform all the functions of a healthy person.
>
> So rejoiced was he at this liberation that he could not find enough to say in praise of the mentor of his health. By turns he marveled at the prowess of medicine and execrated his own distrust because he had so persisted in withholding the faith with which he had finally accepted advice so beneficial.

In short, he was cured.

Anatomy of
a Masterpiece:
The Nightwatch

What was wanted was a really big, festive-looking picture to decorate the wall of a banquet hall. It was commissioned by one of Amsterdam's civic guard companies, and it was to be a group portrait of some of the leading members of the company. Eighteen members had paid to have their portraits included in the group. The main problem for the artist in composing the picture was that he had to adjust the size of each man's portrait to accord with how much each man had paid—so that those who had paid the most were fully visible, and those who had paid least would have only their heads and shoulders visible.

Amsterdam's civic guard companies, like those of other Dutch cities, had been established originally as citizens' militias to defend the independence of their cities, to guard the city gates, and, more modestly, to put out fires and help to maintain civic order. Officially, they were still responsible for those duties, and any member who did not do his share was subject to fine. By the

1600s, however, the members of the companies routinely paid their fines, and let the fines be used to bring in mercenary soldiers and other hired hands to do the work. In rare emergencies, the companies still turned out to do their duty alongside the mercenaries, so that they still had about them some faint whiff of military power and pride, some aura of being the guardians of the city's security and independence, some rightful claim to represent Amsterdam's stance as an autonomous city-republic and world power, although generally, in Rembrandt's day, the companies had become social clubs for well-to-do gentlemen and others who aspired to be gentlemen.

There were twenty such companies in Amsterdam, each one with about two hundred members, or a total membership of four thousand in all twenty companies, which constituted an establishment of some consequence in the city. The twenty companies were organized into three groups, according to the weapons they had traditionally carried in battle: the crossbowmen, the archers, and the musketeers, or *kloveniers*. Each of these three groups maintained a headquarters that contained meeting rooms, banquet halls, an armory where the men could store their weapons, and a shooting range, or *doelen*, where members could conduct target practice. These headquarters were named for their shooting ranges. Thus the musketeers' headquarters was called the *Kloveniersdoelen*.

Rembrandt's commission had come from one of the six companies that composed the *Kloveniersdoelen*, which was in an old pile of buildings on the bank of the Amstel River, on the edge of town near the artists' quarter. The original section of the *Kloveniersdoelen* had been built in the 1480s, and consisted of a fortified tower, which had been built as part of the city's walls along the Amstel, as well as a few smaller structures and the shooting range. In 1631, the *kloveniers* had started construction on an elegant new brick wing for the *doelen*, a wing so grand that when it was finished in 1636 it was the finest and largest structure in the neighborhood. The centerpiece of this new wing, and so henceforth of the entire *doelen*, was the great hall, or *groote sael*, on the second floor. It was about twenty by sixty feet, which made it one of the biggest halls in Amsterdam, and, with six tall windows opening onto a view of the Amstel River, one of the handsomest.

When the *kloveniers* were not using the hall for their own entertainments, they rented it out, and the city government began to hold its annual banquet there and to use the hall to entertain distinguished visitors to Amsterdam. The supervisory body of the Amsterdam militia companies began to use the hall, too, as well as the members of the Order of St. Michael and other groups. A painting hanging in this room, then, had a chance of being seen by nearly everyone who mattered, and so it was worth doing an impressive job.

Not every one of the two hundred members of the company could be jammed into this group portrait. Who was to be in the picture was determined not only by who paid to be in it. Some people must not have been allowed even to buy their way in: These were not a ragtag bunch of foot soldiers having their portraits painted; these were the leading members of the *kloveniers*. And within this group, further social distinctions were clearly made—some men were shown prominently, two men were shown front and center, while others were shown less prominently.

At the head of the group was Frans Banning Cocq, age thirty-seven, a man on the way up. He was not even a resident of this company's neighborhood, but his social connections got him the captaincy of the company. He was the son of Jay Cocq, who had come to Amsterdam from Germany, become the owner of an apothecary shop, and married the daughter of a rich merchant. Frans himself had studied law, taken his doctorate in France, and returned to marry the daughter of another, richer merchant, Volckert Overlander, a former burgomaster and former governor of the *Kloveniersdoelen*.

After Frans' marriage to Overlander's daughter, he began his climb at once: He was appointed the city administrator of marriage contracts at the age of twenty-seven and at age twenty-nine a life member of the Vroedschap, the city's advisory council of thirty-six men. By 1637, at age thirty-two, he had become an alderman, a position he would hold another six times. Eventually, after Rembrandt painted him as captain of his militia company, he would become one of the two colonels in charge of all twenty of Amsterdam's militia companies, and then governor of the archers' *doelen* and finally, ultimately, a burgomaster. He would inherit his father-in-law's townhouse, one of the best houses in Amsterdam, as well as the manor of Purmerland and Ilpendam to the north. Before he died, he would bestow aristocratic lineage on himself, that is, he would have his ancestral coat of arms redesigned to indicate that he had inherited the title Lord of Purmerland not from his father-in-law but directly from his father.

Frans Banning Cocq's lieutenant, the second in command of his company, was Wilhelm van Ruytenburgh, the son of a wholesale merchant who traded with the Indies and, like Overlander, acquired a couple of manor houses and the titles that went with them. Six years older than Banning Cocq, van Ruytenburgh was always a step or two behind his captain. Although he had the same sort of place in society that Banning Cocq did—even slightly better, since it was his father, and not his father-in-law who had acquired the fortune and the lands and titles—he was a bit slow. He became a member of the Vroedschap, too, but not until 1639. He became an alderman, but not until 1641. He married the daughter of a rich and influential man, but not as rich and influential as Banning Cocq's father-in-law. He was never appointed a colonel, never became a burgomaster. If Banning Cocq was on the way up, Ruytenburgh, who had been born a step up, was on his way down. Five years after Rembrandt painted him as a member of the militia company, he quit the feverish competition in Amsterdam and moved to a gentler life in The Hague.

The third-ranking member of the company was the ensign, Jan Cornelisz Visscher. By tradition, the ensign of a militia company had to be a bachelor, perhaps because it was the ensign who traditionally led the company into battle, and it was thought that such a dangerous job should not be given to a man with wife and children. Visscher, age thirty-one, was a well-born young man, but his father died at an early age, leaving him without the sort of assistance a young man could use in this society. An only child, he was raised by his mother, in the home of his grandmother. He had a comfortable childhood; the house was filled with more than fifty paintings and had a considerable library; he was interested in music and drawing, and he eschewed a career in trade. He died in 1650, at the age of thirty-nine, still a bachelor.

The two sergeants were next in rank: Rombout Kemp, age forty-five, and Reijer Engelen, age fifty-four. Both were men getting on in years without gathering the most cherished distinctions. Neither of them were members of the Vroedschap, neither were cut out to be burgomasters. Kemp was a deacon of the Reformed Church, a member of the board of regents of two charitable organizations devoted to the poor, and a well-to-do cloth merchant. He would succeed van Ruytenburgh as lieutenant of the company when van Ruytenburgh went to The Hague, but that is as high as he would rise. He had no rich or powerful relatives.

Reijer Engelen was another cloth merchant, though not as successful as Kemp, and not possessed of such reliable character, either. He had been fined some years earlier for dealing in inferior cloth, and when he had married a woman many years younger than he was he lied about his age in an official document.

The rest of the company members in Rembrandt's painting were, for the most part, well-to-do merchants: Five more of the men were in the textile business; one dealt in hemp and rope; three more dealt in goods from the Indies; two were wine merchants. Jan Visscher was the only man who was not engaged in business of some kind. They all—save Banning Cocq, who lived in his father-in-law's splendid house over on the old Singel Canal—lived in the same neighborhood, a neighborhood, as is apparent from the professions of most of the men, whose main artery was the Nieuwendijk, the street of the drapers. Van Ruytenburgh and a couple of others lived on the stylish, almost suburban, new Gentlemen's Canal, away from the noisy center of town. Visscher lived with his grandmother just one canal closer to the center of town. But most of the men, even including Rombout Kemp and Reijer Engelen were clustered down among the shops in the busy streets of the garment center just off the Dam, where they had made their money and continued to do their business.

(One of the men in the painting, Jan Claes Leijdecker—we know he is there, but we don't know which figure he is—died almost two years before Rembrandt painted the picture. Why he is still in the group is not clear, although the Dutch scholar S. A. C. Dudok van Heel has a guess. Dudok van Heel supposes that Leijdecker paid Rembrandt in advance to be in the painting. After Leijdecker paid, he died. His widow, as it happened, was then in severe financial straits, and probably wanted the money back. If Rembrandt had not put Leijdecker's portrait in the group, he would certainly have had to return the money to the widow. And, as usual, Rembrandt was short of money himself. So Leijdecker stayed in the group.)

Rembrandt faced two problems in thinking how to go about putting these men into a group portrait. First of all, there was the problem of lining all these fellows up so that their faces could be seen and recognized by their friends. Second of all, there was the fact that Rembrandt's painting was not to be the only painting in this hall: Other painters were doing group portraits of the other five companies of the *Kloveniersdoelen* to hang on the walls of the *groote sael*. All of these paintings, like Rembrandt's, were to show the members of the companies more than life size, so that, when all the paintings were finished and hanging in place, the *groote sael*, from wall to wall and from just above the floor right up to the ceiling, would be full of more than a hundred larger-than-life musketeers. The room as a whole would be dazzlingly full of life—spectacular, festive, active, jolly—but Rembrandt's painting could easily get lost in there if he didn't do something special. Moreover, the painters had drawn lots to see which wall spaces they would get. And Rembrandt drew the worst place in the room—away from the door, lost in a dark corner.

There was—in this nation that produced more group portraits than any other nation in the world—a traditional way of doing a group portrait. Ordinarily, the men were lined up in two or three rows—the most important in the front row—a crowd of robust faces looking directly front, as in a school picture. This made for many square yards of intensely boring paintings that covered the walls of civic guard companies and hospital regents' rooms and city halls all over the Netherlands. To be sure, some of the pictures in this tradition were good—especially the later pictures, in which the painter deployed his rows of men around a banquet table or other almost natural settings, and let one or two of them sprawl out in a chair, or lift a glass of wine, and he gave an alcohol flush to their cheeks. Over in Haarlem, Frans Hals got to be superb at this sort of thing. Men turned their heads one way or another, ate, chatted, poured another glass of wine; and Hals dressed the companies up in bright, shining swords and silk sashes, and gave each man a wonderful, hale and hearty, individualistic posture and expression, so that his paintings are enormously dashing and energetic. Still, Hals' paintings did have one little round red face after another bobbing along the horizon line, which gave them a certain predictability.

Of the other painters who had been commissioned to do groups for the *Kloveniersdoelen*, Jacob Backer would do a nice variation on the traditional line-up by having some of the men on the right-hand side stand on a staircase, so the little round heads would swirl across the painting like a waterfall from right to left. Govert Flinck put his company on a set of stairs leading to a balcony, which established several levels for the men to stand on. Nicolaes Eliasz and Bartholomeus van der Helst both lined their companies up in the old left-to-right formation, but they put the men outdoors and dressed them up with some colorful sashes. Van der Helst even added the clever touch of having one of the men in the picture point out at us, the viewers, so that almost the whole company has turned to look at us, which gives the picture a certain focus and vitality. Still, as good as these paintings are—and they were done by some of Amsterdam's leading painters—they all look stagey: There is nothing really spontaneous or lifelike about them. The whole aesthetic convention of group portraiture forces this staginess; after all, the group has gathered to have its portrait painted; it is a contrived moment.

And so Rembrandt—who had never aspired to be a portraitist anyway—threw out all the conventions of group portraiture, and did a history painting. To announce at once and unmistakably that it was a history painting, he put just off center someone who could not conceivably have paid to be included in the group, someone who could not possibly even be a member of the militia, someone who did not belong in a group portrait of a company of musketeers: a little girl in a shimmering yellow dress. And to make sure she was not missed, he picked her out with a shaft of bright light.

And then he did not allow the men in the painting to stand around having their picture painted. In Rembrandt's hands, the men are marching out of their corner toward the center of the room. Banning Cocq and Ruytenburgh are at center. Banning Cocq is gesturing with one hand, and he has turned slightly toward Ruytenburgh to give the marching order. All the men are in motion, pouring out of an archway, about to sweep past to our left. A dog (Rembrandt's ever-present dog) scoots among the men's legs to get out of the way. A drummer marches into the picture from the right. A man loads a musket. The ensign raises the company banner.

Everyone we expected to see is here: Banning Cocq and Ruytenburgh at the front, Jan Visscher at the rear but very visible because he is the one who waves the banner, Sergeant Engelen at the left side with a vicious-looking halberd in hand and an ornate golden helmet on his head, Sergeant Kemp over on the right side, his arm outstretched in a gesture back across the center of the scene, relaying an order down the line. Men turn to speak to one another. Hands are raised to point. A boy runs through the group carrying a powder horn. Spears thrust out at all angles. Capes swirl. Here are the men of imperial Holland: on the move, robust, confident, straightforward men, the men who had dispatched Henry Hudson in 1609 up the river that now bears his name, who had "bought" Manhattan Island from the Indians not quite two decades before this painting was made, who had burrowed into South Africa to stay.

Whereas other painters had dutifully painted the sixteen or eighteen or twenty men who had paid to have their portraits included, taking care to make each face visible, and so trapping themselves into those compositions filled with little round faces, Rembrandt eliminated that problem altogether—by the extraordinary stratagem of *adding* other people. He added the little girl, the little boy, the drummer, and another ten men whose faces didn't need to be seen. He stuck his own face into the painting, too, as some of the other painters of the *groote sael* pictures did as well: a little fellow, lost in the crowd, peeking up over the ensign's shoulder, with no more than one eye and part of his nose and his beret visible.

Whereas other painters had put all their men into dark Calvinist clothes, or, on the other hand, dressed all of them up in bright silks, Rembrandt gave everyone a different costume, so that the group is a riot of individualism, a *coup de théâtre* that suited Rembrandt's tastes. Banning Cocq gets the elegant black of the upper class, a white lace collar, gold brocade on his shirt, a red silk sash with a gold border, and the baton of his command. His gloved right hand holds the glove from his left hand; he is ready to throw down the gauntlet. Ruytenburgh, just next to him, wears a blinding yellow outfit with a blue-white silk sash, yellow leather hose and riding boots, a feathered hat, a pair of spurs. He carries a ceremonial halberd, or partisan. Although his outfit is more attention getting than Banning Cocq's, he is a half-step behind Banning Cocq. Banning Cocq speaks; he listens.

Visscher, the ensign, is in love with his banner. He holds it aloft and gazes at it fondly. Engelen wears his fancy gold helmet, a cuirass and a steel gauntlet. The man loading his musket is all in red, Kemp is all in black. For comic relief, the little boy with the powder horn wears an old beat-up helmet that is too big for him and falls down over his forehead.

The group is better armed with more pikes and halberds and muskets than any of the other companies in the hall. In fact, several of the musketeers are in action: One is putting powder into the barrel of his gun; another is blowing off the powder that presumably remains from having just shot the musket; and one armor-clad musketeer who is racing through the crowd just behind Banning Cocq and Ruytenburgh is actually shooting his musket at this very moment. The picture is filled with sound: the barking dog, running feet, the drummer drumming, the fired shot, and Banning Cocq giving his command.

The picture is called *The Nightwatch*, although it isn't at all a scene of men going out to stand watch at night. No one knows what the painting was called in Rembrandt's time—probably *The Civic Guard Company of Captain Frans Banning Cocq*, if it needed any name at all. It was named *The Nightwatch* at the end of the eighteenth century, after layers of dirt and varnish had made it very dark, and night patrols were the only duties such companies still performed. In any case, the light in the painting is unique. Whereas other painters who did these group portraits lit their pictures with a nice, even light so that each man could be seen equally well, Rembrandt splashed light over the group wherever he wanted to pick someone out. Banning Cocq and Van Ruytenburgh get a splash of light. Visscher gets a warm sunbath. Light flickers across the faces of Kemp and Engelen to pick them out. Several other faces get a bit of sun breaking through the clouds. And the little girl positively glows in her shaft of light. This is not night light, nor quite sunlight. It is Rembrandt's light.

Egbert Haverkamp-Begemann, who is a professor of Fine Arts at New York University, has spent a good deal of time looking at this painting, and he has written a monograph on it with some wonderful observations.

First of all, Haverkamp-Begemann points out, the three men with muskets—the one who loads his, the one who shoots his, and the other who blows the powder from his—are not dressed in seventeenth century clothes; they wear costumes that date from the 1500s.

Secondly, the armor that the other men wear is odd. Nine men wear helmets, none of them the type that was worn in Amsterdam at the time. Engelen's helmet is a Renaissance gilded parade helmet, and his cuirass and gauntlet are old-fashioned, too. A heavy broadsword that some fellow in the background is thrusting aloft above Ruytenburgh's head is an antique. Some

of these militiamen may have had their own collections of antique weapons and costumes and enjoyed putting them on for
parades, but clearly something symbolic is going on here, too.

And what, in any case, are these men doing shooting muskets in the middle of their own men mustering out? Are they
endangering their colleagues' lives? Or are they, perhaps, symbolic? Is it not odd that they demonstrate, as though out of a
manual on weapons, the three basic steps in the handling of a
musket? Without apology, Rembrandt simply throws a how-to
picture into the middle of his group portrait.

And who, finally, is that little girl who so stands out? In fact,
there are two little girls, one barely visible behind the other.
They both wear beautiful brocaded silk gowns. The one we can
see best has a golden band around her head and a pear-shaped
pearl earring. To be sure, boys and girls (and prostitutes) followed armies on their marches, and the boy and girls in this
painting might refer to such camp followers—although camp
followers never dressed like these young girls. The girls, according to Haverkamp-Begemann, must be the sort of children who
sometimes appeared on ceremonial occasions; they must be em-
blem carriers. And, sure enough, hanging upside down from the
belt of the little girl in the front is a chicken, with its claws
sticking up in the air. The claws—originally claws of a bird of
prey—were the symbol of the *Kloveniersdoelen*.

The extraordinary elements in Rembrandt's painting can be
explained as everyday occurrences: The girls are there to join
the parade; the old-fashioned clothes and weapons were the
sort of thing the men might have had; the three musketeers,
however symbolic they might seem, were nonetheless who the
members of this company were. And yet, the mixture of past
and present, symbolic and didactic, the costumes from an earlier
time that appear here so evocatively, the weapons from another
epoch, the little girls who walk through the painting as though
from another picture are not simply coincidental. What is happening here is not merely that Rembrandt is painting present
and past together, not simply depicting the present members of
the company and recalling their glorious past. What is happening, among other things, is that the past is invading the present.

The ghosts are coming back to life. The whole picture is an apparition.

In truth, there is not just one picture here—not just a group portrait, or a history painting. There are four or five pictures going on here, one laid on top of another—a group portrait, a history painting, a symbolic painting, a how-to illustration, a bit of genre painting—one layer placed atop the other so that finally there are a multiplicity of paintings simultaneously occupying the same space. Rembrandt was finally in complete command of his art; he could do whatever he wanted, and he did not hesitate for a moment to take complete liberty. And he makes the other painters in the *groote sael* look agonizingly simple-minded and inhibited. Or, as van Hoogstraten said, whatever other reservations he might have had about Rembrandt, *The Nightwatch* was such an extraordinary painting that it made all those other pictures in the *groote sael* "look like playing cards."

The Crash

J UST AFTER Rembrandt finished painting *The Nightwatch,* his
career collapsed. For the next ten years, as far as anyone knows,
he got no commissions, save for two paintings he managed to
do for Frederik Hendrik. The faces he painted cannot be identified as portraits of any known person in Amsterdam society.
He found no new clients. The paintings he did, again as far as
anyone knows, had no buyers at all—save again for the two
paintings for Frederik Hendrik. For several years, he took in
no new pupils or assistants. Indeed, before long, he closed his
warehouse school on the Bloemgracht.

What brought about this collapse has been a matter of intense speculation among art historians. At first, scholars tended
to blame the failure of *The Nightwatch,* saying that it must
have been so unusual as to have been detested—until it became
clear from further research that *The Nightwatch* had not been
a failure at all, that it had been greatly admired. Then a general
change in fashion was blamed: New, younger painters were do-

ing more elegant, brightly lit, glamorous portraits; Rembrandt's dark old paintings were out of style—until it was discovered that, though fashions were indeed changing, Rembrandt was still regarded as a master.

Others have suggested that Rembrandt's patrons became irritated with his spendthrift ways, his broken promises to deliver paintings for which he had been paid, his constant borrowing of money that he didn't bother to pay back.

Still, though it can't be proved, there is another, or additional, explanation. On September twenty-second, 1641, a son named Titus was baptized—Saskia's and Rembrandt's fourth child, and the only one to survive infancy. (Oddly, there are some coincidences among dates here: The period of Saskia's pregnancy is the period for which there is a gap in any documents or paintings related to Rembrandt—as though he might have been attending full time to Saskia. This, too, is the period in which Dr. Tulp said he was treating an artist for melting bones, for melancholia.) But, although Titus survived, Saskia did not.

She was ill for some months. Then, on June fifth, 1642, she wrote her last will.

> In the name of the Lord, Amen. In the year after the birth of our Lord 1642, on 5 June, in the morning at about 9 o'clock, Saskia van Uijlenburch, wife of the Hon. Rembrandt van Rhijn . . . although sick in bed, yet in full control of her memory and mind, as it appeared outwardly—after commending her soul to the Almighty God and her body to Christian burial— before me declared and appointed hereby as her heirs Titus van Rhijn, her son, together with any other legal child or children she might still bear, and in the event of prior death of one or the other of these, their legal offspring by representation, however, on condition that the aforementioned Rembrandt van Rhijn, her husband, shall retain until his remarriage, or in the event he should not remarry, until his death, the full possession and usufruct of all the testatrix' property she leaves behind. . . .

Some of these provisions have the aura about them of a domineering Rembrandt prevailing on Saskia, even as she was on her deathbed, to get her relatives off his back and make sure he has the use of her money. But the provisions can be read just as easily as something Saskia was eager to do for a husband who had sat by her bed for the past nine months. Saskia and Rembrandt had been married "in community of goods," which meant that she had the right to dispose of half of their possessions. According to law, children were entitled to only a third of a parent's possessions; Saskia left her new-born son everything. It is a measure of her trust in Rembrandt, however, that she left him full possession of her property until such time as he remarried or died. He was also appointed sole guardian of Titus although regulations called for two guardians. In addition, Rembrandt was expressly exempted from any obligation to give "anyone in the world [namely those pesky relatives] an accounting or inventory . . . because she is confident that he will acquit himself very well in good conscience." And finally the Chamber of Orphans, which normally looked after the estates of orphans, was specifically prevented from butting in.

The lawyer that Saskia and Rembrandt engaged to draw up this will did a good job: Rembrandt got the use of the inheritance for his expenses—but the property belonged to Titus, so that it could not be taken to settle any of Rembrandt's debts if he got into trouble. Thus Rembrandt was better protected from his creditors than if Saskia had left her property directly to him. But there was another not-so-hidden aspect to the will: Rembrandt could never marry again without losing the whole estate. It would seem that both Saskia and Rembrandt conspired in her will to enable Rembrandt to support himself and Titus after she was dead.

Ten days later Saskia died. According to custom, when a man or woman was near death, a priest was called in to pray with the dying person; and given Saskia's predilections, if not Rembrandt's, Rembrandt probably called in a priest. After she had died, according once more to custom, mirrors and pictures were turned to the wall. All the furniture, save the bed, was

Saskia in Bed, with a Child. Drawing, about 1636

Saskia Lying in Bed, and a Nurse. Drawing, about 1635

removed from the room. The next of kin, Rembrandt, washed her body, dressed it, and laid it back on the bed; and the vigil of relatives, friends, and neighbors began.

Those who took part in the vigil stood silently, replaced from time to time by others, and the vigil lasted for three days. At the end of the vigil the body was taken from the bed and put in a coffin. The coffin was draped with black cloth and, as the church bell tolled, the pallbearers lifted the coffin and set out in procession down the street. The mourners followed in twos— in long black cloaks, in silence, with Rembrandt and his son in the lead.

Poor people were buried in the churchyard. The rich bought graves in the aisles and chapels of the church, as Rembrandt did. The graves in the church were just under the floor; coffins were placed in several layers there, covered with a foot of sand and sealed with the flat stone of the church floor. Saskia was buried in a grave behind the pulpit, near the organ, in the Old Church (Oude Kerk), over near the Dam. Ordinarily, the tombstone would be engraved with the deceased's name, sometimes with a coat of arms or a family motto. Saskia's grave would never have an epitaph. Rembrandt, whether from depression or for some other reason, evidently could not bring himself to do it. He could not bring himself either to file Saskia's will with the Chamber of Orphans, as the law required, until months after it had been due.

Following the burial, Rembrandt returned home and received visits of condolence from friends. Customarily, drinks were served to guests, and not only friends and acquaintances would come to the house but most of the people in the neighborhood, and tradesmen who had known the deceased, and toasts were drunk with them all until, commonly, everyone had consumed vast quantities of alcohol. A few friends would usually stay on for a big meal, and more drinking, and singing, and the night could become raucous. Not everyone observed this custom, to be sure. Some—it was especially the fashion among the wealthy, in order to avoid such a drunken night—would hand out silver coins to pallbearers and tradesmen and those neighbors they did not know well, and invite them to go on their own to a nearby tavern to have a drink in memory of the deceased, so that they, the next of kin, could be alone, as Rembrandt, with his infant son, was now.

The Difficult Years

AFTER SASKIA's death Rembrandt did not stop painting and drawing altogether, but he did slow down a good deal. He had no lavish commissions or sales to socially prominent patrons, his work was inconsistent, and it was often so bad that his admirers still hope the scholars will come along and decide that a lot of these paintings were not done by Rembrandt at all.

Nonetheless, Rembrandt kept working. For instance, he did a wonderful etching of a pig all tied up and lying just outside the front door of a house. It is the sort of thing an artist might do for his own child. Indeed, in the doorway of this picture of the fettered pig is a small child, who would have been about Titus' age at the time. The child strains forward to get a good look at the pig. Just behind him, sketched in very faintly, is a smiling woman, perhaps a nurse, who has got hold of the child. The child is just learning to walk; he wears a "fall-down cap," a little padded headgear that the Dutch usually had their

The Hog. Etching, 1643

toddlers wear. It is conceivable that the smiling woman behind the child is Titus' nurse, Geertje Dirckx, a young woman who joined Rembrandt's household to take care of Titus just before Saskia's death.

Rembrandt did a pen and ink drawing at about this time, too, of a crowd of children at the front door of a house on Twelfth Night. The man and woman who live in the house have brought their infant to the front door, to hold up to see the revelers. Among the crowd of children in the street is a plump, smiling woman with a young child in her arms. Once again, the child seems to be wearing a fall-down cap. Once again, this could be Titus and his nurse Geertje Dirckx.

If we could read paintings as autobiography, what we would read of Rembrandt's life in these years after Saskia's death would be of a man undergoing an enormous change of life, of a man drawn back into himself, away from the world of dealers and rich commissions, away from the world of boisterous art students, away from social ambitions, away from the rhetorical emotions that had characterized some of his earlier history paintings.

The painting he did closest in time to Saskia's death is of a heartbroken young man being consoled by an older man. The scholars are unable to figure out whether this is David and Absalom or David and Jonathan or David and Mephiboseth; but what is certain is that it is a man being comforted in his sorrow. If Rembrandt did not paint it to express his own sorrow, nonetheless, when he came to paint it, he knew how to express sorrow.

He did a good many sketches of domestic scenes in these years, and he did two paintings of the Holy Family looking very like a cozy scene in a Dutch home—whether done with an eye to the market, or to the life he had in his own home with Titus and Geertje, or to the life he missed in his own home, is anybody's guess.

He did some etchings of friends, too, including a posthumous one of Johannes Corneliszoon Sylvius, Saskia's cousin, the minister of the Groote Kerk in Amsterdam, with whom she had stayed when she first came to town, who had served as a witness at the baptism of their first child and who had baptized their second child.

His sketchbook is filled with quick pen and ink drawings done on walks in the country—not melodramatic like his early landscape paintings, but rather simple, quiet sketches of the countryside, the musings of a man strolling by himself.

He did a beautiful etching of the Dutch countryside at about this time, too, with three trees on a slight rise of land, storm clouds just clearing, a fisherman and his wife beside a stream, an artist sketching from atop a hill, and, hidden almost entirely among the bushes to one side, a couple making love.

He did a painting of a young girl at a window, a painting unlike anything he had done before: simply a pretty, young girl.

He did a number of paintings of working-class people, too, portraits of the sort of anonymous people he had painted as a young man—men and women who have sometimes been doubtfully identified as his mother or father or brothers or sisters, people from the streets, anonymous old men cast in the roles of saints and prophets and astronomers. Rembrandt, having spent some time at The Hague, and among the well-to-do of Amsterdam, is equally at home—perhaps more at home—among ordinary people. He paints them now not as saints or prophets but simply as themselves.

It is some of these paintings that the scholars will no doubt finally throw out of the Rembrandt canon. But many of them were done by a painter of real strength, whoever he was—a painter not only of technical and intellectual virtuosity but of real emotional power, too. There is a painting of a young Jew gazing, lost, into space; a painting, of a few years later, of an old man sitting in an armchair, holding a walking stick, exhausted but still energetic, his cloak heavy with the paint the artist has laid on; there is a picture of a bearded old man wearing a linen headband under a hat, looking as though he might just have arrived from a journey on the road and is still wary of strangers. By now, as is clear from the portraits we can be certain are his, what distinguished Rembrandt as a portraitist was in full evidence: It was the same genius that distinguished him as a history painter. He eschewed vague, gen-

Twelfth Night. Drawing, 1641–42

The Three Trees. Etching, 1643

eralized impressions; rather he burrowed in to capture an instant of deep personal feeling, a unique moment, an internal event, an event that usually remains unknown and mysterious to us outsiders but that is nonetheless specific, exact, and evanescent. Even as a portraitist, especially as a portraitist, Rembrandt was a dramatist.

What Rembrandt did not do much of, and perhaps none at all (some of the paintings are hard to authenticate), were society portraits. Whether he had turned his back on society portraiture again—whether he had decided, after Saskia's death, not to waste his life on anything he detested—or whether he couldn't get commissions even if he tried, no one knows. Possibly he kept running across patrons who tried to tell him how to paint in the smooth new style. At about this time he did a pen and ink sketch of "The Asinine Art Buyer," a gentleman, with ass' horns, sitting amid a crowd of onlookers, viewing what might be a picture of a woman, or a scene of the Holy Family, or a portrait; the gentleman is holding forth, gesturing at the painting with a pipe he holds in his hand, while others smirk with disdain or gaze at him in awe or respect or disbelief. It is Rembrandt's only overtly satirical picture, done in a mood of real disgust. He is done once again with flattering the rich.

These may have been years of great mood swings for Rembrandt. Some bits of gossip that were passed down among his students and hangers-on, some of the stories of the master's sourness and nastiness, may well date from this time. He was, according to Filippo Baldinucci, who got his information from one of Rembrandt's pupils of the time, "a most temperamental man and despised everyone. The ugly and plebeian face by which he was ill-favored was accompanied by untidy and dirty clothes [this was new, if Baldinucci is right: in his days with Saskia he had loved to dress up], since it was his custom, when working, to wipe his brushes on himself, and to do other things of a similar nature." He was rude and snooty, too: "When he worked he would not have granted an audience to the first monarch in the world, who would have had to return and return again until he had found him no longer engaged upon that work."

In Baldinucci's opinion, Rembrandt got no good portrait commissions because he took so long to paint portraits: "He worked
so slowly, and completed his things with a tardiness and toil
never equalled by anybody . . . after it became commonly
known that whoever wanted to be portrayed by him had to
sit to him for some two or three months, there were few who
came forward. [This too was new, if true, since the early 1630s,
when he tossed off a portrait every couple of weeks. Was it because Rembrandt was searching deeper into his subjects now
for some less superficial effect, for some more complex inner
drama?] The cause of this slowness was that, immediately after
the first work had dried, he took it up again, repainting it with
great and small strokes, so that at times the pigment in a
given place was raised more than half the thickness of a finger."
That, at least, was true: He was laying on the paint more thickly
now than he had in his early paintings. As Arnold Houbraken,
the pupil of van Hoogstraten, who had been Rembrandt's pupil
in the 1640s, reported, "It is said that he once painted a portrait
in which the colors were so heavily loaded that you could lift
it from the floor by the nose."

According to Houbraken, Rembrandt spent little time at taverns or parties, and lived simply at home, "often content with
some bread and cheese or a pickled herring as his whole meal."
He "kept company mostly with common people and such as
practiced art." The pretentious costumes of his early self-
portraits, the arrogant posing as a grandee or a man of the court
were gone. He was taking his ease among painters and theater
people and common people.

He was not entirely without friends from Amsterdam society.
Jan Six, a man in his mid-twenties, twelve years younger than
Rembrandt, a partner in a weaving firm, descended from old
money (old as things went in Amsterdam—his grandfather had
founded the firm in 1586), bearing the titles of Lord of Wim-
menum and Vromade, was destined in time to become a burgomaster; he was a lover of art, a collector especially of Italian drawings and paintings and also of ancient statues and reliefs and
other *objets*, and was himself a poet of some talent. He was
a friend of Hendrick Uylenburgh's son, and may have met Rem-

Jan Six. Etching, 1647

brandt through Uylenburgh, or he may have met Rembrandt through mutual friends in the theatrical world. In 1647, Rembrandt did an etching of Six standing at a window, his elbow resting casually on the sill, reading a book. Evidently they became friends. In 1648, Six wrote a verse tragedy, *Medea*, and asked Rembrandt to do an illustration for the title page. But Six did not help Rembrandt to rise to new society commissions; rather the young would-be bohemian joined Rembrandt in the world of painters and poets, actors and playwrights.

Rembrandt had one good commission in these years. Once more, and this time for the last time, he got in touch with Frederik Hendrik and sold the prince two paintings—*The Adoration of the Shepherds* and *The Circumcision of Christ*. This time Rembrandt got the price he had been asking for all these years—1200 guilders apiece—but perhaps he got that lordly sum less because Frederik Hendrik thought the paintings were worth it than because he had heard Rembrandt was on hard times. The paintings are not very good, and the following year, when Huygens began to hire painters to decorate a new palace for The Hague, the Huis ten Bosch, he did not give Rembrandt a commission.

As Rembrandt struggled to keep the money coming in—painting some beautiful pictures, but not consistently, turning out portraits of the sort of low-born people he had fallen among who could not have paid much if anything for them, making etchings for the open market, taking his walks in the country, spending time with his son and his son's nurse, and earning a reputation as a moody, self-involved, even nasty man—Saskia's relatives returned to badger him. In 1647, they demanded—as protectors of Titus' inheritance—that Rembrandt draw up a complete inventory of all his and Saskia's possessions as they had been at the time of Saskia's death. In the view of Saskia's family, Rembrandt was as untrustworthy as ever, maybe worse. Perhaps they had even heard that Rembrandt was giving things to Titus' nurse Geertje Dirckx—clothes and jewelry that had once belonged to Saskia. Some time after Saskia's death, Rembrandt and Geertje had begun to have a love affair.

Not much is known about Geertje Dirckx. She was a peasant

Six's Bridge. Etching, 1645

The Naughty Boy. Drawing, about 1635

woman from the little town of Edam, just north of Amsterdam. She had worked as a waitress at an inn in the nearby town of Hoorn, where she met and married a ship's bugler. Her husband died shortly after their marriage, and Geertje took a job first as a housekeeper in Edam, and then as a helper to her brother, who was a carpenter for the East India Company. From there, somehow, she found her way to Saskia and Rembrandt's house to become nurse to the newborn Titus. She was about thirty-two years old when she joined the household.

How she may have looked is anyone's guess. Rembrandt did do a very few large-scale theatrical paintings in these years, and he might have used Geertje as a model for them—or, as far as that goes, even as an inspiration. He did a beautiful biblical picture of the nearly naked Susanna surprised by the lecherous elders while she is bathing. If this is Geertje, she was a pretty young woman, who looked even younger than she was, and had (or Rembrandt could imagine her to have) an irresistible air of vulnerability and innocence.

He painted a spectacular picture, too—whether to reassure Geertje, or to make some sort of declaration to the world, or merely because there was a market for it—of *Christ and the Woman Taken in Adultery*, in which the innocent young woman (who looks like Susanna), dressed in white, kneels before a compassionate Christ, in the setting of a deliciously corrupt temple with a vast golden throne and golden columns ("He that is without sin among you, let him cast the first stone"). If this is Geertje, she had a capacity, too, for dignity and grace.

And he painted an intimate picture as well in these years, of a young woman in bed, holding back the bed curtain to receive her lover. And if this is Geertje (she, too, looks like Susanna), she was a round, plump, soft woman, and (perhaps this is reading in too much) just a little uncertain of herself or of her situation.

In January of 1648, Rembrandt responded to the harassment of Saskia's relatives: He had Geertje draw up her last will and testament. Geertje appointed as her sole heir her mother, leaving her all the linen, clothing, woolens, and other material in Geertje's possession—but then, specifically excluding from this cate-

gory of clothing "any jewelry." The jewelry, and all other property, "moveable and immoveable, securities and credits, and
legal rights, to the exclusion of nothing," she left to Titus.

What strain the writing of this will may have caused between Rembrandt and Geertje is impossible to know. Maybe
there was no strain. Maybe Rembrandt had already promised to
marry her, and that made it easy for her to write such a will,
leaving the things that Rembrandt had given to her to her step-
son. Or maybe, in order to persuade her to write the will, Rembrandt now promised to marry her. By 1648 they had been
living together for six years; their neighbors probably already
regarded them as common-law husband and wife. But, when
Geertje wrote her will, she would have been thirty-eight years
old, an age at which she might have begun to feel frantic about
having children of her own, and about having something to
leave to them as well. Perhaps she too, like Saskia's relatives,
was pressuring Rembrandt.

Possibly it was a rumor that Rembrandt and Geertje were
about to marry that had roused Saskia's relatives in the first
place. If they heard such a rumor they no doubt feared that
Rembrandt would be giving something of Saskia's estate to
Geertje's children. Whatever the case, by making a fuss, they
reminded Rembrandt that, if he remarried, he lost all claim to
Saskia's property, which would certainly include the house he
was living in.

Aside from financial difficulties, remarriage might cause other
troubles, too. There was the possibility, for instance, that other
guardians would be appointed to look after Titus if Rembrandt
remarried, interfering not just with Titus' inheritance but with
Rembrandt's manner of raising his son. The Chamber of Orphans might assert some authority over Titus. Clearly Rembrandt was not going to get married again. But by this time
he had evidently let Geertje believe he might, a belief that was
now stirring up suspicions and hard feelings on all sides.

Just how Rembrandt himself was bearing up under all the strain
he had created can best be guessed from a self-portrait etching
that he did in 1648. He has shown himself seated at a window, his lips pursed tight, his mustache neatly clipped. He wears

Rembrandt Drawing at a Window. Etching, 1648

a white shirt under his painter's smock and a stovepipe hat with a squat crown. (He doesn't look as untidy as the gossips were saying.) He has a pen in one hand and a sheaf of papers in front of him on which he draws.

What is remarkable above all about this etching is that this is Rembrandt without frills—without any pose as a courtier or cavalier, without any attempt to look the part of a merchant-prince or Italian count, without any swagger, without any boisterous tavern setting. After all these years of posturing here is Rembrandt, for the first time, as a working man. He is middle-aged, forty-two years old, at home at his work table: the picture of a man working to support a household. He has the beginnings of a double chin, a little puffiness around the eyes, and his complexion does not look very healthy. His eyes bear the traces of a good bit of past and even present sadness, but he looks straight ahead, with a steady, unflinching gaze—no worse than a king, but no better than a commoner.

The Nadir

WHEN EXACTLY the twenty-two-year-old Hendrickje Stoffels joined the household is not clear. Nor is anything much known about her. Like Geertje, she was from the country and from the lower classes. She was born in Bredevoort, a little village far to the east of Amsterdam, the daughter of an army sergeant. Both of her brothers were in the army, and her sister was married to a soldier. She moved in, probably sometime in 1648, as the new housekeeper—very likely with Geertje's approval, perhaps at Geertje's urging, now that Geertje had taken on the role of Rembrandt's wife. By January of 1649 the household was in such a state that Rembrandt had evidently stopped drawing and painting altogether. For the whole year of 1649, there is not a single dated Rembrandt etching or painting.

For the first six months of 1649, the records are silent. Were Rembrandt and Hendrickje spending all their time making love? Was there tension in the house all this time? Or did Geertje only discover what was happening in June? In June of 1649, according to a deposition that Hendrickje delivered before a notary, there was a loud, ugly scene in the kitchen, with Geertje, Hendrickje, Rembrandt, and a neighbor woman present. Geertje, according to Hendrickje, "wanted to depart and leave." And Rembrandt did not stand in her way. He agreed at once to pay her 160 guilders outright and sixty guilders a year for the rest of her life, and, if necessary, he might give her more "at his discretion, according to her actual needs," providing she would promise that the will she had drawn up in Titus' favor back in January of 1648 remain inviolate.

Apparently, then, Geertje moved out at once and took up residence in a rented room.

By September, however, she had thought about it, and decided she had settled for too little, or else, brooding about the young woman living with Rembrandt, she decided she had settled too easily. On September twenty-fifth, she appeared before the Chamber of Marital Affairs. There she accused Rembrandt of breach of promise. Rembrandt was summoned to appear before the Chamber to defend himself.

But Rembrandt, having no taste for appearing before courts, arranged another meeting at his house. This time, October third, Geertje came with a friend, a young, twenty-nine-year-old shoemaker from the neighborhood. On the one hand, the young shoemaker must have been impressed, and even intimidated, by the great temperamental painter in his palatial home. On the other hand, the young man was ready to stick up for his friend against the old (age forty-three) lecher. Maybe the young man was Geertje's lover; maybe he was just a friend.

Geertje and the shoemaker, named Octaeff Octaeffszoon, got Rembrandt to raise his settlement: a payment of two hundred guilders outright and the sum of 160 guilders a year for the rest of Geertje's life.

But by now there was another complication. While they had been arguing over this financial settlement, Geertje had spent whatever money Rembrandt had given her and had nothing to live on. Evidently Rembrandt had got wind of the fact that Geertje had been pawning Saskia's jewelry (that jewelry he had given her with the understanding she would leave it to Titus) to meet her current expenses, and he was alarmed and enraged at that. So, in addition to everything else, the new settlement called for Geertje to use that two hundred guilders to redeem the pawned jewelry so that it would again be in her possession to pass down to Titus.

On October fourteenth, Rembrandt and Geertje and Octaeff appeared before a notary to formalize their agreement. By this time, however, Rembrandt had had second thoughts. Apparently he had begun to suspect that Geertje would not redeem the jewelry she had pawned. And so he added a couple of tough clauses to their agreement: He himself would redeem the jewelry and deduct the cost of redemption from the lump sum of two hundred guilders. Furthermore, he insisted that Geertje swear "to conduct herself in a proper manner, so that the ring with the cluster of diamonds, and all other property in her possession, including the items [redeemed] with the aforementioned sum of money, will be left behind by her in free and unencumbered condition at the time of her death," so that it could pass to Titus in accord with her will of January, 1648. If Geertje did not abide by this condition, Rembrandt would cease paying her 160 guilders per annum and Geertje would be obliged to return everything she had received from him immediately.

At this, Geertje lost whatever self-control she had left. Whether she felt her integrity had been impugned or whether, in fact, she wanted to be left free to pawn the jewelry in the future for money—and had not earlier quite realized the implications of her promising to abide by her will of 1648—she now "inveighed very vehemently and unreasonably" against Rembrandt, and said she didn't want even to listen to a reading of the agreement, much less sign it.

The notary tried to explain the agreement to her, but she steadfastly refused to sign it—arguing now, desperately, that "in the event of illness or other infirmity a maid or nurse would require more than 160 guilders annually." It is not hard to imagine tears. Rembrandt, touched perhaps, but still cautious about committing himself, said that he was willing to adjust the annual payments, providing it were left to his discretion. That was not good enough. Geertje refused to sign.

Two days later, Geertje summoned Rembrandt again to appear before the Chamber of Marital Affairs. Once again Rembrandt failed to appear. Then, seven days later, a third summons went out to Rembrandt and, at last, he appeared.

The hearing got right to the heart of the matter, as the record shows. The plaintiff, Geertje, "declares that the defendant has made oral promises of marriage and given her a ring [as pledge] thereof. Furthermore, that he slept with her on several occasions, and she demands that the defendant marry her or else support her."

Rembrandt, cold (it must have been frightening to Geertje), replied: He denied ever having made promises of marriage; as for the allegation that he had slept with her, "the plaintiff . . . will have to prove it."

The court deliberated only briefly. It awarded Geertje two hundred guilders in a lump sum and raised the annual payment from 160 to two hundred guilders and ended by enjoining her to abide by all the other provisions of the previous agreement drafted by the notary.

Financially, Geertje scored a victory. At least she got more than Rembrandt had originally promised her back during the scene in the kitchen. But money seems not to have been what she was after. Whether Geertje had always been given to suspicion and rage, or whether she had been driven to it by Rembrandt, whether this public rejection pushed her over the edge or she was destined for collapse in any case, she fell apart.

Apparently she began to pawn Saskia's jewelry again at once. And evidently Rembrandt retaliated by cutting off his payments to her. In April 1650 she gave power of attorney to her brother Pieter—in a document filled with expressions of anguish. She appeared before a notary and "declared most vehemently" that she appointed Pieter "to take charge of, prosecute, and further her cause, rights, and just claims against and toward anyone; to take action and defend her in and out of court, and also to demand, claim, and receive from any and all whatever such debtors owe her . . . to give service and notice in courts, to protest, demand, attach persons and goods, make claims, draw conclusions, choose domicile, contest lawsuits, reply, counter-plea. . . ."

Pieter dutifully went to Rembrandt's house to collect the money—and then the most astounding thing happened. Before he left Rembrandt's house, Pieter apparently agreed to collect testimony from the neighbors against Geertje, so that Geertje could be sent away to an insane asylum. He did collect the testimony. The testimony was presented in court. And Geertje was sent off to an insane asylum—for twelve years. Then Pieter went to the pawnshop, redeemed Saskia's jewelry, and presumably turned it over to Rembrandt.

Why did Pieter do such a thing? Had Rembrandt bribed him? Or threatened him with a lawsuit over the jewelry? Or manipulated him into some perverse view of his sister's condition? Or had Geertje by this time become so consumed with rage, so unhinged with anguish, that even her brother and her neighbors thought it best for her to be locked up? Was it compassion or some dreadful betrayal that caused her to be sent away? Whatever the case, Rembrandt paid 140 guilders, the cost of the procedure to have Geertje sent to the insane asylum, where she spent her time spinning and listening to religious sermons and instruction.

This was not the end of it. When it appeared that Geertje might be released from the asylum, Rembrandt hired an agent to collect more evidence against her, to make certain that she stay locked up. This sordid move on Rembrandt's part finally provoked some of Geertje's women friends to petition to have her released. At last, in 1655, she was released. She revoked at once the power of attorney she had given to her brother, and, since Rembrandt had not paid her any alimony in those five years, she sued Rembrandt once again. This time the lawsuit failed to go to its conclusion because, in the latter half of 1656, Geertje died.

The Hundred Guilder Print. Etching, 1649

The Hundred Guilder Print

URING THE TIME that Rembrandt was living with Geertje, he did a good many pictures. Without doubt, however, the most famous picture he did in those years was not a painting but a print. The business of printmaking—though in terms of prestige it ranked beneath history paintings, beneath portraiture, beneath flower paintings, beneath genre paintings—was a good way for an artist who needed money to do a picture fast and sell a lot of cheap copies. And in the hands of such artists as Dürer and Lucas van Leyden, printmaking had even been a distinguished art. Rembrandt was the best there was in the business of printmaking in his own day, and he was better known to many people for his prints than for his paintings. It is odd, then, that his print of Christ healing the sick, which was to become his most famous print of all, violated the most basic tenets of printmaking: It took ten years to do and, according to legend, it sold for the outrageous sum of one hundred guilders.

The print shows Christ in front of a town wall preaching to

multitudes of devout poor on one side, and indifferent rich on the other. It is based on Matthew 19, which tells the story of Christ traveling to the coast of Judea, followed by great crowds, many of whom were sick or dying, and on whom Christ laid his healing hands.

When Christ reached Judea, the Pharisees came out to meet him and to try to trap him into preaching unorthodox lessons. They asked him, for example, whether it was lawful for a man "to put away his wife," to which Christ replied that man and wife are one flesh. "What therefore God hath joined together, let not man put asunder."

Small children were brought to Jesus, and his disciples tried to keep the pesky little children away; but Christ said, "Suffer little children, and forbid them not to come unto me: for of such is the kingdom of heaven."

A young rich man asked Jesus what he might do to gain salvation, and Christ replied that the young man must "sell that thou hast and give to the poor, and thou shalt have treasure in heaven." But when the young man heard this radical suggestion he turned away depressed, and that was when Christ said to his disciples that it was easier for a camel to pass through the eye of a needle than for a rich man to get into heaven.

In Rembrandt's etching, all the characters out of Matthew are present: At the far left, the Pharisees cluster in conversation, trying to think up clever questions; to the right an endless swarm of poor, desperate, sick people descend on Jesus for help and cure. Just in front of Jesus is a young woman holding up her baby—and Peter, standing next to Jesus, puts out his hand rudely to push the woman away. Just to the left of this young woman is the rich young man, sunk to the ground in depression, his head in his hand. (And to the right, coming out of the town gate, for those who like to see everything in a story illustrated, is a camel—not the big rope that modern translators say is meant by a "camel," but the one-humped dromedary of everyone's childhood imagination.)

Rembrandt has improved on Matthew with a few touches of his own: In the left foreground is a well-to-do gentleman, quite indifferent to the preachings of Christ, chatting amiably with a couple of bystanders. A little boy and a dog are playing nearby, and the dog has a good grip on the toddler's left foot. Most of the rich people are talking among themselves; the poor, having nothing else, depend on Christ's every word.

Until the 1510s, when the first etchings were made in Germany, prints like this one of Christ were made by engraving. An engraver carves deep channels in a copper plate. These channels hold ink which is, in turn, soaked up by paper when the paper is pressed onto the plate.

An etcher on the other hand coats his copper plate first with wax and then, with a sharp point, scratches lightly through the wax to expose the copper. The plate is then put in an acid bath, and the acid eats into the plate wherever it is exposed, to make the channels for the ink. Corrections were simple enough: a plate could be burnished smooth in a particular area, re-coated with wax, and etched again. Whereas an engraving is composed only of lines, an etching plate, given a quick dip in an acid bath, can add areas of tone to the lines. In the hands of the right artist, certainly in Rembrandt's hands, an etching has a kind of fluidity and spontaneity impossible to achieve in an engraving.

What, then, took Rembrandt so long to do this picture? The subject was spelled out in Matthew. The composition, while complicated, is no more difficult than compositions Rembrandt had done in the past with ease. There are about forty people in the picture, a lot of people, but not as many as in his drawing of St. John preaching. What was so difficult to get right about this picture that it took Rembrandt the whole decade of the 1640s to finish it?

To go back to the subject of the picture, Matthew 19 is about the rightness of a man putting away his wife, about whether it is better to be rich or poor, about achieving salvation in the company of children, the poor, the sick, the outcast, and the desperate—and about healing.

As always, we have no idea whether Rembrandt did the print out of some personal feeling or out of some judgment about the art market. But it is inconceivable that as he worked on the print he did not think about his own life—about putting away his common-law wife Geertje, about his own confusions and troubles about money, about his new life with his son and his low-born neighbors, and about healing his own wounds. He could hardly have been unaffected by all these associations which the picture calls up. The composition could not have felt right until it caught just the right emotion. And getting a feeling just right is the hardest thing of all. A slight change of light or shadow will alter a scene from gloomy to hopeful or from stupidly optimistic to somber. The subtlest change of pose will put energy, or lethargy and depression, into a picture. And it may be that Rembrandt found it hard to finish the picture when he had not settled all these matters in his own mind. Whatever may be the case, he finished the picture in 1649, the year that he finally broke with Geertje.

Money Trouble

Rembrandt van Rhijn p. Christoffel Thijsz   350

                                                               43.15

1650   13 Maart 1652 p. Mr. van Rhijn   43.15

1651   43.15

1652   27 januario 1653. Christoffel tijsz   43.15

                 —from the Amsterdam municipal archives

In 1639, Rembrandt had bought his palatial house in Sint Antoniesbreestraat from Christoffel Thijs and so assumed an obligation to pay 350 guilders in taxes on the purchase of the house. Evidently, he made a payment of 43.15 guilders and then fell behind on the taxes immediately. Here he was in 1652, thirteen years later, still in arrears on his taxes, and with the municipal authorities becoming impatient.

Such were Rembrandt's powers to get others to do things for him that he got Christoffel Thijs himself, the previous owner of the house (to whom Rembrandt still owed a large part of the purchase price) to come up with three more tax payments on Rembrandt's behalf. Presumably it was in Thijs' interest to keep the tax collectors at bay, to keep Rembrandt afloat so that he could eventually come through on the full purchase price of the house. But in fact, this is the earliest warning that we have—and that Rembrandt ignored—that, financially, Rembrandt had begun to sink.

The taxes had not been stiff as such things go. There had been many times in the 1640s that Rembrandt had had a spare forty-three guilders for taxes. But he had let the taxes slide—as he generally let all demands from bureaucrats slide, as he declined to meet his legal obligation to file Saskia's will with the Chamber of Orphans, as he did not bother to answer summonses from various city courts. He spent the city's money on art, no doubt, or on props for the studio, or on some other accouterments to which a famous artist and prosperous member of the upper classes felt he was entitled, whether he could afford them or not. He had been living beyond his means for years. The tax collectors were only the first to catch up with him.

Money troubles seemed to run in the family. While Rembrandt's father had been a prudent man with money, his children were less dependable. In the mid-1640s, Rembrandt's brother Adriaen and his sister Elysabeth had had to go outside the family to borrow five hundred guilders from a farmer near Gouda. A couple of years later, according to a document from the archives, Adriaen owed another man interest on another loan. His brother Willem, meanwhile, owed interest on a loan he had managed to get from a widow, and pledged his house and garden in Leiden as security. In 1652, when the tax collectors were coming after Rembrandt, his sister Elysabeth was being hounded for yet another debt.

But Rembrandt was tremendously resourceful. Getting Thijs to come up with the payments was only his first maneuver. In 1653, Thijs began to lose patience and sent a notary around to Rembrandt's house to present him with some threatening papers. The notary, "being told that said person was not home, handed my writ to a certain housemaid and . . . she declared that she would report it to her master upon his return home."

When that failed to produce a result, a second writ was delivered to Rembrandt's house two days later. And then Rembrandt began to scramble a little more frantically. Within two weeks he managed to secure a loan from Cornelis Witsen, a man of considerable substance and standing, soon to be nominated to be one of Amsterdam's burgomasters. Rembrandt may have come to know Witsen because Witsen had been a member of the *kloveniers* and no doubt admired Rembrandt's painting in the hall of the *Kloveniersdoelen*. Witsen advanced Rembrandt a loan for the handsome sum of 4180 guilders, far more than Rembrandt needed to pay those taxes.

As bad as things got for Rembrandt, as financially undependable, as devious and manipulative, as generally untrustworthy as he was known to be, there were still people who believed in his talents, and so with their help he was able to dig himself even deeper into debt.

Anatomy of
a Masterpiece:
Aristotle with
a Bust of Homer

Half-length figure of a philosopher made in
Amsterdam by the painter named Rembrandt (it seems
to be an Aristotle or Albertus Magnus)
—from the inventory list of
Don Antonio Ruffo of Messina

Don Antonio didn't know what he had, although he had paid
five hundred guilders for it, eight times what he would have
paid a first-rate Italian painter, and as much as ten times what
Rembrandt could have gotten from a Dutch collector, for a
single figure. That Rembrandt sold a painting to a Sicilian
nobleman for five hundred guilders in 1654 proves three things:
that Rembrandt was hard up for patrons in Amsterdam, that
he was world-famous, and that he still had a lot of nerve.

Don Antonio, though he had paid extravagantly for a painting by the hard-bargaining Rembrandt, was no fool. He was a
worldly man in his mid-forties, the descendant of a family that

had been prominent in Calabria for centuries. He lived in a palace decorated with frescoes, tapestries, sculpture, gold and silver objects, a library that was worth a fortune, and nearly two hundred modern paintings from all over Europe. He also, like many other wealthy householders of the seventeenth century, had a hall set aside for pictures of illustrious people, and it was evidently for his Hall of Fame that he asked Rembrandt to paint something appropriate. He left the choice of the exact subject to Rembrandt.

Rembrandt chose Aristotle, and proceeded to paint him in a way no classical Greek would have recognized him. Aristotle's contemporaries left very clear and exact descriptions of the philosopher: He was a short, bald, paunchy fellow with spindly legs and tiny eyes, a cynical expression around his mouth, and a stutter. Clearly, this would not do for Rembrandt's purposes; and he adopted the more up-to-date fashion of depicting philosophers, no matter who they were, as men of noble stature, with impressive beards and long mustaches. Though Aristotle was something of a dandy, who loved to wear a lot of rings, Rembrandt put him (with a single, simple ring) in a long, dignified, flowing white gown of a sort that, so far as anyone knows, was never worn by anyone in any period of history. Rembrandt gave him a style of beret that appears indiscriminately on the heads of many of the older men Rembrandt painted in these years. He also put Aristotle in some sort of apron that goes from the philosopher's chin to the floor. The beret and the apron are black, as befits a philosopher, because black is the color of melancholy, and all philosophers were, by definition, melancholics. The black was especially suited to Aristotle, since he was popularly (though incorrectly) said to have written: "Why is it that all those who have become eminent in philosophy or politics or poetry or the arts are clearly melancholics?"

In Rembrandt's view of him, Aristotle is lost in thought, as, indeed, a lot of Rembrandt's people are, both philosophers and ordinary men and women. There was a vogue in the 1650s for philosophers lost in thought, and Rembrandt was the best of the painters at turning them out. Even as a young man, Rembrandt had painted old men and women gazing sadly into space; and, after the fad passed, Rembrandt would still be painting the same sort of pictures. He had become the master of depicting introspection, of showing people alone with their private thoughts and sensations—and, even more, of showing men's and women's ultimate loneliness and isolation.

It may be that men and women of the seventeenth century responded to this sort of thing because they had become increasingly impressed by the fruits of scientific investigation, secular thought, and some sense of awe before the depth of *human* mystery; and they may have felt, too, after the Protestant Reformation, and Luther's preaching that each individual faces God alone, that they were lonelier and more isolated than they had ever been before. But the resonance Rembrandt himself felt with these themes seems likely to have come from a more personal source. Many of Rembrandt's early paintings are filled with dramatic interactions among people caught up together in an event. In the early portraits he painted there was often a sense that the subject of the portrait had just noticed the viewer entering the room. But in nearly all of Rembrandt's paintings of the 1650s and 1660s there is an overwhelming sense that these people, even when they are in a group, are alone.

Aristotle stands in a library, which is certainly the right setting for him. There are a few books in the background. It is a gloomy library, which is in keeping with the general atmosphere of melancholy. Over his black apron is a spectacular gold chain. Gold chains were worn simply as jewelry in Rembrandt's day, but such gold chains had sometimes been awarded to illustrious persons in the ancient world as symbols of honor, a practice which had been revived in the Renaissance. Artists were given them sometimes. Titian got one from Charles V in 1533. Paolo Veronese got one. Rubens got three of them on three different occasions. The chain betokens honor—and, of course, it also betokens a tie, even a shackle, to a patron. (In Rembrandt's self-portraits, he awarded himself a gold chain more than a dozen times, taking the decoration without shackling himself to anyone.)

Suspended from Aristotle's gold chain is a little gold medallion portrait of his patron, Alexander the Great. Alexander's father King Philip of Macedonia had brought Aristotle in to tutor his son. Aristotle tutored the young Alexander for nine years and, on Alexander's accession to the throne, Aristotle returned to Athens. According to Plutarch, Alexander "admired Aristotle at first, and loved him, as he himself used to say, more than he did his father. . . . Later, however, he held him in more or less suspicion. . . ."

Indeed, in later years, Alexander had a man named Callisthenes—a friend, perhaps even a nephew, of Aristotle's—executed on suspicion of treason. The moral of the story was clear not just to Aristotle but also to Rembrandt and his contemporaries: A prince may give you a gold chain one day and come close to killing you the next. In Rembrandt's painting, Aristotle is fingering his gold chain, as though he might be thinking about honor, wealth, and the fickleness and uncertainty of fortune.

While Aristotle fingers his medallion with his left hand, his right hand rests on a bust of Homer, who was, in Aristotle's view, the "divine" master of poetry and thus, because poetry was the highest art, the sovereign of all art. No mortal could be more exalted than this. Nor was Aristotle alone in his worship of Homer. Once Aristotle had finished instructing Alexander, Alexander worshiped Homer, too. In fact, according to Plutarch, Alexander carried with him at all times a copy of the *Iliad*, edited by Aristotle, and slept with it under his pillow at night.

Although Rembrandt's painting has been known as *Aristotle Contemplating the Bust of Homer*, it might more properly be called Aristotle recognizing that, while the prince is instructed by the philosopher, the philosopher is instructed by the poet (or artist).

Don Antonio Ruffo, not knowing whether he had a painting of Aristotle or of Albertus Magnus, hardly got Rembrandt's message, although he did love the painting (it is beautiful and moving no matter what it means) and knew that, with a Rembrandt, he had a treasure. Nonetheless, however much he loved it, it had been expensive, and he was not eager to pay another five hundred guilders for another painting for his Hall of Fame.

Homer Dictating to a Scribe. Drawing, 1663

Evidently he wanted to hang the Aristotle where it required a companion piece to balance it, and so he got in touch with the Italian painter Guercino, who was then sixty-nine years old, a workmanlike painter with a touching and admirable appreciation for his more inspired fellow artists.

To Don Antonio's request that he do something to accompany a Rembrandt, Guercino replied, "As for the figure in half-length by Reimbrant which has come into your hands, it cannot but be completely perfect, for I have seen various of his works in print which have reached these parts. They are very beautifully executed, engraved in good taste, and done in a fine manner, so that one can assume that his work in color will likewise be entirely exquisite and perfect. I sincerely esteem him as a great virtuoso."

Guercino was complimented to be asked to do something to accompany the Rembrandt and asked Don Antonio to send him the measurements of the Rembrandt and to have some local artist do a sketch of the Rembrandt. With the sketch in hand, Guercino would be better able to think of a proper companion subject and know how to handle the light in his painting so that it would accord well with the Rembrandt.

Once he received the sketch of the Rembrandt, Guercino had no doubt what to do. He did his painting at once. As he wrote Don Antonio, it looked to him as though Rembrandt had painted a physiognomist (a man feeling the lumps on another man's head), and so Guercino thought a cosmographer would provide an excellent companion piece: one picture representing the study of mankind, the other representing the study of the heavens. Accordingly, Guercino had done a painting of a cosmographer and was dispatching it under separate cover. "I shall remain here," Guercino concluded, "anxiously attending to your every wish and consider myself fortunate to have acquired in some way the good will of your lordship by showing you that I am more than ever ready and desirous to obey your commands. I close with a deferential bow." This deferential bow certainly distinguished Guercino from Rembrandt. In another letter to Don Antonio, Guercino concluded by saying, "With the prayer that you continue holding me in your affection, I reverently kiss your hand." In part Guercino showed how Italian he was with all his bowing and scraping and hand kissing; in part, however, he showed how far apart Rembrandt stood from almost all other artists in his relationships with his patrons.

Guercino's painting has disappeared, so it's not possible to see how well he did. Whether Don Antonio liked it or not, he decided before long to commission yet another inexpensive companion piece to the Aristotle, this time from one of Guercino's former pupils, Mattia Preti. Either Don Antonio was searching for the perfect companion piece, or he was just trying to fill up his Hall of Fame with more paintings that matched Rembrandt's high standard. In any case, he evidently failed twice to match the quality of the Aristotle to his satisfaction, and so, within a few years, he was back in touch with Rembrandt himself to ask for a companion piece, and Rembrandt was happy to oblige. Very soon, Rembrandt despatched the only possible companion piece to the Aristotle: a painting of Alexander.

Rembrandt's portrait of Alexander has gone astray. Over the years there have been a couple of pictures of noble, armor-clad men, holding spears and shields, who have been identified as the Alexander. But one minor objection or another—to their authenticity or their date or their composition—has kept the scholars from declaring in favor of them. Both, however, suggest the sort of picture the Alexander may have been: an image of a strong but civilized leader who would easily understand the value of art and artists.

Along with the portrait of Alexander, Rembrandt included yet another companion piece: Homer. The painting of Homer was not finished, and was sent on approval to entice Don Antonio to commission its completion.

Don Antonio did not hesitate a moment before sending off a letter to his agent in Holland, instructing him to inform Rembrandt how "little pleased" Don Antonio was with the painting of Alexander. Don Antonio spoke with as much restraint as he could muster, but he was enraged. The picture "was painted on four pieces of canvas sewn together. These four seams are horrible beyond words. Besides, in time they will crack and consequently the canvas as a whole will be ruined." The agent was instructed to tell Rembrandt that Don Antonio (far from being the ignorant provincial Rembrandt might take him to be) "does not own a single painting with patched canvas among his 200 examples of the best subjects in Europe. Rembrandt—maybe in order to save work or perhaps crushed by his many tasks—in order to transform this 'Alexander' (since at the start it was nothing more than a Head on a single canvas) into a half-length figure, decided to add canvas to it." (Could it be, in fact, that Rembrandt had had an old picture of a helmeted man lying around the studio and, to make it seem like a companion piece to his Aristotle, with his customary cavalier attitude toward his patrons, had tacked on a few pieces of canvas to make it as large as the earlier painting?)

"He first added it lengthwise, but then, seeing that the painting was too narrow added another one widthwise. In order to make up for both of these deficiencies, he sent along with the 'Alexander' a half-completed painting of 'Homer.' "

Had a patron seen through Rembrandt at last?

Don Antonio was angry—but not blind. He understood he was dealing with a scoundrel, but he recognized how uncommon a scoundrel Rembrandt was. He did not want to sever relations. He wanted the Homer, and he wanted Rembrandt to fix the Alexander.

The Homer, Don Antonio told his agent, was being returned "in order to be completed." The Alexander was being returned to have the extra strips of canvas removed and the painting finished up in its diminished size. But let Rembrandt not think he could cheat Don Antonio endlessly. Don Antonio would pay only half what Rembrandt was asking for these paintings—250 guilders, not five hundred—because the Alexander is really only a head, not a half-length, and the Homer is already half-finished. (Maybe Don Antonio thought the Homer was just something Rembrandt had lying around the studio, too.) And five hundred guilders is, anyway, at least four times the amount "the best known Italian painters would ask for." And, in case Rembrandt did not agree to repair the Alexander as Don Antonio specified, then Don Antonio would insist on having his money back, "since we need not keep in our house such an expensive painting with so many defects." Finally (this should prove a sufficient bribe to get Rembrandt to behave like Guercino), if Rembrandt should please Don Antonio in all this, the agent was to drop the hint that a pleased patron would be likely to ask for quite a few more paintings—"at least half a dozen." Rembrandt should send Don Antonio sketches of his ideas for some paintings "on paper, in pencil, red or black, whatever he prefers" so Don Antonio "may be able to choose from these."

Rembrandt was faced with a choice, as he had been so often in the past: He could admit that his patron was right, and apologize; or he could try to bluff his way out.

"I am very amazed," Rembrandt replied brazenly, by what was being said about the Alexander, "which is very well done. I don't think many people like it at Messina [that is, the provincial Don Antonio must be too easily swayed by the rubes who hang around his palace]. I am also astonished that your Lordship should complain as much about the price as about the canvas [proving how vulgar he is, thinking as much about money as about art]." Nonetheless, Rembrandt added blandly, he would paint another Alexander if Don Antonio wished (gone were the days he could pretend total indifference to money). It would be no trouble at all—although, really, this fuss was about nothing at all. "As for the canvas, I did not have enough of it while I was painting and I therefore needed to lengthen it [if Don Antonio understood anything at all about painting, he would understand that painters do this sort of thing all the time, completely routinely]. However, if the panel is hung well in daylight [if there were anyone in Italy who knew anything about hanging paintings at all], one will not notice anything."

In any case, said Rembrandt, the price was six hundred guilders for the Alexander, five hundred for the Homer, not a guilder less. And Rembrandt was too proud even to deign to mention the suggested bribe of further commissions.

In the end, Don Antonio settled for keeping the Alexander as it was, paying the price Rembrandt demanded for it, and accepting the Homer also at Rembrandt's price. And he considered himself lucky. Don Antonio, as it turns out, was not an ignorant provincial or a man of insecure ego; he didn't allow his judgment to be misled by Rembrandt's behavior. In the late 1660s, Don Antonio put in an order with his agent to buy almost two hundred etchings from Rembrandt, and some years after that, when he drew up his last will, he included the three Rembrandt paintings in a list of works that his descendants must never sell from his collection.

The third painting, the Homer, is more moving than the first two. It shows an old man, poor, worn down by his travails—and, of course, blind, utterly alone and adrift in his own thoughts. This canvas, too, is not perfect; it was damaged by fire in the eighteenth century and was cut down slightly. In its original state, it seems to have had Homer placed in the town of Cumae.

According to legend, when Homer arrived in the town of Cumae to sing his famous poems, he noticed that some of the townsmen seemed especially pleased with his performance; and so he made them a proposition. If henceforth they would take him in and support him, he would make the town of Cumae famous.

The proposition was brought before the town council, where it had a great deal of support until one of the councilmen said that if Cumae began to take in the Homers of the world—that is, the blind—soon the town would be overrun with them. And so the town, to its everlasting shame, refused to take Homer in. (Homer did make the town famous after all.) It was a story well-known in Rembrandt's time, particularly well-known among the painters of the Netherlands, so many of whom would die poor.

The story of a great artist, the story of a great and unappreciated artist, the story of a blind man, the story of a man whose art came of an inner vision, the story of a man who was not universally admired because it was said that his work was often base and vulgar: This is the story of Rembrandt.

But Homer alone, fine as he is, is not as powerful as he becomes in the company of Aristotle and Alexander. It is the three of them together that set up the real resonance of the mysteries of worldly success and failure, friendship and betrayal, greatness and neglect, the need to preserve a town's balanced budget compared to the need for compassion, and the value of an immortal song.

Hendrickje Summoned
for Fornication

REMBRANDT was besieged on all sides.

Mr. Diego d'Andrada, a Portuguese merchant here, went and visited Mr. Rembrandt van Rijn, painter, and notified and announced to him the following:

The aforementioned claimant asserts that some time ago he asked you, the respondent, to paint a portrait of a young girl, for which he gave you an advance of 75 guilders. . . .

And because the claimant is of the opinion that the aforementioned painting or portrait shows no resemblance at all to the image of the head of the young girl . . . the claimant advises through me, the notary, his request that you are to alter and retouch the aforementioned painting. . . . And that, in case you fail to do so, he will have you keep the aforementioned

painting as it is of no use to him, but demands that
you . . . reimburse the amount paid in advance. . . .

This is the first time we know of that anyone objected that
one of Rembrandt's portraits was not a good likeness. In the
past, everyone had wanted to be complimented, not shown a
likeness; and it is not clear that Rembrandt was ever skilled at
making a likeness of a person anyway: Too many of his portraits of women look alike to imagine that they are all good
likenesses. And too many of his portraits of Saskia look different to imagine that he could or wanted to capture the same likeness time after time. Feeling, not verisimilitude, was his strong
suit. But being recognized as a master was no insurance against
constant squabbling about your work.

Meanwhile, Daniel Pinto, Rembrandt's next-door neighbor,
was having his house shored up by a contractor. All these
houses, built as they were on wooden pilings, tended to sink,
but in the Breestraat area they may have tended to sink more
than most. This whole part of town was built along a dike
where the sand was not as firm as in other parts of town, and
where the water level tended to rise and fall, exposing the
wooden pilings to rot. Pinto's house seemed to be in real danger:
He had to have it raised a full three feet.

It may be that Rembrandt's house was in equal danger. Indeed, it may be that the previous owner unloaded a problem
house on Rembrandt. As it happens, the market value of Rembrandt's house was declining—perhaps not only because the
house was sinking but also because the neighborhood was becoming less fashionable. In any case, it appears from documents
in the municipal archives that Pinto and Rembrandt were both
doing work on their houses, possibly in common. They needed
at least to cooperate on one project: They shared a common
wall. Either both houses had to be lifted up together, or Pinto's
house had to be slid up that common wall and reattached at a
higher level. The inconvenience of this operation, the mess of
construction, the endless banging and dropping of things must
have been insufferable. By February of 1654, the two neighbors
were fed up with one another.

On February ninth, Arent Reyessen, master mason, and Jan
Janssen, master carpenter, appeared before a notary to tell their
story about a quantity of lumber purchased in part for Rembrandt and in part for Pinto. The lumber had not been cheap.
A bill was owing of 729 guilders and some change. Rembrandt,
of course, refused to pay anything, and Pinto wanted to know
why the lumber merchant had not drawn up separate bills, one
for him and one for Rembrandt. The lumber merchant was
maintaining he knew nothing about Rembrandt; the lumber had
been ordered on Pinto's account, and he wanted to be paid. And
master carpenter Janssen, who had evidently made the mistake
of telling the lumber merchant to just charge it all to Pinto
(had Rembrandt told him to?), was trying to shift the blame
somewhere else—demanding to know why the lumber merchant
had charged a price two or three times higher than that charged
by other lumber merchants.

Evidently Janssen was fired, because several months later,
when Rembrandt and Pinto were having another dispute, Arent
Reyessen was back in court, but this time with a co-worker
named Mordechay D'Andrade. This time Pinto was angry because he could not get to some things that he had stored in
Rembrandt's basement. Pinto was engaged in trade in the Middle East and had apparently rented a section of Rembrandt's
basement to store some merchandise while renovations were
going on. Now, the masons and carpenters had so blocked up
the front of Rembrandt's house (at Rembrandt's encourage-
ment?) that Pinto couldn't get at his goods.

Nor were these all Rembrandt's problems. He was still scrambling desperately for money to pay off the principal on his
house—even, it seems, as his house was declining in value—
and he was hitting up everyone he could for loans. The loan
from Cornelis Witsen sufficed for only a couple of months before Rembrandt was scrounging for more money—4200 guilders
from Isaac van Hertsbeeck (a loan Rembrandt would never repay), one thousand guilders from his friend Jan Six.

As collateral for his loans, he put up "all his possessions,"
and it seems, even as he pledged his possessions, he was trying
to sell off the most valuable of them for cash. In a couple of

years, when a complete inventory was taken of Rembrandt's possessions, not a single copper plate that he had etched would be found. Possibly, as "workman's tools," they were excluded from an inventory of his possessions; more likely he had sold or transferred them to put them beyond the reach of the creditors who were even at this moment advancing him money.

A good many of the portraits Rembrandt painted in the fifties were portraits of his creditors. It worked like this: Rembrandt would borrow a sum of money against a promise to paint a lender's portrait. In this way he could get and spend the money for a portrait even before he painted it, and so fall even more deeply into debt and even further behind in his work.

Yet, out of this relentless, depressing, debilitating pressure came wonderful work, including a spectacular portrait of Jan Six—looking not like the soulful poet of the etching Rembrandt had done back in the 1640s, but like a prosperous businessman capable of granting large loans.

The portrait is done with bold, dashing brushstrokes—in places, the sort of brushstrokes commonly associated with nineteenth century impressionist work. Six is putting on a glove, and the blurred brushstroke catches the glove in motion. He has a brilliant red cloak thrown over one shoulder, a cascade of buttons coming down the front of a handsome, well-made jacket, and his whole posture and attitude, the tilt of the head, the level gaze suggest a character that is sensitive, intelligent, stylish, and ruthless. Six must have loved the portrait; he kept it all his life, and passed it down to his descendants; it is still in his family, in their house on the Amstel, in Amsterdam.

He turned out another handsome portrait—of a man who can no longer be identified, dressed in a fur-trimmed coat, of the same size (and unique presence) as the portrait of Six; and an elegant portrait of the well-to-do Floris Soop. He did more than a half-dozen heads of Christ (if all of them are authentic). He dashed off more than a half-dozen unknown old men and women. He did a large picture of a richly costumed Saul, listening to David play the harp. He did two very beautiful and dramatic pictures of Joseph and Potiphar and Potiphar's wife gathered around a bed—pictures based on the story that Poti-

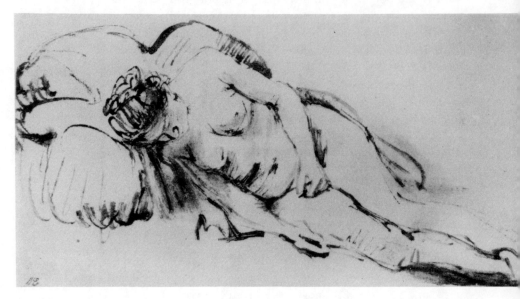

Female Nude Asleep. Drawing, about 1657–58

phar's wife tried to seduce the young household servant Joseph, and when he refused her, she accused him of trying to rape her. There was a play based on this story playing at a theater in Amsterdam, and these paintings look almost as though they were done as posters to hang in the lobby, or in some way to promote the play. Why did Rembrandt do two paintings? The young fellow in Joseph's role is different in each painting; perhaps there was a cast change in mid-run and Rembrandt ground out another poster for a second fee. He seems, in these years, to be refusing no opportunity for money. He accepts any commission, paints any subject—portraits, history paintings, religious subjects, anything that will bring in money.

Even so, he could not escape vexation. It was in the midst of all this that Hendrickje received a summons from the council of the Reformed Church:

> Hendrickie Jaghers, residing on Breestraat, having acted like a harlot with Rembrant, the painter, will be summoned to appear within eight days.

Is it conceivable that the neighbors in this community of artists could have entered a complaint? Is it conceivable that Pinto arranged this to retaliate against Rembrandt? Someone must have put the church council up to it—or perhaps it was just that Hendrickje had become too noticeable. When she got the summons, as it turns out, Hendrickje was six months pregnant.

Since it mentions Rembrandt, the summons could be interpreted to mean that Rembrandt, too, was summoned before the council. Needless to say, Rembrandt had no intention of answering the summons, and he must have convinced Hendrickje to ignore it, too, although she was a member in good standing of the church.

A week later, Hendrickje got another summons—this time without mentioning Rembrandt's name. And two weeks later she got a third summons:

> Hendrickie Jaghers, residing on Breestraat with the
> painter Rembrant, having acted like a whore, has been
> summoned three times and has failed to appear. The
> Brethren of her district shall call her to account.

At last, after some brethren of the church came to call at her home, Hendrickje appeared before the council and there "admitted that she has lived with Rembrant like a whore." For this she was punished: She was admonished to penitence and banned from the celebration of the Lord's Supper.

Three months later she gave birth to a baby girl, a child who would survive into adulthood. Evidently Rembrandt, however distracted he might have been with work and debts and the intrusions of church councils, was not indifferent to the baby. He and Hendrickje named her Cornelia, after Rembrandt's mother.

Hendrickje Naked

WHEN REMBRANDT painted a nude, it was an event, because he painted so few of them. In 1654, when he painted Hendrickje as the naked Bathsheba, it was not possible to mistake it for anything but an event: The painting, five feet by five feet, is the largest history painting Rembrandt had made in more than fifteen years, and so it stands out emphatically.

Hendrickje sits on the edge of a couch or bed that is covered with linens and silken covers, with an old woman kneeling at her feet giving her a pedicure. Hendrickje holds in her hand a letter (in the biblical story, Bathsheba received a letter from King David asking her to come to him). She has let the hand that holds the letter fall to her knee, and she gazes into space with an expression that seems to mix some regret (some tug of conscience) with some sense of pleasure at the compliment, some sense of daydreaming about how such an affair might be. She has been tempted.

She is a beautiful young woman, no mistake about that—with

only a modest share of the plumpness that was fashionable then in Holland—a delicious body and a lovely face: an arched eyebrow, a quiet, composed air, an ease and warmth in the eyes and mouth, and a grace in her posture that suggests some innate sense of equilibrium. She has smooth, healthy skin, and Rembrandt has tossed in a casually suggestive whirlpool of diaphanous silk to cover her quim. There is no question why David might have been tempted to begin with.

For whom Rembrandt might have done this painting is a question. It is a large painting to have done for the open market, in the vague hope that someone would have a wall big enough for it. It might have been ordered by Rembrandt's friend Jan Six, though there is no record of Six ever having owned it, and no record of its having gone through the hands of any other friend or collector of the time. As always, it is hard to know whether there is an autobiographical motive in Rembrandt's paintings, or just what it might be, but it is hard to imagine that he did not at least notice the resonance between his own life and the story of David and Bathsheba.

The story of King David and Bathsheba appears at II Samuel 11, 1–27. One evening David was walking on the roof of his house. From the roof he looked down and saw a woman bathing, "and the woman was very beautiful to look upon." David sent to find out who she was, and learned that she was the wife of Uriah the Hittite. Then David sent a messenger with a letter to her, asking her to come to him. She did, "and he lay with her," and fell in love with her. And then the story takes its truly villainous turn. David has Uriah the Hittite sent out to battle, and instructs the commander to put Uriah in the front lines so that he will be killed. Uriah is killed, and David sends once more for Bathsheba, "and she became his wife."

The Lord was displeased with what David had done, as the Bible story concludes, to have committed a terrible sin for the sake of a beautiful woman; but David—like Rembrandt—was not inclined to make any apology to God or his neighbors. This painting of a beautiful, composed, and graceful woman proclaims why.

A Girl Sleeping (Study After Hendrickje). Drawing about
1655–56

Self-Portrait (In Studio Attire, Full-Length). Drawing, about 1655–56

Portrait of the Artist
as an Artist

A**T SOME** point Rembrandt must have realized that he had no talent as a merchant or real estate investor or financial manager or social climber or master of human relations, that his talent was that of an artist. That, at least, was how he pictured himself in his self-portraits of the 1650s.

What is an artist, according to Rembrandt? In his self-portrait of 1655, an artist is a man who dresses modestly in an old floppy beret and an old smock. He is leveled at last, without pretension, without class, without social aspiration, neither swayed nor limited by a wish to be acceptable. He is, at age forty-nine, already an aging man, a man whose body is beginning to disintegrate. He is not ill, but he is not in good shape either. He has put on more weight than is good for him. His double chin is fleshier than it was just a few years before. He is under enormous stress. He seems extremely, chronically, worried.

An artist is one who looks intently, and who depicts what he sees exactly.

Around the eyes, the frown, the beginnings of crowsfeet, the bags under the eyes are the look of exhaustion.

If one takes stock of his face fragment by fragment, his left eye, in pain, is penetrating; his right eye, also in pain, is taken aback by what it sees, and invites sympathy.

But if the frown is removed, if the eyebrows are removed, and both eyes are taken together, they are calm, detached, even cold, and frankly observing.

If the face is divided into quadrants, the lower right quadrant of jaw and cheek has the set of one who is alert and devouring. The lower left quadrant has the delicacy of one who is discerning and possessed of unerring taste.

The lips, mouth, and jaw are determined.

Altogether, through him, you see what it is to have life take its toll and to go on.

Bankruptcy

NO ONE knows how deeply Rembrandt had gotten himself into trouble. Most Dutch couples kept detailed household accounts; indeed, those who had enough space in their houses generally set aside a little room upstairs exclusively for managing the household affairs—but as far as anyone knows, Rembrandt never kept household accounts. When he had borrowed from Witsen, Heertsbeeck, and Six, he had promised to repay them within one year. Several years passed, and the creditors began to grow impatient. The house still carried a massive mortgage. Other little debts accumulated. By 1655, it was clear that Rembrandt's finances were about to come apart. Once more, Rembrandt began to scramble.

By this time, Rembrandt had few options left. He could not let his taxes slide; he had already done that. He had no debts he could ignore for a while: He had already ignored them all. He evidently had no new sources of money he could turn to for loans. Inclined to grab at anything, he grabbed finally at his fourteen-year-old son and dragged the boy into the midst of his problems.

Titus seems to have been a sweet boy and a dutiful son. If Rembrandt's portraits of him are reliable, he was a good looking boy who was given the comforts—or at least the clothes—of a well-born young man. Rembrandt shows him more than once at his studies, reading and writing; it seems he was having the sort of childhood Rembrandt had had, with a little added prosperity. He looks like an agreeable young man, the sort of young man who knows he need not work too hard to be assured of a good enough career. Rembrandt, like his own father, slotted his first-born (as it turned out, his only) son to take over his own business. Rembrandt taught Titus some drawing and painting, and, presumably, later on, buying and selling. No paintings from Titus' hand survive, which suggests that, in the long run, he had a better head for business than for art and so, eventually, came to concentrate on dealing rather than painting.

In 1655, when Titus was still only fourteen, Rembrandt's first plan for him was to have him write a last will and testament. According to this will, Titus left all his earthly goods—"including those he might have inherited from his late mother"—and, more especially now, *"any he might yet come into possession of now and again"* to his father. Emphatically, "the testator does not wish that any of the goods he leaves behind shall come into the possession of or be inherited by any of his relatives on his mother's side."

Thus, having made sure that anything of Titus' would revert to him, Rembrandt proceeded with the rest of his plan. Within a few days, he rented some rooms at the Emperor's Crown Inn where he held a Christmas sale of his art collection. For the month of December he held an exhibition of works from the collection. At the end of the month, he conducted an auction. The exhibition and auction came in that festive time of year between the two most important family holidays in Holland: the Feast of St. Nicholas on December sixth, and Twelfth Night on January sixth. Although the Calvinist Church had tried to squelch these old Catholic feast days, the Dutch celebrated them anyway. The Feast of St. Nicholas was an occasion given over to children, who put their wooden shoes by the chimney to have them filled by St. Nicholas and his helper Zwarte Piet ("black Peter," who got that way by spending so much time in chimneys). On Twelfth Night, each family chose a "king" at breakfast (customarily a bean or silver coin was baked into a loaf of bread, and when the loaf was shared at the table, the person whose piece contained the coin was king). The king, with candle in hand, led a procession of children (dressed in grotesque costumes, with baskets on their heads) out into the streets to sing songs and make their way, finally, to a tavern. In some homes, the family followed the ancient custom of putting a row of candles on the floor, and the small children had to leap over the candles ("Jack be nimble, Jack be quick . . ."). In some neighborhoods, the children went out as early as five o'clock and went from door to door carrying satchels and begging for bread and cheese and money.

No one knows how much of Rembrandt's enormous collection he put up for sale during these holidays, how much of it he auctioned off or what the proceeds were. More particularly, no one knows where the proceeds of this auction went while everyone was distracted with children's presents and parades. None of Rembrandt's creditors were paid, none of his taxes were settled, the mortgage on his house was not paid. In fact, he didn't even pay the 130 guilders he owed the Emperor's Crown Inn for the rental of the auction rooms. He kept every last bit of the proceeds himself.

But this was not the end of Rembrandt's plan. On the very last day of the sale, Rembrandt made a deal to buy a new, and inexpensive, house some blocks away from his house in Sint Antoniesbreestraat. Presumably he meant to sell the big house in Sint Antoniesbreestraat, take the proceeds from the sale, buy a cheaper place, and settle the family into this new house along with a fresh supply of cash.

In fact, not even this was the end of the plan: Rembrandt thought he would buy the new house not with cash but with paintings and a mortgage and a promise to make an etching of the current owner. In this way, he would have the total proceeds from the sale of the Sint Antoniesbreestraat house for cash. Of course, he may have meant to use this big chunk of cash to pay off his long-suffering creditors—but that would only be an assumption.

Whatever Rembrandt's intentions, he did not move quite fast enough. The purchase of the new house fell through for some reason, and Rembrandt evidently felt the creditors were closing in on the house in Sint Antoniesbreestraat. In May of 1656, he transferred ownership of the house to Titus to put it safely beyond the reach of his creditors. So Rembrandt was no longer the owner of the house, although, of course, he and Hendrickje and Cornelia and Titus continued to live there as though nothing had changed.

Having put his house in Titus' hands, and the cash from that December sale in some safe place, Rembrandt then proceeded to declare bankruptcy. Not quite bankruptcy: To be precise, he applied to the High Court of Holland, at The Hague, for a *cessio bonorum*, a surrender of goods, a dignified form of liquidation that was granted to those who had been unlucky in their financial dealings rather than fraudulent (strictly speaking, perhaps Rembrandt had not committed fraud; at least the court didn't know of it when he applied for a *cessio bonorum*). A *cessio bonorum* ceded ownership of all Rembrandt's property to his creditors. An inventory would be taken, his property sold. Whether or not the sale of property satisfied the claims of his creditors in full, Rembrandt would owe them nothing more.

In his petition for a *cessio bonorum*, Rembrandt referred plaintively to "losses at sea," a phrase the commissioners must have heard often. Perhaps Rembrandt meant he had actually had investments in some trading company. Perhaps not. After all, in a nation of traders, what financial reversal was not ultimately the fault of the sea? In any event, "losses at sea" sounded much better than spendthriftiness.

So Rembrandt got the *cessio bonorum* and avoided jail, but this was hardly the end of his vexation. These debts were held by friends or business associates who did not simply vanish after the court reached its decision. To take just one of his debts, the thousand-guilder loan from his old friend Jan Six, how did Jan feel about Rembrandt stiffing him after all these years? Or did Rembrandt give his friend Jan some advance warning? As it happened, Six did sell the debt to a well-to-do man named Gerbrand Ornia *before* Rembrandt applied for his *cessio bonorum.* So then how did Ornia feel about Six stiffing him? Or had Six told Ornia in advance that it was likely to be a bad debt—and all these old friends had just decided to spread the losses around? Whatever the arrangement, someone somewhere along the line experienced some bad feelings, because, before too long, Ornia demanded payment from Lodewijk van Ludick, who had co-signed the Jan Six loan, and Ludick had to pay up. Then, not long after that, perhaps out of old friendship, and despite the *cessio bonorum,* Rembrandt promised to pay Ludick back. But, of course, more years passed, and Rembrandt paid Ludick nothing, though he did give Ludick a cut of a commission he received for a painting. And so, eventually, in trade for a quantity of cloth he didn't really want, Ludick passed on the loan to a man named Harmen Becker who began to pester Rembrandt for the money. Becker, it turns out, was no stranger to Rembrandt: Becker held the paper on two other loans of Rembrandt's and, as collateral, Becker was keeping nine paintings and two albums of prints and drawings. Rembrandt said he would pay the Six-Ludick debt if Becker would return this collateral on the other loans. Becker replied that he would return the collateral if Rembrandt would finish a painting of Juno that he had promised and never delivered. Rembrandt balked. Becker hired a lawyer. This was now ten years after Rembrandt was given his *cessio bonorum.* A committee of arbitration summoned Rembrandt, who refused to respond to the summons. On and on the dispute went. Becker was never paid.

No one knows how Jan Six felt about the way his friend Rembrandt treated him. But when Jan married the daughter of Dr. Tulp in 1655, and commissioned a painter to do her portrait in 1656, he did not commission Rembrandt to do it; he commissioned Govert Flinck.

Rembrandt, meanwhile, was thrown into the lengthy process that follows on a grant of *cessio bonorum.* A representative of the Chamber of Insolvent Estates (the *Desolate Boedelskamer* as it is gloomily styled in the Dutch) appeared at Rembrandt's house to make an inventory of all his goods. Rembrandt conducted the fellow from room to room, pointing out the furnishings, providing titles or identifications for the works of art hanging on the walls and stuffed into storerooms. It took two days to go through the whole house, and the list of items worth putting on the inventory ran to 363 separate entries. There was a vast quantity of things—of paintings and sculptures and studio props, of shields and helmets and musical instruments, Indian hand weapons and book after book after book of prints and drawings, painting after painting on the walls, gourds and bottles, a harp, plaster busts of Roman emperors, baskets full of architectural drawings, a collection of shells, coral branches, a pair of East Indian cups; and yet one does come away from the list wondering: Where is all the good stuff? In the front room there are seven nice Spanish chairs and a walnut table, but is that all? In the kitchen there are a few old chairs and a table and a coat stand and a copper kettle—but nothing else? In the linen cupboard there is nothing but three men's shirts, six handkerchiefs, twelve napkins, three tablecloths, and a few collars and cuffs. The house seems more than half empty! The long, long inventory list of Rembrandt's possessions seems to tell two stories simultaneously: that he was a man who had an enormous number of things, a man of really impressive material possessions; and that he was a man of even greater wealth than the representative of the *Desolate Boedelskamer* ever knew. This guided tour Rembrandt gave the man through his house, meticulously pointing out one thing after another, appears to have been something of a charade: A lot of his possessions seem to have been already gone. How much may have been gone, neither the *Desolate Boedelskamer* nor Rembrandt's creditors nor we will ever know.

The point of taking inventory was to see just what there was to put up for sale, and the *Desolate Boedelskamer* sold off Rembrandt's possessions in several auctions over the coming months. The first auction fetched a scant 1322 guilders, slim pickings for the art collections and household goods of one of Amsterdam's richest artists.

There is no way to know how Rembrandt was feeling during all this. Even if he was managing still to keep some of his money and his furniture out of the hands of his creditors—and we don't know for sure that he had squirreled away all the money and possessions that seem to have vanished without record— this sort of thing is horribly depressing. Yet, even in the midst of the depositions and appeals and inventories and auctions, Rembrandt made an etching of Thomas Jacobszoon Haringh, the very man who was responsible, as warden of the Amsterdam Town Hall, for carrying out the sale of Rembrandt's possessions. Technically, the etching is one of Rembrandt's finest. He went over the etching with both drypoint and an engraving burin to perfect the shading and to add accents to the darkest parts of the picture. He worked over the picture with great care, and obviously for many hours. What sort of man could face the auctioneer of his household goods with such cool skill?

In Rembrandt's hands, Haringh is certainly not a cheerful man. He does look a little like the grim reaper. His hands fall loosely onto his lap like crab's claws. He looks slightly unshaven. One side of his face seems a little larger than the other side, and one eye cants up and off at an odd angle. He could not be called a handsome man. But even so, Rembrandt has not savaged him; Haringh, one suspects, could have looked worse. Rembrandt has not tried to pretty him up; but he has not tried to denigrate him either. More than anything, the etching has the sense of an artist trying to see the truth exactly.

Still, something caused Rembrandt anxiety about the arrangements he had made. What if Titus actually were to die and leave his possessions to Rembrandt, and then Rembrandt's creditors would seize what he had? And so Rembrandt dragged his infant daughter into his troubles along with his son. He had Titus draw up a new will, leaving everything to his half-sister Cornelia, but specifying that Rembrandt "shall for the rest of his life reap and enjoy the benefits and the annual income derived from the goods and the assets . . . which benefits and income shall serve and are to be used for the alimentation and sustenance of the testator's father, with the condition that these abovementioned benefits will not at any time or to any extent be subordinated, serve as collateral, or be used in connection with any debts or obligations by the father of the testator to be

placed upon him, nor that he may transfer these benefits to sat-
isfy his debts or give them to anyone as if they were his property." There. That should do it.

In November of 1657, the *Desolate Boedelskamer* conducted
another sale of Rembrandt's goods. This time the proceeds
amounted to 2516 guilders, more than the first auction, but
still slim pickings. Historians have tried frantically to explain
these paltry sums paid for Rembrandt's possessions. Perhaps
just when these auctions occurred there were no dealers in town
from abroad to keep up the bidding. Perhaps the Amsterdam
dealers actually got together and agreed to keep the bidding
down out of a sense of revenge against Rembrandt for having
tried to manipulate the market in his own work all these years.
Perhaps the sale of Rembrandt's possessions produced such a
glut on the market, or such a fear of a glut, that prices stayed
low. No one likes to think that Rembrandt had already maneu-
vered the good things out of the clutches of the auctioneers.

And yet, the more Rembrandt thought about it, the more he
thought he could still improve the provisions of Titus' will. The
day after the auction that netted 2516 guilders, he had Titus re-
write his will yet again. Once more Rembrandt was made the
sole heir of Cornelia's property, but this time another key pro-
vision was added: "The aforementioned father shall control and
administer the property left behind, at his discretion and desire"—but this time he was allowed not only to live off the income from the property, he was allowed, too "in case of need,
to dip into, take, and use the principal sum . . . taking such
action in an appropriate manner."

Rembrandt had finally found the key: to possess his property,
but not to own it. To be able to dip into whatever he wanted, to
take it, to use it, to sell it, but to have it forever not his own,
forever beyond the reach of creditors. Clearly this was the safest
way for a compulsive debtor to live, safe not only from old debts
but from any new debts he might accumulate in the future, forever out of the reach of creditors.

Of course, when Saskia's relatives heard about this, they
would be livid to see how Rembrandt had absconded with Titus'
inheritance. And so a pointed few sentences were added to the

Thomas Jacobszoon Haringh, Warden. Etching, 1656

will: "It is explicitly willed that the testator's father need not give access to anyone in the world to the property left behind by the testator, nor give an account or provide an inventory thereof. . . . In fact, the latter is expressly forbidden and relieves him of such action herewith."

Was all this legal? No. Rembrandt might get away with some of it, but in February, 1658, his house was taken from him—no matter what paper he had drawn up to give it to Titus—and sold at auction to pay his creditors. The house fetched only 11,218 guilders—two thousand guilders less than Rembrandt had paid for it almost twenty years before. So perhaps the neighborhood had gone down or the house was sinking into the water, or Rembrandt simply hadn't taken care of it.

But not even this was the end of Rembrandt's trouble. Still another auction of his possessions was held in April of 1658 (proceeds: a minuscule 432 guilders). And even another auction was held in September of 1658 (proceeds: 470 guilders). And when it was all over, Rembrandt had been stripped of his art collection; the dozens of paintings and drawings on the walls and stacked in unused rooms and in corners of the studio, the books of engravings of Rubens and Titian and Lucas van Leyden were gone; the walls of Rembrandt's house were bare.

From all the auctions, including the house, the *Desolate Boedelskamer* received 16,182 guilders, a far cry from what Rembrandt had paid for all these things when he first got them. Even if Rembrandt had rescued some of his wealth from the auctioneers, few experiences are as depressing as the sight of one's remaining treasures—acquired originally with such anticipation, kept through the years until they have become imbued with personal associations—going down under the auctioneer's gavel at prices ordinarily paid for junk.

The heirs of Christoffel Thijs—Christoffel himself had evidently died—received 1168 guilders. Cornelis Witsen got his 4180 guilders back. A man named Gerrit Boelissen, from an old Amsterdam family, got 848 guilders. Isaac Vrancx got back ninety-five guilders on a loan of 116 guilders. Isaac van Heertsbeeck almost got four thousand guilders—and then the Chamber of Orphans intervened on Titus' behalf, and diverted 6952 guilders into Titus' estate—and so back into Rembrandt's hands. Other small debts, taxes, and fees consumed the rest.

And so, Rembrandt got away with it in some narrow, diminished sense, although for more than ten years he had to endure endless court documents, appearances before notaries, answering complaints, filing papers, conducting examiners through his house, scheming up underhanded financial maneuvers, plotting evasions and deceptions, hiding property, pretending to summons servers not to be at home, and facing, in the end, the fact that he had not succeeded in this society of clever, solid, dependable, reliable, resourceful merchants of good character—that he had been, on the contrary, forced in the end to recognize that he was just a struggling painter.

The Self-Portrait
of 1658

WHILE REMBRANDT's house was being sold, while the city clerk was giving a share of the proceeds to Cornelis Witsen, while Thomas Jacobszoon Haringh was taking possession of Rembrandt's furnishings and household effects to auction them off, while Hendrickje was appearing before the commissioners of the *Desolate Boedelskamer* to claim that a cupboard they were taking was actually hers, while sales were being conducted of Rembrandt's paintings and prints, while an appeal was made to the courts to save 4200 guilders from these sales to put into Titus' estate, Rembrandt painted a self-portrait.

He shows himself in three-quarter length, facing almost directly front, seated in a large chair, wearing a white shirt, a gold-yellow smock with a richly brocaded gold and yellow collar, a large black velvet hat, and a fur mantle thrown over his shoulder, covering his left arm, and falling to his thigh. Around his waist he wears a knotted cord with a tassel and gold ball.

The man in this picture is no longer the brash, bragging art student of the 1620s, no longer the arrogant, overconfident young man of the years with Saskia, no longer the famous society painter, no longer even the stoic sufferer of the 1640s; the man in this picture has been battered. The forehead now is thoroughly creased; the bags under the eyes are palpable and permanent; the skin has lost its healthy blush; the face has begun to collapse into jowls and double chins and frailty. There is a puffiness about the face that suggests heavy drinking (though not necessarily alcoholism). This is a man who has been through the wars; he is even ever so slightly wary.

But the man in this picture is, at the same time, hardly beaten. In the first place, he occupies an enormous canvas, nearly three and a half feet wide by five feet high, a portrait of grand dimensions, the largest self-portrait Rembrandt ever painted, a picture that does not shrink from staking a claim to attention. It is hard to imagine who could have bought such a huge picture, or where it might have been hung; any portrait hung next to it would seem puny, except perhaps that of a monarch. Indeed, it is a painting that could only truly be at home in a royal portrait gallery, where it would take its place as an equal. The pose itself is monarchical: Rembrandt sits in a large, throne-like chair, his right hand resting easily on one arm of the chair, and his left hand holding a silver-topped cane as though it were a scepter. It is the picture of a man who, though his kingdom may have been taken from him, is still, like Lear, assertively, the king.

The New House

I_N 1658, R_{EMBRANDT}, Hendrickje, Titus, and Cornelia moved to a new (rented) house in the Jordaan, one of the poorer neighborhoods of Amsterdam, filled with the houses of the lower middle classes, of artisans and small shopkeepers. This was the part of town that was usually hardest hit when the plague made its periodic sweeps through Amsterdam. This area had originally been set aside, when it was still outside the center of the city proper, for flower gardens; and many of the streets and canals were named after plants and flowers. Rembrandt and his family lived on the Rozengracht, the rose canal.

By the time Rembrandt arrived there the neighborhood was conscious of a distinctive character; the people who lived there thought of themselves somewhat as outsiders; they spoke their own argot; eventually the Jordaan would become the Jewish quarter; and Anne Frank would live in the Jordaan. In Rembrandt's day, because of the cheap rents, it was becoming the new artists' neighborhood. More than a half dozen painters lived no more than one canal away on the Lauriergracht, as did Uylenburgh's son Gerrit, and Rembrandt's former pupil the successful Govert Flinck, who had a palatial house on the Lauriergracht with a spacious studio and a handsome salesroom for his paintings. Rembrandt and his family lived in six small rooms, for which they paid 225 guilders a year.

In Rembrandt's ceaseless wriggling to avoid creditors, he had established a new business, a new art factory—or, perhaps, more a cottage industry than a factory. Rembrandt set up Hendrickje and Titus as the partners in a new business, designating himself as a mere employee without salary, on an expense account. The business was chartered to trade in "paintings, graphic arts, engravings, and woodcuts, as well as prints, curios, and all related objects." According to the contract drawn up by Rembrandt, Hendrickje, and Titus and signed before a notary, all household effects currently in the possession of the three were declared to have been purchased by Hendrickje and Titus and were henceforth to be considered invested as their joint property in the business. Similarly all of Titus' other property—including baptismal gifts, savings, his own earnings, and other possessions—would be invested in the business. In return for this investment, each party (that is, both Hendrickje and Titus) would be entitled to half the profits of the business.

And Rembrandt? Rembrandt "would live with them, receive free board, and be exempt from housekeeping expenses and rent on condition that he will aid the partners in every respect to the extent possible, and promote the business." Let the creditors take notice: "Rembrandt van Rijn shall not own any part of the enterprise [was this perfectly clear?], nor have anything to do with the furniture, household goods, art objects, curios, tools, and related items which would be found at their house at any time."

Did he still own any scrap or shred of any property to which any creditor might still lay claim? "He also cedes and transfers . . . to the parties mentioned above whatever he might be found to possess or might still acquire or bring in now and then without having or reserving thereupon any rights, claims, or demands, under any pretext."

Of course, he would need a little spending money and, in the contract, he honestly acknowledges receipt from Titus of nine hundred guilders and from Hendrickje of eight hundred guilders "for his necessities and food, which he promises to pay back to them respectively as soon as he will have earned something by painting." Spending money of 1700 guilders (and surely Hendrickje took care of food at home) was a tidy sum, being more than the equal of the annual income of three entire families among his neighbors in the Jordaan.

Some of Rembrandt's admirers have choked a bit on this arrangement he made to drag his son and mistress even deeper into his financial troubles. But what was he to do? The best hope for his family lay in getting Rembrandt back to work, bringing in income, making it so that the uncontrollable Rembrandt could not run up new debts with new creditors who would have a claim against his household. Had he not made this arrangement, the lawyers might descend on him again, take what he had managed to rescue, and leave him with his mistress and son and daughter out in the streets. Hendrickje and Titus must have realized that this arrangement was the best they could do for themselves as well as for Rembrandt. And, if Rembrandt peeled off an excessive sum of spending money right there in the presence of a notary, well, one doesn't change one's whole character overnight.

In truth, Rembrandt seems to have been relieved finally—like a compulsive thief locked up at last—to have all financial responsibility taken away from him, to be allowed finally just to paint and to be taken care of by Hendrickje. The moment he signed the contract for this new business arrangement, his productivity soared once again: He began to turn out paintings in numbers he had not achieved since way back in 1634, in the days with Saskia, when her money and social position protected him.

To be sure, more than simply a newfound sense of security, or even elation, must have motivated his productivity: He had a new business to stock with pictures; his company had no inventory; and he began to churn out pictures of the apostles, the evangelists, and other saints at a great rate. (These paintings are of such uneven quality that some scholars have suggested Rembrandt let Titus help him.) He had kept up doing some history paintings in the years right after his bankruptcy—a couple of versions of Christ and the woman of Samaria, Tobit and Anna waiting for Tobias to return home, Jacob wrestling with the angel, Moses with the tablets of the Ten Commandments—and he did not stop doing histories just because he was turning once again to establishing a business. He did a particularly beautiful and touching picture of the return of the prodigal son.

And he also filled his sketchbooks with drawings, some that were preparatory drawings for paintings but others that seem to have been done for no reason but his own pleasure: quick pen-and-ink renderings of a woman suckling a child, two men chatting on the street, a nude woman stretched out in bed asleep, a woman with a boy pissing, three beggars (two of them with wooden legs), a young man and his dog, three men in intimate conversation, an old man at his desk, a group of hovering grownups helping a child to walk, a young man in a large hat sitting by a window with a book, a couple of quick little self-portraits, a nude woman sitting on a stool and reaching down as though to remove a stocking, a cheerful nude woman on a chair with a veil partly covering her arm and shoulder, a slender nude woman with erect nipples stretching languidly, a nude woman sitting on a chair turning slightly to one side and turning back to look at the viewer, a seated nude woman with a big belly and thighs and a strong back. These nude women may have been studio models, though they look a lot like Hendrickje. Whoever they are, Rembrandt is once again in a frame of mind to do erotic drawings.

He is also in a mood to make money again by doing portraits, and he began to paint them once more with his old alacrity. He did a splendid portrait of the eighty-six-year-old Jacob Trip, the patriarch of the family that had made its fortune in iron, tar, and the arms trade. Rembrandt endowed Trip with some of the monarchical trappings of the self-portrait of 1658—a throne-like chair, a scepter-like cane, and even added a robe-like cloak. (Once Rembrandt got hold of a good idea, he didn't let it go.) Trip has a cool, unhurried, appraising expression on his face; one eyebrow is raised in the barest suggestion of skepticism. Altogether Rembrandt has given Trip a regal bearing—this is the king of the arms dealers—although Trip's portrait is not on quite as large a piece of canvas as Rembrandt's self-portrait was.

Rembrandt did a portrait of Trip's wife, Marguerite de Geer, too. Marguerite, though she was only seventy-eight years old at the time, looks far more frail than her husband, even though Jacob died in the year his portrait was painted, and Marguerite lived another eleven years. She looks like a woman who has been dipped into fire and seared. Her skin is parchment thin and white with red blotches; her eyebrows are faint; her teeth are gone. But she sits absolutely straight, and looks directly front, and she looks like a woman of tested mettle and clear intelligence. The de Geer family, too, were arms dealers; the marriage of Jacob and Marguerite had been a model alliance.

Marguerite wears a black gown and a vast starched and pleated white ruff collar that seems a century out of date and that is, at least, several decades old. These were old-fashioned people; and, when they came to commission their portraits in their old age, they commissioned someone who was by this time one of Amsterdam's most old-fashioned painters.

Rembrandt also did a pair of portraits of a younger man and woman, whom one scholar has identified as the grandchildren of Jacob and Marguerite. Whoever the woman is, she is strikingly beautiful. She wears a black dress with broad white cuffs and stole-like collar, and she holds a large white ostrich feather fan. Her hair is pulled straight back from her face. In conventional parlance she would have to be accounted homely. She has a weak chin and a nose that is too large, and there is a suggestion about her mouth of an overbite. She looks as though her face has been too thoroughly scrubbed. But she has a most composed, gentle, and sensitive expression, and gorgeous, dark, heavy-lidded, partly closed eyes, and her lips are—well, slightly parted. It is an adulterous portrait. We may not know what she

Het Ledekant (*The French Bed*). Etching, 1646

was thinking while she sat for it, but we can't help suspect what Rembrandt was thinking.

Despite his commissions for these portraits of people at the very center of Amsterdam society, Rembrandt was living less in the heady atmosphere of rich merchants and entrepreneurs and their wives than he had been back in the 1630s. Not that he was isolated: He was living in the company of the odd characters and low lifes with whom he had come to feel at home in the past decade. Among others who passed through his life now was Lieven Willemszoon van Coppenol who specialized in self-promotion and marrying wealthy women. The son of a French teacher and calligrapher, Lieven became a teacher and calligrapher too, but his passion went into commissioning famous artists to do engravings or etchings of him, which he would send to famous poets and pay to have the poets write poems about him and his fine penmanship. Armed with these handouts, he would set off in a wagon on tours of the countryside to display samples of his calligraphy and drum up business. No one, surely, ever had a better maker of publicity pictures than Coppenol: He got Rembrandt to knock out several of these handouts, and Rembrandt made Coppenol look as dignified as a cardinal.

Another of the companions of these days was Jeremias de Decker, who may indeed have been Rembrandt's oldest, perhaps best, friend, a friend from the 1620s who remained a friend. De Decker had been one of a group of poets around Jan Six, a hanger-on around the edges of the Amsterdam theater world, a friend of the playwright and producer Jan de Vos. He seems to have been something of a loner, and a lonely man, a bachelor who worked diligently at his poetry all his life without ever achieving much success, often sick and in financial need. But he was, like Rembrandt, though not a member of any organized church nonetheless a great reader of the Bible, and his poetry—and no doubt his conversation—appear to have influenced a number of Rembrandt's pictures, especially a number of pictures related to the crucifixion. From time to time he wrote poems about Rembrandt's paintings, and in the 1660s, to his deep pleasure, Rembrandt did his portrait and gave it to him. In

Rembrandt's portrait he seems a soft man, a washed-out man with a soft shadow falling across his face, with tired eyes and a mouth settled in disappointment, a melancholy man, but sweet, defenseless and loyal. It is not hard to imagine him seated at Rembrandt's dinner table, or hanging about Rembrandt's studio, or to see the two men strolling along a canal to a local tavern.

Among Rembrandt's other faithful friends was Aert de Gelder, his last known pupil—a sweaty-looking, unkempt man according to his self-portrait—who joined Rembrandt in 1661 and stayed for about six years. De Gelder fairly worshipped Rembrandt; in that unkempt self-portrait he holds a copy of Rembrandt's Hundred Guilder print, turning it so that the viewer can look at it with him, as much as to say: Isn't this Rembrandt an extraordinary piece of work? Even after de Gelder left Rembrandt and went off to live on his own, he seems to have tried to make his house resemble Rembrandt's as closely as he could. As one of his acquaintances said, de Gelder's house "is a rubbish heap of all sorts of clothing, hangings, shooting and stabbing weapons, armor, and so on, including shoes and slippers, all brought together; and the ceiling and walls of his studio are hung with flowery and embroidered lengths of silk cloth and scarves, some of them whole, others tattered just like the flags of conquered armies that hang in the hall of the Hague Court. From this rich supply he selects the equipment for his pictures."

No matter what the Trips and de Geers and de Decker and de Gelder thought, however, by this time, as van Hoogstraten's pupil Houbraken would report, "Before Rembrandt's death, the world had its eyes opened by true connoisseurs to imported Italian painting, and bright, clear painting came into fashion again." The master of dark, mysterious, inward-looking paintings was definitely being replaced by the practitioners of a lighter, glossier, more "finished" style—led by Ferdinand Bol and van der Helst and Govert Flinck. Rembrandt was still well-known, and still admired. Indeed, to some he had become a virtual standard of excellence. One playwright in that old circle of theatrical acquaintances, searching for the highest praise to heap on a piece of gold embroidery on the clothes of a character

An Actor Seated. Drawing, about 1636

in his play, said that the embroidery eclipsed even the art of Rembrandt. Poems were written in praise of Rembrandt's Hundred Guilder print. Jan Vos, when he came to write some verses celebrating the painters' guild of St. Luke's, and to mention the illustrious members of the guild, placed Rembrandt in the first rank. Rembrandt could pull down an occasional commission from as far away as Switzerland, France, Genoa, or Rome. Two of his self-portraits were in the collection of the English royal family. One was in the royal collection in Copenhagen. And yet, he had never become nearly as famous a painter as, say, Rubens. He counted no kings among his patrons. The grandest patron he ever had in Amsterdam was a mere alderman. Today his paintings are scattered over the world; less than fifty of them remain in the Netherlands; London has more than thirty; Berlin, New York, and Leningrad each has about two dozen; Kassel and Washington, D.C., each have about a dozen. But in his own time nearly all the buyers of Rembrandt's paintings lived within a few streets of Sint Antoniesbreestraat. The artists in other countries who knew his work knew it from his etchings. And the young artists who were interested in the new work that painters were doing, such fellows as Filippo Baldinucci, tended to dismiss Rembrandt as locally famous but hardly great.

Gerard de Lairesse arrived in Amsterdam in the 1660s, an aspiring artist in his twenties, just starting out. He came from a family of Liège businessmen who had dealt with the Trips for more than fifty years. In Amsterdam, he landed a place at once in the establishment of Hendrick Uylenburgh's son Gerrit. In the beginning, he admired Rembrandt greatly; but then he caught on to what was being purchased in Amsterdam and he wholeheartedly embraced the rules of clarity, classicism, finish, and fashion. "Away with fumbling, grubbing, and messing," he wrote: "touch your work with a manly hand. Not like Rembrand or Lievensz, however, so that the sap runs down the Piece like dung."

Rembrandt painted Lairesse's portrait when he had first arrived in town, and Lairesse should have displayed a more longlasting gratitude. In fact, Lairesse was already, at his young age, showing the first ravages of syphilis. He had almost no nose or eyebrows. When he had first arrived at Gerrit's studio, the other assistants there had "gazed in horror at his sickening appearance." In Rembrandt's skilled hands, the disfigurement almost disappears amidst a general impression of stylishness, worldliness, and dash. Lairesse holds some papers in one hand and has his other hand thrust inside his cloak. He wears a large black hat, and long blond curls fall to his shoulders. And his eyes are so luminous, so sincere, and so tender that one looks past the disfigurement to the young man within.

Lairesse may well have liked the portrait, but he did not allow it to influence his judgment that, in the end, Rembrandt was really "hopelessly old fashioned."

Anatomy of

a Masterpiece:

The Oath

of the Batavians

B Y THE MIDDLE of the seventeenth century, Amsterdam, the center of the world, needed a new town hall. The little old town hall, built in 1395, had been damaged by fire and rebuilt twice in the fifteenth century. Like everything else in Amsterdam, it was crumbling and sinking and then, in 1637, it was struck again by fire. In 1639, the burgomasters decided to let it go and build a new, larger municipal building. Two blocks of old buildings on the Dam were demolished, and on January twentieth, 1648, the first wooden piling for the new building was driven down into the sand. The new town hall, an enormous five-story palace, with hundreds of windows all around and two large interior courtyards, handsome offices for the Amsterdam bureaucracy and grand public halls and a vaulted entrance lobby covered with marble walls, required a total of 13,659 pilings to hold it all up above water level.

As it happened, the town hall was built at just the time that the Eighty Years' War was coming to an end—the Treaty of

Westphalia was signed in the same year that the first piling was driven for the town hall—and so even as it was being built the town hall was transformed into a monument to the end of the Eighty Years' War. The merchants of Amsterdam had long been advocates of making peace. The nature of the war had gradually changed during its course. The Dutch fight for independence from Spain had been swallowed up in a more general European war, led by France, against Hapsburg domination of the continent. This war was not relevant to the merchants of Amsterdam; and it was bad for their European trade.

And so, as construction on the town hall neared an end, the burgomasters began to commission decorations that would celebrate the end of the war and the independence of Amsterdam. Having fought off the Spanish monarch, however, the burgomasters did not see themselves as a new breed of emperors and kings to be glorified in a public monument. Rather, they saw themselves as distinctly different from all those who ruled the neighboring monarchies of Europe and Britain. They conceived of themselves instead as the natural heirs of the consuls of the ancient Roman Republic, as representatives of the people, bound by civic duty to serve the common good. And so, in their commissions for the new town hall, they ruled that no living person could be depicted, and they looked for paintings that would recall the heroes of the ancient Roman Republic.

There was no lack of painters for the burgomasters to choose from: The empty walls of the new town hall attracted a swarm of painters looking for a piece of the public largesse, and the relative standing of Amsterdam's artists can be quickly judged by seeing who got the jobs. In the first set of commissions, Rembrandt was not even considered. For the plum commission to decorate the burgomasters' own assembly chamber, with its prominent empty spaces just above the two beautiful marble fireplaces at either end of the room, the commissions went to those two former pupils of Rembrandt: Ferdinand Bol and Govert Flinck, both of them masters of the fashionable new glossy style. Bol did a picture of *The Intrepidity of Gaius Fabricius Luscinus in Pyrrhus' Army Camp*. According to Plutarch's *Lives*, the Roman consul Luscinus went to the enemy king

Pyrrhus' camp to negotiate peace terms. Pyrrhus first tried to bribe the consul and, when that failed, tried to frighten him by arranging the sudden appearance of an elephant. "Neither your gold yesterday," said Luscinus, "nor your monster today can sway me"—a good moral tale for the public servants of Amsterdam.

Flinck did a picture of *Marcus Curius Dentatus, Who Scorned the Enemy's Gold and Chose a Meal of Turnips Instead*, another story from Plutarch. As the title suggests, Dentatus not only spurned bribery, but lived a simple, frugal life as well—like his Calvinist Amsterdam admirers.

But the best commission of all was the one to decorate the vast *Burgerzaal*, or Hall of Citizens, where there was room for twelve huge paintings. The central theme chosen for these paintings came from the *Historiae* of Tacitus, in which he tells of a Germanic tribe known as the Batavians, who rose up to fight for their independence from Rome in AD 69–70. The Batavians had lived just north of the Rhine delta, in territory well within the borders of seventeenth century Netherlands, so that their story could be read as a story of Holland's ancestors; and it seemed an appropriate parallel to the recent history of the Dutch war of independence from Spain. The Amsterdam burgomasters were not the first to think of this parallel. Way back in 1609 Otto van Veen had painted twelve scenes from the story of the Batavians for the assembly room of the States-General in The Hague. In 1610 Grotius had written an immensely popular history of the Batavians as spiritual precursors in the war against Spain. In 1612 an Italian artist did a book of etchings based on van Veen's paintings. In 1619, the East India Company had given the name Batavia to their principal trading post in Java, present-day Jakarta. For the Hall of Citizens in the new town hall, the grandest commission given in the history of Amsterdam, the burgomasters chose not a splendid collection of the city's best artists but rather one man, the man they knew to be the single best artist in the Netherlands: Govert Flinck.

Before Flinck was able to do much more than some preliminary studies and start on one painting, he died. The burgomasters were evidently thrown into terrible consternation. Presumably no one was great enough to take on the whole of Flinck's commission, and so the town fathers divided up the commission: They gave some of it to Rembrandt's former partner Jan Lievens; they gave some of it to Jacob Jordaens, a Flemish painter who had done a spectacular *Triumph of Frederik Hendrik* for Huygens in The Hague; and then, almost grudgingly it seems, they peeled off one piece of the commission and gave it to Rembrandt.

The burgomasters provided Rembrandt with a huge piece of canvas, almost eighteen feet by eighteen feet square, of a special herringbone weave that was commonly used in large paintings in Venice but was rarely seen in Holland in Rembrandt's day. And they assigned him a space like those they had assigned to Lievens and Jordaens: high up under an arch at one end of the vaulted lobby, a dark recess of a dark lobby that was illuminated only by the fitful sunlight that came from the courtyard—hardly the best place to put a painting.

Rembrandt was always good at research. The town fathers wanted to memorialize their similarity to the Batavians, and Rembrandt evidently went back to see what Tacitus had to say about them. He had been asked to paint the moment at which Julius Civilis (Tacitus mistakenly called him Claudius Civilis), the chief of a tribe of Batavians, called together the leaders of neighboring tribes and persuaded them to join him in revolt. Tacitus described the moment this way:

> Civilis called the leaders of his tribe and the boldest of the common people into a sacred grove under the pretext of giving a banquet, and when he saw that the night and revelry had fired their spirits, he began to speak of the honor and glory of their tribe, then passed on to count over their wrongs. His words won great applause, and he bound them all by their national oaths and barbarous rites.

In this passage, and another, Rembrandt was evidently struck by three things: Civilis was blind in one eye; the meeting took place in the middle of the night; and the chieftains were bound

Study for the Oath of the Batavians. Drawing, about 1660–61

together by oaths and "barbarous rites," not by the polite hand-shake that had been the tradition since the appearance of Otto van Veen's pictures in The Hague.

Apparently Rembrandt got the commission in the autumn of 1661, because he did a sketch of his idea on the back of an invitation to a funeral that took place on October twenty-fifth for an acquaintance named Rebecca de Vos. Possibly the funeral invitation was simply the piece of paper closest to hand when a thought occurred to Rembrandt about the commission. Or perhaps he happened to be thinking about his painting when he attended the funeral and the somberness of the funeral was on his mind when, on the back of the invitation, he sketched out a composition for the largest picture he would ever paint—a ghostly gathering of men in the night, in a huge, dark, sepul-chral vaulted room with arches opening out onto the murky, black outlines of the trees in the darkness outside.

When the finished painting was put in place in the dark vault at the town hall, it must have made an astonishing impression: In the center of the deep, deep murk, four broadswords shimmer in an unearthly white light. The table itself seems to glow. A group of men are seated around the table in the wild and eerie shadows. Some raise their transparent crystal goblets. Others raise their arms. Others thrust out their swords to lay them across the heavy luminous blade of Julius Civilis, who sits far to the left of center in sumptuous robes, the lid of one eye closed over an empty socket, the other eye glaring straight out—seeming very like the ghost of Hamlet's father who calls insis-tently from the grave to Hamlet's fellows in conspiracy to swear, to swear by his sword, and again: swear.

Rembrandt laid the paint on with broad, bold strokes; indeed, he laid it on with both brush and palette knife—smears and gobs and jabs and flowing swaths of reds and yellows and browns all infused with that cadaverous incandescence. Just to Julius Civilis' right is a bearded old man, who looks as though he might be a Druid priest there to give his blessing to war; he reaches out to put two fingers to the hilt of Julius' sword. To Julius' left is a well-dressed young nobleman with a pearl in his ear and a golden chain around his neck. He reaches out with his open hand to lay it on Julius' blade. From behind the young nobleman, a shifty-eyed fellow in a flat, wide-brimmed hat reaches around the young nobleman's back to put his sword across Julius'. (In fact, there is an extra sword here: There is the shifty-eyed man's sword and then another sword just above it that belongs to no one. Rembrandt didn't paint this second sword; it was added to Rembrandt's original four swords by a restorer in the eighteenth century who evidently felt Rembrandt's painting needed improving.) In the foreground, on our side of the table, a cluster of men surges forward to join in the oath. A fat, elderly fellow who is seated on a low bench raises a shallow drinking bowl to Julius' sword. Behind him a young man, who is coming up to the table from some steps below, holds out his upraised hand. And to the old man's right, a young fellow in a slashed sleeve Burgundian outfit rises from the low bench to touch his sword to the (real) sword of the shifty-eyed man in the flat hat. Farther down along the table to Julius' left is another cluster of three men, including an old man at the end of the table who is bent forward toward his goblet, drunk and laughing. Altogether, as one art critic of delicate sensibilities later wrote, this looked like a bloodthirsty rabble. "Druids drink from flat bowls, mercenaries from looted chalices. . . . Giant primitive drinking vats block the steps. Rising over his barbaric partisans the one-eyed Claudius Civilis sits enthroned with the arrogance of the rebel . . . and all the hands and all the bodies reach out for the chieftain during the swearing of the wild oath."

Evidently, the burgomasters agreed with the critic: This was not a suitable painting for the town hall. This was not a patriotic celebration of the esteemed founding fathers of the free and independent Netherlands; this was a crude, violent piece of work that almost seemed to say that politicians were, at base, barbarians (surely this was not intended? surely Rembrandt did not mean to suggest that the men who had only given him this one small commission were barbarians?)—or at least that the earliest leaders of the Netherlands were barbarians—that Julius Civilis, hero that he was, was also a votary of naked power, and that the origins of the free and independent city of Amsterdam were rooted in infernal, drunken oaths, in short that the Netherlands had been born in the tomb of power and violence. And this was the painting that Rembrandt thought to present to the town fathers.

In addition to everything else, Rembrandt had ignored several well-established conventions with his painting: First of all, he had shown Julius Civilis from the front. No one had done that before. It was universally accepted among Dutch painters that Julius was to be shown in profile. Indeed, it was a matter of long-standing practice that went back even to classical antiquity: As a matter of decorum, all one-eyed people were shown in profile. To show any one-eyed person from the front was a breach of taste; to show a national hero in this way was incomprehensible.

Secondly, Grotius had demonstrated in his history that the Batavians were not crude barbarians at all. They had, early on, entered a treaty with the Romans that recognized their equal standing as a people; they were entitled, therefore, in any paintings that were done of them, to wear classical armor and to be seen as behaving like gentlemen.

Furthermore, before Rembrandt, painters had shown this oath of the Batavians as occurring in daylight, not in the dark of the middle of the night—whatever Tacitus said—and they had shown it as taking place outside, in a sacred wood, a setting of sylvan wholesomeness. Rembrandt had not only moved it into a dark, cavernous hall, the vaulting of Rembrandt's hall actually corresponded to the vaulting in the new town hall—as though these barbarians were conspiring within the very building where the burgomasters now met.

It can hardly be surprising that the burgomasters told Rembrandt to take the picture back and fix it up before he brought it in again. Why the town fathers had ever let him hang it in the first place is a mystery: Perhaps they had all been too busy to notice it when Rembrandt first brought it in, and then their friends began to question them about it and they took a good look at it for the first time. In any case, there was hardly anything Rembrandt could do to fix it: Everything that was wrong was wrong in the very conception of the piece. If the burgomasters could not stomach drunken laughter and death-laden oaths and other suggestions of ambiguous values along with reverence for the birth of the Netherlands, there was nothing much Rembrandt could do about it: He had never been what one might call a political painter; he had not gone out of his way to put personal political messages into his pictures; and he had not suddenly become a political satirist—but he was not interested in painting any other vision than his own.

So Rembrandt took the picture home, and cut it down. In its original size, it was far too big for anyone to buy; so he cut away the vast hall and the arches opening out into the night and kept just the scene of the men around the table, a picture a fifth the size of the original. He retouched it a bit here and there to remove any awkward effects that this cutting down had caused—and he took the hunks of canvas that he now had left over and painted other things on them. The burgomasters naturally refused to give him the 1200 guilders they had originally agreed to pay, so all Rembrandt got out of it was some free scraps of canvas.

Back at the town hall, meanwhile, the burgomasters seem to have been in a swivet. They realized soon enough that Rembrandt was not going to repaint the picture for them. But they were in a hurry to get the empty space filled in the Burgerzaal. Perhaps, once again, visitors were coming, and that gaping black hole was an embarrassment. So the town fathers turned to Juriaen Ovens, a former assistant of Govert Flinck (and a former pupil of Rembrandt), who evidently finished up the picture Flinck had begun. He knocked it out in four days and took, in payment for it from the burgomasters, only forty-eight guilders—perhaps because Flinck had already taken the painting close to completion. Ovens' painting is still there in the town hall today—mercifully hard to see up there in the dark.

As far as anyone knows, Rembrandt was never able to sell his *Oath of the Batavians*, even the cut-down version of it. The archives contain no record of the picture until 1734, when it appeared in an auction as lot 17 and was sold to a Swedish merchant for sixty guilders—barely enough by that time to keep an old couple in butter and eggs for the year—dirt cheap for a picture six and a half by ten feet that is certainly one of the greatest political paintings ever done.

Anatomy of
a Masterpiece:
The Syndics of
the Drapers' Guild

F IVE MEN SIT around a table covered with a Persian rug. One of the men is half rising out of his chair. Another holds a pair of gloves, as though he had just arrived, or is just leaving. Two of the others are going through a large book together—and one of these two has his right hand upturned as though to say, 'What do you make of this?' A sixth man stands inconspicuously in the background. All of the men have turned, at this same moment, to look at us.

However ignominious Rembrandt's failure with his town hall painting, he was still able to get commissions—though not many more: This was to be his last group portrait of members of the Amsterdam business establishment. These are the syndics, or sampling officials, of the Drapers' Guild—the men responsible for ensuring that the cloth marketed by members of the Amsterdam Drapers' Guild was up to guild standard. They gathered to do their duty every Tuesday, Thursday, and Saturday in the guild's *Staalhof*, or sampling hall, which was in the center of a complex of buildings devoted to the textile business, across the canal from the *Kloveniersdoelen*. Cloth samples of blue and black cloth (the only kind inspected by this guild) were brought to them there, and they would look over the samples and put their seal on those that passed muster. The sampling hall in which this business ritual was carried out was already hung with four group portraits of earlier boards of sampling officials—each group portrait showing five men seated and one man standing—and Rembrandt was charged with doing a picture in exactly the same manner.

The man all the way to our left is Jacob van Loon, at age sixty-six the oldest man in the group, who had a shop at the corner of the Kalverstraat just at the Dam. The man who is half rising from his chair is Volckert Jansz, a merchant and art lover who was well known for his collection of shells, stuffed animals, and rare books. The man with his hand upturned in a gesture of inquiry is Willem van Doeyenburg, the chairman of the group, a well-to-do cloth dyer who had been a member of the syndics since 1649. (It is odd that Doeyenburg sits at the table and Jansz gets all the attention by rising from his chair. Doeyenburg, as chairman, should be the center of attention but isn't.) The man who is going over the books with Doeyenburg is Aernout van der Mye, a cloth merchant. And the last man, holding his gloves, is Jochem de Neeve, at age thirty-two the youngest man in the group, a cloth merchant, the offspring of a wealthy family. The man who stands in the background is Frans Hendrickszoon Bel, a servant.

Rembrandt may have painted the picture on a piece of canvas he had left over from the *Oath of the Batavians* (he was still hard up for cash); the syndics are painted on the identical, relatively rare, sort of canvas as the town hall picture—and X-rays may yet reveal some remains of Batavians underneath the syndics. X-rays have already revealed that Rembrandt struggled with the syndics before he got them quite the way he wanted them. Originally he painted Volckert Jansz standing straight up, and only later made Jansz half sit, or half rise. He painted Chairman van Doeyenburg over and over, three times in all, changing that hand gesture each time before he got just

Study of Three Figures for the Syndics. Drawing, 1661

the right tone of inquiry or challenge. He did not trouble much with the servant, or with van der Mye, but the X-rays show a complete whirlwind of heads and collars before Rembrandt settled on just how to show young Jochem de Neeve with his gloves.

What was it Rembrandt was trying to get just right? Evidently something is happening here, but it is not clear just what. First of all, it is clear that we are actually present at this occasion. This is not a picture of an event in some remote time or place that Rembrandt is showing us; he has brought us into the picture. We are in the room. Nor has he simply brought us into the picture as bystanders or observers of a dramatic moment in which other people are taking part. It is a dramatic moment in which we are participating. We are part of the event. All of these men are reacting to our entrance.

Were they expecting us? Have we been called in before the syndics to explain some inadequacy on our part, some sample of cloth that has failed to pass inspection, some juggling of the books? Has there been a scandal? If this is the case, judging from the expressions on these men's faces, we are in trouble: The two men to the right look pleasant enough, as though they might take up our side; but the two men to the left do not look pleased. It looks as though the vote might be two to two, with Chairman van Doeyenburg casting the deciding vote. And how does van Doeyenburg look? Van Doeyenburg's expression might be impartial, and Rembrandt may have tried hard to rework that hand gesture until he got just the right impression of reserving judgment until all the evidence is in—but still, it does not look good for us. The servant in the background is tense; he is expecting the worst.

Or perhaps we have done nothing wrong. We were not expected at all. We have simply, in our wanderings through this complex of textile buildings, stumbled into a private meeting and intruded on some piece of confidential business. Volckert Jansz rises at once to ask us to leave. We have done nothing wrong, but we are out of place. Whatever the case, from the moment we stepped into this room it has been clear that we have entered a special chamber: This is not any ordinary corridor or hall; this is the room of the judges.

Rembrandt knew well the experience of entering a room full of judges, having been so often summoned to appear in such a room—before a panel of church elders, or a commission of the *Desolate Boedelskamer*, or, more recently, a panel of judges who requested and then rejected his *Oath of the Batavians*.

And having had such relentless experiences with panels of judges, having just slandered the Batavians, how does Rembrandt feel about this group? Remarkably enough, he shows these judges completely straightforwardly and objectively. He neither glorifies them nor vilifies them. They are neither gods of judgment nor ignorant fools; rather they are individual men with their own (largely unknowable) thoughts and feelings, quirks and histories, openness of understanding and prejudices.

Of course, there is another explanation for the picture, but it is too outrageous to be true. It fits the picture too perfectly, and has no basis in the conventions of Dutch painting. Nonetheless, suppose the painting captures the moment not that we appeared before the syndics of the Drapers' Guild but that Rembrandt did—the moment when the syndics had just been discussing whether or not it was a good idea to give him a commission to paint their group portrait. Volckert Jansz rises to meet Rembrandt because, as the art lover in the group, he was the one who convinced his colleagues to commission Rembrandt. That would explain why he rises and not van Doeyenburg, and why he looks a bit tense. Van Doeyenburg is checking the books to see how much previous painters were given for such commissions, and his gesture indicates he thinks they may be paying Rembrandt too much. The syndics are not all agreed that this commission is a good idea; it is not certain they are going to give it to Rembrandt. Jochem de Neeve has his hand on his gloves because he has made up his mind; he has had enough of this conversation, and he is about to leave. Still, the vote could go either way. And the painting itself is a picture of the moment Rembrandt enters the room to speak to the syndics about the commission to paint the painting. In the end, Jochem decides to stay and hear what Rembrandt has to say; the syndics vote in Rembrandt's favor—and despite all this uncertainty on their part, Rembrandt paints them all with complete understanding and respect.

The Plague

THE BLACK DEATH came out of China and travelled down into India and across central Asia so that, by the early 1300s, it had reached the Middle East and the Mediterranean Basin. According to some epidemiologists, the plague bacillus, *Yersinia pestis*, travelled with the horsemen and supply trains of Genghis Khan's Mongol Empire. According to others, the sirocco blowing out of the Sahara brought gradual desiccation to central Asia, so that the marmots and susliks and other rodents moved west in search of food and water. Some say that it struck hardest in places where populations were overcrowded and sanitation was poor; others say that such a view is too anthropocentric, that its progress had to do with the exigencies of the rodent population, not the human population, and that its spread was entirely beyond human control. In any case, by 1347, the plague entered the Sicilian port of Messina, evidently brought ashore by the black rats that climbed down the hawsers of the ship when it tied up at the dock, and from there it spread through

Europe, killing a third or a half or even two-thirds of the populations of the towns and cities it passed through.

Humans share sixty-five different diseases with dogs, fifty with cattle, forty-two with pigs, thirty-five with horses, thirty-two with rats and mice. The plague bacillus is transmitted from rodent to human by the parasitical fleas—the *Xenopsylla cheopis*—that travel on the rats' bodies. On occasion, the plague bacilli that the flea sucks in with the rat's blood multiply in the flea's stomach—so much so that the engorgement of bacilli blocks the flea from taking in more nourishment, and threatens the flea with starvation. And so, in order to be able to take in more blood, the flea regurgitates the bacilli back into the host's body before it takes a fresh supply of blood.

Most hosts can tolerate some bacilli in their systems, but, when the bacilli multiply greatly, the host succumbs—and the flea moves on to a new host, another rat, or a human being. The first symptom is a blackish pustule just where the flea has bitten. Then, as the bacilli multiply, there is a swelling of the lymph nodes of armpits, groin, or neck. Then, just below the surface of the skin, little hemorrhages occur, causing the purple blotches or buboes which give the bubonic plague its name. Because of the hemorrhaging, the body's cells begin to die, and the host begins to exhibit both neurological and psychological disorders. It may be from the symptoms of the plague itself that the convulsive Dance of Death took its choreography. Bubonic plague is fatal in fifty to sixty percent of all cases.

The bacillus Y. *pestis* can also be transferred directly from person to person as pneumonic plague. When the infection moves into the lungs, a person's sputum contains the bacillus and so, with coughing and spitting up, the plague becomes airborne. Pneumonic plague is fatal in ninety-five to one hundred percent of all cases. Finally, the bacillus can be carried from host to host by the human flea P. *irritans* or even by the human body louse. In this case, in what is known as septicemic plague, the bacilli are transmitted in massive numbers. A rash forms within hours of the insect's bite, and death comes within the day—before the buboes have even had time to form.

When the plague hit Siena in the 1340s, as the chronicler Agnolo di Tura wrote,

> It seemed that almost everyone became stupified by seeing the pain. And it is impossible for the human tongue to recount the awful truth. Indeed, one who did not see such horribleness can be called blessed. . . . Father abandoned child, wife husband, one brother another; for this illness seemed to strike through breath and sight. And so they died. And none could be found to bury the dead. . . . Members of a household brought their dead to a ditch as best they could. . . . And in many places in Siena great pits were dug and piled deep with the multitude of dead. And they died by the hundreds, both day and night, and all were thrown in those ditches and covered with earth. And as soon as those ditches were filled, more were dug. And I, Agnolo di Tura . . . buried my five children with my own hands.

The Black Death struck Europe with its greatest force in the 1340s—but that was not the end of it; before it had entirely spent its force, it came back again and again during the next 350 years. In 1665, it struck London and killed fully 70,000 people, enough to make some believe that God in his wrath meant to bring an end to the world. In Amsterdam in 1663 it killed perhaps 10,000 people, and, after a mild winter, it returned and killed perhaps another 24,000—a sixth of Amsterdam's population. By this time, piles of bodies were no longer accumulating in the streets; the civil authorities had learned better how to cope with the depredations of the Black Death, though the blow of having a husband or wife stricken by the plague cannot have been much softened.

Evidently the outbreak of the plague in 1663, among the thousands of victims it claimed, killed Hendrickje and, when it did, Rembrandt stopped painting almost entirely.

He had had a great burst of energy in the few years just

before this, when he and Hendrickje and Titus and Cornelia had moved into their new, small home, and he and Hendrickje and Titus had formed their company. Now, with Hendrickje's death, that was over. Nothing else is known about Hendrickje's death; there are no letters, no diary entries, no recollections of friends to say how Rembrandt felt about it. Rembrandt buried her in a rented grave in the Westerkerk, and virtually stopped working.

He did do one wonderful painting not long after Hendrickje's death, however (if the assumed date of the painting is correct): a painting that is sometimes called *The Jewish Bride*, sometimes identified as a double portrait of the Jewish poet Don Miguel de Barrios and his wife Abichael de Pina, sometimes thought to be the biblical figures Isaac and Rebekah, or Jacob and Rachel, or Boas and Ruth. What is certain is that it is a man putting his hand very lightly on the breast of a woman, who raises her own hand to hold his hand in place—a moment of incredible intimacy and tenderness.

The couple is shown in the sort of rich clothes a bride and groom might wear for their wedding—thus the title of *The Jewish Bride*—and Rembrandt has painted them with the same sort of technique he used for Julius Civilis: Great swaths of glistening paint have been laid on with a palette so that the picture dematerializes even as it takes shape, and so that it has an unearthly light—not the cold light of Civilis this time, but rather a hazy warm glow.

In the most recent interpretation of the painting, the man and woman have been identified as King Cyrus of Babylon and the shepherdess Aspasia. As it happens, a play about these two was performing in Amsterdam. In the play, King Cyrus is in the habit of fondling women of the court, and, when he first sees the beautiful Aspasia, he tries the same with her. She gently but firmly fends him off—and so, presumably as a result, he falls in love with her and vows not to touch her again until they are married. By the end of the play they are married, and presumably he does touch her again, this time with real tenderness and love. It may be that Rembrandt was once again knocking out a publicity picture for one of his theatrical producer friends.

If so, once again, the producer was blessed in the poster artist who was available to him; Rembrandt infused the moment with an extraordinary depth of personal feeling. The couple seem to appear in a dream or vision, or memory, and the moment is one of purest love, the only such moment Rembrandt ever painted.

That he was painting so little now could scarcely have made his life easier to finance. He was still beset with money troubles, still borrowing when he could find some collector willing to take paintings and drawings as security for a loan. The year before Hendrickje died, Rembrandt had had to sell Saskia's grave in the Oude Kerk. Just a few years after Hendrickje's death, a notary's records in the Amsterdam archives indicate that he was in arrears for his rent. The archives show, too, that Rembrandt remained incorrigible: Just four months after his landlord had taken action to collect back rent, and without any indication that he had gotten his financial affairs in order, a document shows that Rembrandt was trying to get his hands on a portrait by Holbein for the princely sum of a thousand guilders.

As poor as he was, as out of fashion, as depressed or otherwise disoriented and unable to work as he was, he was still recognized throughout Europe as a great master. When Cosimo de Medici, the Grand Duke of Tuscany, visited Amsterdam in 1667, he made it a point to call at the home of "Reinbrent the famous painter." He bought nothing, however: Rembrandt had nothing finished to show him. Possibly Rembrandt was no longer able to finish a painting. Or perhaps the fact that he had no finished work was a sign that, while his productivity might have slacked off, still, everything he did was sold at once—and meanwhile, as usual, he was in the midst of a number of different pictures, taking his time, reworking things again and again.

In February of 1668, Rembrandt's son Titus, now twenty-seven years old, became engaged to Magdalena van Loo, age twenty-six, one of thirteen children of Anna Huisbrechts and Jan van Loo, jeweler and silversmith. Anna and Jan had been close friends of Saskia and Rembrandt. Jan's brother Gerrit was married to Saskia's sister Hiskia. No doubt Magdalena and Titus had been lifelong friends.

An engagement was taken seriously, and celebrated solemnly, as Paul Zumthor, a professor at the University of Amsterdam and an observer of these things, has recorded. One custom called for an engaged couple to sit side by side on a bed, with both families present in the room, and exchange their first public kiss. They exchanged rings, too—large, heavy, unmistakably significant gold rings, often engraved with little allegories. In well-to-do families, the prospective father-in-law gave the bride-to-be a box made of silver or gold containing four essential items: a scissors, a knife, needles, and a mirror.

Engagements were often short, but between the engagement and the marriage were a round of parties and banquets. Rembrandt was a widower, Anna a widow, and they would have escorted one another at these parties. Friends of the prospective bride and groom were chosen to be 'playfellows' and to help with preparations. Bridesmaids were chosen; the bridal wreath and robe were made. The robe was the proper wedding dress: a Rembrandtesque robe of heavy velvets and silks, dramatically contrasting colors, crimson and pale green, or violet and cerulean, indigo and amethyst. The young couple was to live with Magdalena's mother in her house on the Singel Canal just opposite the apple market. The best room in Anna's house would have been decorated with flowers and greenery and colored paper, all the mirrors of the household brought into the one room and hung on the walls, wreaths and angels and cupids suspended from the ceiling.

The wedding took place at the end of February in the New Church, which was itself dressed up in oriental carpets and flowers and greenery. There, in front of the altar, when the young couple exchanged their vows, Titus would have taken the ring from his own hand and added it to the engagement ring that Magdalena already wore, so that she would now wear two rings on the second finger (or perhaps the thumb) of her right hand.

At the end of the ceremony, the wedding party made their way in procession—led by the bride and groom, with a gaggle of small children they had chosen to scatter flowers in front of them—back around the two short blocks to the Singel, to

Anna's house opposite the apple market, into an entrance hall filled with greenery, past little statues of Cupid and Venus, past the candelabra reflecting in all the mirrors, and into the reception room where the bride and groom took their place in throne chairs at the center. A carpet would have been hung up behind the couple, or a canopy mounted over their chairs. Family and friends would come to them there, bringing gifts. The small children and friends would gather around them there, and a decorated pipe would be brought to the groom so that he could begin at once to assume the patriarchal manner.

Biscuits and jam and other sweets were served right away. In the evening, the whole wedding party would sit down to a marathon banquet of as many as fifty courses, all washed down with copious lashings of beer and gin. An original poem would be recited—preferably one composed in Latin or Greek, or at least French or Italian. No doubt Rembrandt was able to provide one of his theatrical friends for this duty. Song books were taken out, and everyone sang in chorus, accompanied by an orchestra. (Wedding celebrations were evidently getting out of hand in Amsterdam. In 1665, attempts were made to limit the noise with new municipal ordinances: Orchestras were restricted to three musicians who might play such instruments as the cello, the harpsichord, the viola da gamba, and the lute.)

When the dinner was over, the 'playfellows' would usually close in for a last bit of raucous comedy and try to sneak the married couple out of the room without anyone noticing; the other guests would, of course, notice and try to prevent the departure with wild and noisy struggling. The bride might be kidnapped and hidden until the groom promised to treat all his friends to a dinner. Or, as Zumthor reports, someone might decide that the husband's shoes were worn out and needed repairing, and all his friends would grab hold of him and take off his shoes and, using the shoes like hammers, get down on the floor and hammer the floorboards furiously.

Sometimes the 'playfellows' would take hold of the bride and blindfold her and thus blindfolded she would take the wreath from her head and spin around and put it on the head of another—who would then be the next to marry. Sometimes the

entire wedding party would accompany the bride and groom
to their bed, where the bride's mother would be waiting to say
goodbye. With that, the young couple was left alone at last,
to climb into bed in their nightshirts—nightshirts that, by long-
standing custom, they would wear only twice, this first time
on their wedding night, and the second time for their burial.

Within five months, Magdalena was pregnant.

Then, a recurrence of Caravaggio, the chiaroscuro of daily
life: When Magdalena was three months pregnant, Titus died
of the plague.

Rembrandt, still short of money, could not afford to buy a
grave for his son, and so Titus was buried temporarily in a
rented plot, with the thought that he would later be moved to
the van Loo family grave. In fact, no one ever got around to
moving him.

Six months after the death of her husband, Magdalena gave
birth to a baby daughter, who was named Titia in honor of
Titus. She was baptized in the Reformed Church, in the presence of her surviving grandparents, Anna Huisbrechts and Rembrandt.

Then, seven months after Titia was born, Magdalena, too,
died—either from the lingering effects of childbirth, or from the
last flickerings of the plague.

And soon after all these terrible illnesses and tragic deaths,
on October fourth, 1669, Rembrandt, too, died of unknown
causes—perhaps he, too, of the plague—at the age of sixty-
three. Of course, there was no money for a big funeral, or any
sort of monument. He was buried somewhere in the Westerkerk, in an unmarked and unrecorded grave.

Epilogue

THE DAY AFTER Rembrandt died, a notary came to his house to conduct an inventory of his possessions. It was the house of a modest craftsman. The great art collection was gone. In the entrance hall—still the place for the merchant to display his wares—were twenty-two paintings, some finished, some unfinished. In the parlor were four unfinished paintings. In the next room were three "modest paintings"—not much for a painter who had been so prolific in earlier years, who had usually had a studio full of works in progress.

The notary did not bother to record any of the painter's props he may have seen around the house, no ancient helmets, swords and halberds, plaster casts of noble Romans, baskets full of musical instruments, books of prints of the work of other great artists. Rembrandt had precious few of these things left: a couple of helmets, a helmet's visor, four pieces of flayed arms and legs anatomized according to the teachings of Vesalius. The bankruptcy of 1656 had stripped him of most of these things;

nearly all of what he had had left, it seems, he had gradually dispersed to one creditor or another. Just the year before he died, he had put up an album of Lucas van Leyden prints and drawings as collateral for a loan.

For the rest, the house contained the accouterments of middle-class comfort—a very modest collection of things, though more than Rembrandt had left around for the notary to see in the bankruptcy inventory of 1656: a bed and a bolster, five pillows and a bolster, six silk curtains, four green lace curtains, an oak table and tablecloth, two pewter platters with pewter candlesticks, six cloth cushions, five plain chairs, a small square table, a Bible, a brass basin and pitcher, two copper candlesticks, a warming pan, a flatiron, a pothook, seven earthenware dishes, a few bowls, six pillowcases, eight neckties, ten men's caps, eight handkerchiefs, an old mirror with a clothesrack.

Rembrandt's last act of financial mismanagement had been a loan he had taken from his fifteen-year-old daughter. In the weeks before he died, in order to meet the household expenses, he had been dipping into the little bit of savings that were left from Cornelia's inheritance from Hendrickje. After Rembrandt's death, Cornelia's guardian found the last of the money, a few gold coins in a money bag, in a cupboard.

Cornelia herself lived to marry a painter (and jailkeeper— such was *his* need to have some income) named Cornelis Suythof. They went together to live in Batavia, in the Dutch East Indies, where they had two children, Rembrandt and Hendrick, neither of whom survived to adulthood. Titus' daughter Titia grew up and married a jeweler named François van Bijler. Titia died at the age of forty-six, without children.

No one knows what finished and unfinished paintings were found in Rembrandt's house after his death. Perhaps Julius Civilis was still there, perhaps some other history paintings, perhaps a picture of Hendrickje. There seem to have been no self-portraits still in the house; evidently he could still sell those as quickly as he finished them. In hindsight, as we look at the self-portraits he did in his last years, we imagine we can trace the beginnings of his decline right to his death. In fact, it is not quite so simple as that.

In one self-portrait of 1660, dressed in his smock and a silly white working hat, he looks withdrawn and feeble, as though one could see the start of his slipping toward death; in another portrait of the same year, wearing a jaunty black beret tipped to one side, with his shoulders squared back, he looks like a pugnacious forty year old. He could still move from role to role like quicksilver.

Still, there are certain roles he slips into these days and others he does not. Evidently, he no longer feels the need to paint himself in fancy dress, in the costumes of courtier, dandy, or grandee—not even in the understated elegance of the Amsterdam merchant. He belongs to the class of workingmen, and he shows himself time after time in his plain brown working clothes. He no longer has the need to make faces, pulling looks of mockery or insolence, insufferable self-possession, arrogance, obstreperousness, assertiveness. He no longer places a distance between himself and his neighbors.

One self-portrait is an exception to this—it is an assertion of the old ego that has sustained him through all his hard times: a portrait of himself done in 1660—perhaps as an advertisement for his new business with Hendrickje and Titus—in which he stands facing directly front, wearing a massive cloak with a fur collar, a white cotton cap on his head, a palette and maul and brushes in his hand, and on the wall behind him are two perfect half circles.

The key to the portrait lies in those two half circles. Those circles must refer to Apelles, the court artist to Alexander the Great and regarded in Rembrandt's time as the greatest artist who ever lived. According to legend, Apelles once travelled to Rhodes to meet one of the great ancient masters, Protogenes, an artist Apelles had long admired but never met. When Apelles arrived at Protogenes' house, the master was out. Rather than leave a message with the housekeeper, Apelles picked up a brush and, on a prepared canvas, drew a fine line. (Whether or not the fine line was a circle, the original sources do not say; as the story was passed down through the Renaissance, the line was assumed to be a perfect, free-hand circle.) When Protogenes returned home and saw the line on the canvas, he knew at once that Apelles had come to call. And so Protogenes joined the game: He picked up the brush and drew an equally fine line or circle on the same canvas. Thus, when Apelles returned and saw that his feat had been equalled, he picked up the brush once more—the moment at which Rembrandt has shown himself in his self-portrait—and bested Protogenes by drawing a third line or circle that perfectly bisected the other two. The message of Rembrandt's self-portrait is clear enough: He is the Apelles of his age, the greatest Dutch artist living—a good claim to make if you are about to launch a new painting business, or even if you only want to buck yourself up in the face of a lot of discouragement so that you can go on working. It takes a huge and powerful ego to live through the punishment any artist does—and Rembrandt especially put himself in the way of— and continue to turn out fresh, powerful work.

With the sole exception of this self-portrait as Apelles, however, Rembrandt practiced modesty—not self-effacement, but modesty. He painted himself without vanity or boasting, without swagger or haughtiness, without conceit or bluster or self-glorification. He painted himself, too, without self-deprecation or obsequiousness, without sniveling or cringing, without self-pity or despondency. He painted himself directly, front on, without flinching, plain and rough-edged, as he was, with all of his weaknesses and foibles showing.

The year that he died, he did two self-portraits that were, finally, unquestionably the work of a man who was not well. In both of them, he has still that same penetrating, compassionate and soul-searching gaze. But one of the self-portraits especially is the picture of an ailing man; he has gotten not simply fat; he has gotten alarmingly puffy, either from drink or from some illness. He is pasty-faced and pallid, his eyes are watery. He looks as though he might break out in a cold sweat. There is no resilience left.

Just before he died, Rembrandt did one more self-portrait, the last glimpse we have of him, in which he appears in the guise of another renowned artist of Alexander's time, the painter Zeuxis. According once more to legend, an odd-looking, wrinkled old woman came to Zeuxis and asked him to paint a portrait of

Venus. Zeuxis agreed, and then the old woman asked if he would use her as his model. Zeuxis burst out laughing. Or else, according to another version of the story, as he was painting her, thinking of the everlasting vanity and vainglory of human beings, who never tire of having portraits painted that show them to their best advantage, who never cease wishing to be beautiful and immortal, he burst out laughing. Indeed, he became so caught up in his paroxysm of laughter that he died laughing. This, the moment of Zeuxis' death, is the moment Rembrandt has painted. There is the profile of an old woman to one side of the self-portrait, but Rembrandt is not looking at her. He is looking in the mirror at himself, and he, more than anyone, with his little white cotton cap and the shawl thrown over his bent shoulders, and his wrinkled, puffy face, looks like a vain old woman laughing herself to death, as she does her own last self-portrait.

Bibliography

NOTE: *The principal sources for this book are the works of Rembrandt himself and the few documents related to his life that are, for the most part, collected in* The Rembrandt Documents *cited in the Bibliography below under Strauss and van der Meulen (and referred to in the Notes as Docs). Among secondary works, I am repeatedly indebted to the very recent and controversial book by Gary Schwartz, to Anthony Bailey's informal recounting of Rembrandt's domestic life, and to the two books about Rembrandt's work and his times by Bob Haak cited in the Bibliography. For Rembrandt's paintings up to 1634, the Rembrandt Research Project has published the first two volumes of* A Corpus of Rembrandt Paintings *under Bruyn (referred to in the Notes as Corpus), which gives the most thorough analyses of individual paintings for his early years.*

BOOKS

Alpers, Svetlana. *The Art of Describing.* London, 1983.
Bailey, Anthony. *Rembrandt's House.* Boston, 1978.

Barker, Francis. *The Tremulous Private Body*. London, 1984.

Benesch, Otto. *The Drawings of Rembrandt*. London, 1954–57.

Blankert, Albert, et al. *Gods, Saints & Heroes, Dutch Painting in the Age of Rembrandt*. Washington, D.C., 1980.

Boon, K. G. *Rembrandt: The Complete Etchings*. London, 1963.

Boxer, C. R. *The Dutch Seaborne Empire, 1600–1800*. London, 1965.

Bredius, Abraham. *The Complete Edition of the Paintings of Rembrandt*, revised edition by H. Gerson. New York, 1969.

Broos, B. P. J. *Index to the Formal Sources of Rembrandt's Art*. Maarssen, 1977.

Brown, Christopher. *Images of a Golden Past*. New York, 1984.

Bruyn, J., B. Haak, et al. *A Corpus of Rembrandt Paintings*. Boston, 1982–.

Buchbinder-Green, B. J. *The Painted Decorations of the Town Hall of Amsterdam*. London, 1976.

Burke, G. L. *The Making of Dutch Towns*. London, 1956.

Clark, Kenneth. *Rembrandt and the Italian Renaissance*. London, 1966.

Durantini, M. F. *The Child in Seventeenth Century Dutch Painting*. Ann Arbor, 1983.

Fowkes, Charles. *The Life of Rembrandt*. London, 1978.

Fromentin, Eugene. *The Masters of Past Time*, ed. by H. Gerson. Ithaca, 1981.

Gerson, H. *Rembrandt Paintings*. Amsterdam, 1968.

———. *Seven Letters by Rembrandt*. The Hague, 1961.

Goldscheider, Ludwig. *Rembrandt*. London, 1960.

Haak, Bob. *The Golden Age*. New York, 1984.

———. *Rembrandt, His Life, His Work, His Time*. New York, n.d.

Haley, K. H. D. *The Dutch in the Seventeenth Century*. London, 1972.

Haverkamp-Begemann, Egbert. *Rembrandt, The Nightwatch*. Princeton, 1982.

Heckscher, William S. *Rembrandt's "Anatomy of Dr. Nicolaas Tulp," An Iconological Study*. New York, 1958.

Held, Julius S. *Rembrandt's "Aristotle" and Other Rembrandt Studies*. Princeton, 1969.

Hodges, Devon L. *Renaissance Fictions of Anatomy*. Amherst, 1985.

Hofstede de Groote, C. *A Catalogue Raisonné of the Works of the Most Eminent Painters of the Seventeenth Century*. Cambridge, 1976.

Landsberger, Franz. *Rembrandt, the Jews and the Bible*. Philadelphia, 1946.

Münz, Ludwig. *The Etchings of Rembrandt*, 2 vols. London, 1952.

Murray, John J. *Amsterdam in the Age of Rembrandt*. Norman, Oklahoma, 1967.

Museum het Rembrandthuis. *Rembrandt and His Sources*. Amsterdam, 1986.

――――. *Rembrandt as Teacher*. Amsterdam, 1985.

Nash, J. M. *The Age of Rembrandt and Vermeer*. Oxford, 1979.

Nordenfalk, Carl. *The Batavians' Oath of Allegiance*. Stockholm, 1982.

O'Malley, C. D. *Andreas Vesalius of Brussels*. Los Angeles, 1964.

Regin, D. *Traders, Artists, Burghers; A Cultural History of Amsterdam in the 17th Century*. Assen, 1976.

Rosenberg, J. *Rembrandt*. New York, 1968.

Rosenberg, J., S. Slive, and E. H. Ter Kuile. *Dutch Art and Architecture 1600–1800*. Baltimore, 1966.

Schupbach, William. *The Paradox of Rembrandt's Anatomy of Dr. Tulp*. London, 1982.

Schwartz, Gary. *Rembrandt, His Life, His Paintings*. New York, 1985.

Slive, Seymour. *Rembrandt and His Critics*. The Hague, 1953.

Stechow, Wolfgang. *Dutch Landscape Painting*. Ithaca, 1966.

Strauss, Walter L. and Marjon van der Meulen. *The Rembrandt Documents*. New York, 1979.

Sumowski, W. *The Impact of a Genius. Rembrandt, His Pupils and Followers in the Seventeenth Century*. Groningen, 1983.

Valentiner, Wilhelm Reinhold. *Rembrandt and His Pupils*. The North Carolina Museum of Art, 1956.

――――. *Rembrandt and Spinoza*. London, 1957.

de Vries, A. B. et al. *Rembrandt in the Mauritshuis*. Alphen aan de Rijn, 1978.

van de Waal, H. *Steps Toward Rembrandt*. Amsterdam, 1974.

Weisbach, Werner. *Rembrandt*. Berlin-Leipzig, 1926.

White, Christopher. *Rembrandt and His World*. New York, 1964.

――――. *Rembrandt as an Etcher; A Study of the Artist at Work*. London, 1969.

Zumthor, Paul. *Daily Life in Rembrandt's Holland*. New York, 1963.

Articles, Dissertations, and Papers

Bloch, E. M. "Rembrandt and the Lopez Collection," in Gazette des Beaux-Arts, S.6, V. 29, 1946.

Brown, C. "Rembrandt's Portrait of Hendrickje Stoffels," in Apollo, CVI, 1977.

――――. "Rembrandt's 'Saskia as Flora' X-Rayed," Essays in northern European art presented to Egbert Haverkamp-Begemann on his sixtieth birthday. Doornspijk, 1983.

Bruyn, J. "Rembrandt and the Italian Baroque," in Simiolus, IV, 1970.

Gerson, H. "Rembrandt and the Flemish Baroque: His Dialogue with Rubens," in Delta, XII, 1969.

Haverkamp-Begemann, Egbert. "The Present State of Rembrandt Studies," in The Art Bulletin, LIII, 1971.

Held, Julius S. "Flora, Goddess and Courtesan," in De Artis Opuscula XL, Essays in Honor of Erwin Panofsky, ed. by Millard Meiss. New York, 1961.

Levine, David A. "William Schupbach, The Paradox of Rembrandt's 'Anatomy of Dr. Tulp' " in The Art Bulletin, LXVIII, 1986.

Martin, W. "The Life of a Dutch Artist in the Seventeenth Century," in Burlington Magazine, 7, 1905.

Montias, J. M. "The Guild of St. Luke in 17th-century Delft and the Economic Status of Artists and Artisans," in Simiolus 9, 1977.

Pope, Joan E. "Rembrandt's Conspiracy of Julius Civilis and the Concept of Sovereignty in the Dutch Republic after 1648," Department of Art History, McGill University, unpublished master's thesis, 1981.

van de Waal, H. "Light and Dark: Rembrandt and Chiaroscuro," in Delta, XII, 1969.

Notes

1. Prologue

For Rembrandt's self-portraits, see Christopher Wright. See also *Corpus*, both for notes on individual self-portraits and for a wonderful section in Volume 2 about how Rembrandt painted lace and how the rendering of lace can be used in helping to authenticate his paintings.

2. A Three-Hundred-and-Fifty-Word Biography

The Orlers biography is from *Docs* 1641/8. Schwartz gives very interesting genealogical charts. For general observations about children see Durantini. Parival is quoted in Murray. For general background on the Netherlands at this time, see Boxer and Haak's *Golden Age*.

3. The Landscape

Tony Bailey has a wonderful sense of the Dutch landscape. (See also his book *The Light in Holland* and Stechow's book on Dutch landscape painting.) For background on Dutch history, see the early chapters of Haak's *Golden Age* as well as C. R. Boxer.

4. The Cityscape

See Haak's *Golden Age* and Murray's *Amsterdam in the Age of Rem-*

brandt. The remark on Dutch tolerance is quoted in Murray, page 25. For observations on genre paintings of markets and street life in Amsterdam see Brown.

5. THE STREET OF ARTISTS

For the neighborhood of Sint Antoniesbreestraat, see Murray and Haak's *Rembrandt*. The flourishing market for Dutch art is recorded in *Docs* 1640/16, among other places. For observations about Rembrandt and chiaroscuro, see H. van de Waal's article in Delta. For the basic distinction between Italian narrative painting and Dutch descriptive painting, see Svetlana Alpers.

6. REMBRANDT'S EARLIEST KNOWN PAINTING

See the *Corpus* edited by Bruyn et al. See also Schwartz, and Haak's *Rembrandt.*

7. THE YOUNG FAILURE

The subject of Rembrandt's father's blindness is treated in some detail in Held's study of "Rembrandt and the Book of Tobit," published in his *Rembrandt's "Aristotle" and Other Rembrandt Studies.* Also see Schwartz for this chapter, especially for his observations on Lievens's standing and reputation.

8. CHRIST AT EMMAUS

See *Corpus.*

9. ALMOST A CAREER

Huygens' observations on Rembrandt are *Docs* 1630/5, and Schwartz gives a good commentary on Huygens' relationships with artists generally.

10. THE PICTURE BUSINESS

The opening quotation is from *Docs* 1631/4 as is the record of Rembrandt's purchase of property near Leiden (*Docs* 1631/1). For the economics of a painter's life, see Haak's *Golden Age.* See also W. Martin and J. M. Montias.

11. SOCIETY PORTRAITS

Once again, the *Corpus* gives the most complete account of these early paintings, although Schwartz is also very good on Rembrandt as a portraitist and on Rembrandt's earliest subjects. The status of portrait painters is eloquently described in Haak's *Golden Age* (at page 98, especially). Rembrandt's attempt to pass for a merchant is recorded in *Docs* 1634/7.

12. An Anatomy of *The Anatomy Lesson*, Rembrandt's First Great Painting

For the most complete study see Heckscher's superb monograph, and then, for the most up-to-date notes, see de Vries et al. See also Schupbach and Levine; and, for more general historical and philosophical considerations, see Devon Hodges and Frances Barker. Vesalius is quoted from the appendix of C. D. O'Malley's study.

13. Rembrandt's Signature

See the first two volumes of *Corpus*, passim.

14. The Woman He Loved

See Brown's "Rembrandt's 'Saskia as Flora' X-Rayed." It is Bob Haak (page 101 of his *Rembrandt*) who says that Saskia appears naked under the armor of Bellona. Walter Liedtke of the Met, where the painting is today, says this is nonsense. For genre paintings of taverns and prodigal sons in general see Brown's *Images of a Golden Past*.

15. Independence

The story about Rembrandt and Uylenburgh and Grossman comes from *Docs* 1634/6. For Rembrandt and the Jews, see Franz Landsberger. Gary Schwartz takes a more skeptical view of Rembrandt's friendship with the Jews.

16. How to Handle a Patron

The first letter to Huygens is in *Docs* 1636/1, the second in *Docs* 1636/2.

17. The Dealer

The opening quotation is in *Docs* 1637/7. Sandrart is quoted from Goldscheider (who reproduces the three very brief recollections of Rembrandt by Sandrart, Baldinucci, and Houbraken in the front of his book). The record of Rembrandt's dealings is from *Docs*, passim.

18. The Teacher

For Rembrandt's relationship with Hoogstraten, see Schwartz (especially, page 232). Bailey is good on Rembrandt's studio. The best concise study of Rembrandt as a teacher is the one published by the Museum het Rembrandthuis. The student gossip, including the story of the dead ape, is quoted in Goldscheider.

19. On Top of the World

The description of Rembrandt's house is reconstructed largely from the inventory made when he sought a *cessio bonorum* (*Docs* 1656/12).

The list of Saskia's jewelry is in *Docs* 1659/13. The lawsuit with Saskia's relatives is recorded in *Docs* 1638/7. For Rembrandt's house, see both Bailey and Zumthor. The financial arrangement is found in *Docs* 1639/1.

20. LETTERS TO HUYGENS
Docs 1639/2–7. Strauss and van der Meulen have a good brief discussion of "lifelike emotion" at page 162.

21. THE SELF-PORTRAIT OF 1640
For Lopez, see Bloch. See also *Docs* 1639/8.

22. HIS MELTING BONES
Tulp's record of the case is quoted in full in Appendix I of Heckscher.

23. ANATOMY OF A MASTERPIECE: *The Nightwatch*
Haverkamp-Begemann's monograph is the indispensable source. Haak has written on other civic guard paintings in his *Golden Age* (especially, page 292, where he discusses the other paintings in this hall).

24. THE CRASH
Rembrandt's lack of commissions is noted in Schwartz. Saskia's will is in *Docs* 1642/2.

25. THE DIFFICULT YEARS
The gossip of students and fellow artists is quoted in Goldscheider. Geertje's will is in *Docs* 1648/2.

26. THE NADIR
See *Docs* for June of 1649 and after.

27. THE HUNDRED GUILDER PRINT
See Haak's *Rembrandt*, especially at pages 214 ff.

28. MONEY TROUBLE
The opening quotation is in *Docs* 1652/1. Other money troubles are recorded in *Docs* 1646/2, 1648/3,5,6, 1652/5, 1653/2–7.

29. ANATOMY OF A MASTERPIECE:
Aristotle with a Bust of Homer
The opening quotation is in *Docs* 1654/16. For a detailed study of the painting, see Held. The Guercino commission is recorded in *Docs*

1660/7,9,14, and later correspondence with Ruffo is in *Docs* 1662/11, 12. Gary Schwartz is especially good on the Homer.

30. Hendrickje Summoned for Fornication

Hendrickje's ordeal is recorded in *Docs* 1654/11,12,14,15. The troubles with Pinto are in *Docs* 1653/9, 1654/3, and 1654/8. The Witsen and Six loans figure in *Docs* 1653/5,11. In this connection, see Strauss's footnote #6 on page 479 for the suggestion that Rembrandt was removing his etching plates from the hands of his creditors.

31. Hendrickje Naked

See Gary Schwartz, especially pages 292ff.

32. Portrait of the Artist as an Artist

This is the self-portrait that is in the Kunsthistorisches Museum in Vienna.

33. Bankruptcy

The documents on this begin in 1655 (*Docs* 1655/6) and run through the next several years, intermingled with interesting side issues. Schwartz traces the fate of the Jan Six loan on page 287.

34. The Self-Portrait of 1658

This picture is in the Frick Collection, New York. Schwartz noted that it would only have been at home in a royal portrait gallery.

35. The New House

On Rembrandt's new business, see Schwartz, pages 297 ff. Both Schwartz and Haak's *Rembrandt* are good on Rembrandt's work and friends in these years.

36. Anatomy of a Masterpiece:
The Oath of the Batavians
See Nordenfalk and Pope.

37. Anatomy of a Masterpiece:
The Syndics of the Drapers' Guild
See the essay on the syndics in H. van de Waal's *Steps Toward Rembrandt*.

38. The Plague

The recent interpretation cited of *The Jewish Bride* is from Schwartz. Rembrandt's money troubles are shown in *Docs* 1662/9,13 and 1666/

2,3. Cosimo's visit is recorded in *Docs* 1667/6. Rembrandt's death is recorded in *Docs* 1669/4.

Epilogue

The final inventory is recorded in *Docs* 1669/5. Gary Schwartz is good on the final self-portraits.

Illustration Sources

Etchings on pages 4 and 258 by permission of Rembrandt-Huis, Amsterdam. (Marburg/Art Resource, N.Y.)

Etchings on pages 15, 20, 24, 45, 53, 59, 73, 82, 92, 95, 100, 138, 149, 156, 163, 176, 184, 210, 214, 217, 219, 223, 230, 269, 279, photographed directly from *Collected Etchings of Rembrandt*, 3 Vols. Vol. 1 edited by Jaro Springer; Vols. 2–3 edited by H. W. Springer, New York, E. Weyhe, nd.

Etching on page 19 by permission of the Ashmolean Museum, Oxford. (Marburg/Art Resource, N.Y.)

Etchings on pages 32, 220 by permission of the Kupferstichkabinett, Berlin-Dahlem. (Marburg/Art Resource, N.Y.)

Etching on page 34 by permission of the Kobberstiksamling, Copenhagen. (Marburg/Art Resource, N.Y.)

Etchings on pages 37, 182 by permission of the Albertina, Vienna. (Marburg/Art Resource, N.Y.)

Etchings on pages 40–41, 282. Devonshire Collection, Chatsworth. Reproduced by permission of the Chatsworth Settlement Trustees/ photograph courtesy of the Courtauld Institute of Art.

Etchings on pages 46, 127, 135, 297.

Kupferstichkabinett, Staatliche Museen, Berlin-Dahlem.

Etchings on pages 49 and 213. British Museum, London.

Etchings on pages 56, 171, 257 by permission of the British Museum, London. (Marburg/Art Resource, N.Y.)

Etching on page 132. The Hague, Koninklijke Bibliotheek. ms. 112 c 14, f.233. r-v

Letter on page 143. By permission of the Houghton Library.

Etching on page 155. Hessisches Landesmuseum, Darmstadt.

Etching on page 169. Kobberstiksamling, Statens Museum for Kunst, Copenhagen. (Photo: Hans Peterson)

Etching on page 205. Fogg Museum of Art, Paul J. Sachs Collection, Harvard University.

Etchings on pages 206, 289 by permission of the Staatliche Graphische Saamlung, Munich. (Marburg/Art Resource, N.Y.)

Etching on page 242. Nationalmuseum, Stockholm.

Etching on page 252 by permission of Rijksprentenkabinet, Amsterdam. (Marburg/Art Resource, N.Y.)

Index